Inclusive Education

This book combines modern Artificial Intelligence (AI) and inclusive education learning systems methodologies. The book also provides an extensive discussion and methodologies related to STEM education to enhance future educational opportunities.

Inclusive Education: STEM in the Age of Modern AI explores and provides an educational support system for students with special needs within the STEM education framework. The book is composed of five chapters. Chapter 1 introduces the evolution of inclusive education during the last two decades. This chapter also discusses the importance of having an equal education and current challenges in inclusive education. Chapter 2 discusses the AI methodologies that can provide solutions to inclusive education. Furthermore, it discusses how modern AI approaches, such as Generative AI (GenAI) and Large Language Models (LLMs), are integrated into inclusive education support systems. Chapter 3 introduces AI-supported systems for analyzing emotional and behavioral aspects in STEM education. Enhancing STEM learning for visual and hearing impairments has been discussed in Chapter 4. Finally, Chapter 5 introduces the Metaverse approach as a methodology for inclusive learning support in distance learning education.

The book is written for a wide audience, such as STEM module learners, teachers, researchers, system developers, medical professionals, and industrial professionals, who interact in modern AI and education support system development.

AF736502

Inclusive Education

STEM in the Age of Modern AI

H.M.K.K.M.B. Herath
S.L.P. Yasakethu
B.G.D.A. Madhusanka
Chaminda Hewage

CRC Press
Taylor & Francis Group
Boca Raton London New York

CRC Press is an imprint of the
Taylor & Francis Group, an **informa** business

Designed cover image: © Shutterstock

First edition published 2026
by CRC Press
2385 NW Executive Center Drive, Suite 320, Boca Raton FL 33431

and by CRC Press
4 Park Square, Milton Park, Abingdon, Oxon, OX14 4RN

CRC Press is an imprint of Taylor & Francis Group, LLC

ISBN: 978-1-041-07634-6 (hbk)
ISBN: 978-1-041-07632-2 (pbk)
ISBN: 978-1-003-64149-0 (ebk)

DOI: 10.1201/9781003641490

Typeset in Times
by SPi Technologies India Pvt Ltd (Straive)

Dedication

Dedicated to my loving father
H.M.K.K.M.B. Herath

Contents

About the Authors

Eng. H.M.K.K.M.B. Herath is a lecturer-higher grade in the Department of Mechatronics Engineering at the Sri Lanka Technology Campus (SLTC). He not only imparts knowledge to students in advanced course modules, such as Artificial Intelligence, Robotics Engineering, Bionics, and Modern Control Systems, but also leads pioneering research initiatives as the co-investigator at the Computational Intelligence and Robotics (CIR) Research Laboratory at SLTC. His research has a profound impact, inspiring the next generation of engineers and roboticists. Herath's academic journey began with his Bachelor of Technology Honors Degree in Mechatronics Engineering from the Open University of Sri Lanka (OUSL) in 2019. Demonstrating a commitment to advancing his knowledge and expertise, he pursued and completed a Master of Science degree at the University of Moratuwa (UoM), Sri Lanka, in 2023. Herath's professional affiliations reflect his dedication to the engineering community. He holds memberships with several prestigious organizations: he is an associate member of The Institution of Engineers Sri Lanka (AMIESL), an Associate Engineer (AEng) with the Engineering Council, Sri Lanka (ECSL), and a Member of the Institute of Electrical and Electronics Engineers (MIEEE).

Dr. S.L.P. Yasakethu is a senior lecturer at the Department of Electronics and Telecommunications, Faculty of Engineering, Sri Lanka Technology Campus. He is currently serving as the Principal Investigator of the Computational Intelligence and Robotics (CIR) research lab. Dr. Yasakethu received his BSc. Engineering degree (First Class Hons.), with a perfect GPA, in Electrical and Electronic Engineering from the University of Peradeniya, Sri Lanka, 2007. He was awarded the prize for best performance in Electronic Communication Engineering by the University of Peradeniya for his achievements in undergraduate studies. After graduation, he joined Dialog Telecom (Pvt.) Ltd., Sri Lanka, as a Core-Network Engineer (2007). In October 2007, he was awarded the Overseas Research Scholarships Award by the Higher Education Funding Council of England to pursue a PhD at the University of Surrey, UK. After completing his PhD, he worked as a research engineer for Technicolor Research & Innovations (formerly known as THOMSON R&D) in Rennes, France (2010–2012). Dr. Yasakethu worked as a research fellow and a senior research fellow at the University of Surrey, UK, and Kingston University, London, UK, respectively (2012–2014). Afterward, he worked as a senior lecturer at the Department of Mechatronics, Faculty of Engineering, SAITM, Sri Lanka (2014–2016) and the Department of Electrical and Electronic Engineering, Faculty of Engineering, University of Peradeniya, Sri Lanka (2016–2018). His areas of expertise are 3D Video Communication, Quality of Experience (QoE) modeling in visual media, Artificial Intelligence, Machine Learning, and Cyber-Security. Dr. Yasakethu has worked on several European Commission projects under FP6, FP7, Horizon 2020, and Erasmus+ frameworks. He is a senior member of IEEE (SMIEEE) and an author of numerous publications.

Dr. B.G.D.A. Madhusanka is a senior lecturer in the Department of Mechanical Engineering at the Open University of Sri Lanka (OUSL) and a distinguished member of the academic and professional community. He earned his bachelor's degree in Mechatronics Engineering from OUSL in 2010, an M.Sc. in Industrial Automation from the University of Moratuwa in 2017, and a PhD from the Malaysian University of Science and Technology (MUST) in 2022. His research focuses on Service Robotics, Ambient Assisted Living (AAL), Image Processing, Artificial Intelligence (AI), and Computer Vision. Dr. Madhusanka's exceptional academic performance was recognized with a gold medal as the Best Student in Mechatronics Engineering. Under his leadership, his Soft Robotics Research Team achieved runner-up status in the high school soft robotics design competition at Harvard University in 2016, showcasing the team's excellence. Dr. Madhusanka is also a professional member of the Institution of Engineers Sri Lanka (IESL), the Engineering Council Sri Lanka (ECSL), and the Institute of Electrical and Electronics Engineers (IEEE). He has contributed to OUSL as a lecturer in the Department of Mechanical Engineering for over 13 years.

Dr. Chaminda Hewage is a reader (associate professor) in Data Security at the Cardiff School of Technologies, Cardiff Metropolitan University, UK, where he also serves as the Associate Dean of Research for the school. He is the Founding Director of the Cybersecurity and Information Networks Centre (CINC) at Cardiff Metropolitan University. He received a B.Sc. Engineering (First Class Honors Degree) in Electrical and Information Engineering from the Faculty of Engineering, University of Ruhuna (Sri Lanka) in 2004, and a PhD in Multimedia Communications from the University of Surrey (UK) in 2009. He was awarded the Gold Medal for best performance in Engineering (2014) by the University of Ruhuna for his achievements in undergraduate studies at the General Convocation held in 2004. After graduation, he joined Sri Lanka Telecom PLC (Sri Lanka) as a Telecommunication Engineer (2004). In September 2005, he was awarded the Overseas Research Scholarships (ORS) scholarship by the Higher Education Funding Council of England (Universities UK) to pursue his PhD at the University of Surrey, UK. Upon completing his PhD, he worked as a researcher at the University of Surrey, UK, and Kingston University, London, UK. In 2015, he joined Cardiff Metropolitan University in the United Kingdom as a senior lecturer in Networking and Cybersecurity. In 2014, he received a post-graduate certificate in higher education (HE) teaching and learning from Kingston University, London. He is a fellow of the Higher Education Academy (HEA), UK. He is a senior member of the IEEE, IET, and the Chartered Institute of Information Security (CIISec). His research interests include data security, data protection, and the use of AI and ML to protect personal and confidential business data.

Preface

Inclusive education in Science, Technology, Engineering, and Mathematics (STEM) is not just about fairness; it's the foundation for sustained innovation. Solving today's grand challenges, from climate resilience to biomedical breakthroughs, demands insights from learners with diverse cognitive and cultural perspectives. Yet, barriers still hinder participation for students with sensory, emotional, or behavioral differences. Without intentional inclusion, STEM risks reinforcing exclusion and limiting collective creativity.

Generative AI (GenAI) marks a decisive shift, utilizing multimodal understanding that integrates text, visuals, speech, and gestures to personalize learning experiences, clarify abstract concepts, and seamlessly translate content across different languages and modalities. Thoughtfully designed, GenAI becomes a cognitive collaborator, expanding accessibility and amplifying human potential for discovery.

Chapter 1 traces the evolution of inclusive education from integration models to Universal Design for Learning (UDL) in digital contexts. It analyzes research, policy, and empirical studies across policy, pedagogy, and STEM. Findings highlight the shift to strength-based, technology-enhanced inclusion, addressing policy-practice dynamics, implementation challenges, and innovative, evidence-based approaches that promote authentic belonging and equity in education.

Chapter 2 examines Artificial Intelligence (AI) for inclusive STEM Education. It demonstrates how AI and Machine Learning (ML) expand participation across four key pillars: personalized learning, AI-enabled assistive technologies, assessment and feedback, and teacher support. A pragmatic review of near-term classroom tools is paired with governance guardrails that address issues of opacity, privacy, fairness, accessibility, and human oversight. With strong UDL alignment and robust safeguards, AI expands opportunity while keeping teachers at the center.

Chapter 3 links persistence on demanding STEM tasks to coupling cognition with continuous insight into effect and behavior. The authors introduce a four-layer architecture: multimodal data ingestion, emotion and behavior analytics, a generative feedback engine that produces hints, explanations, and nudges, and delivery through chat, dashboards, and voice. The chapter details disciplined data practices, contrasts GenAI with conventional ML, demonstrates learner-archetype clustering and synthetic traces, and addresses risks and privacy.

Chapter 4 reframes access for learners with visual, hearing, and speech impairments from accommodation to integrated multimodal design. After mapping barriers, it presents solutions including tactile-ready diagrams and 3D models, data sonification, context-aware audio description, STEM-robust speech recognition with math-aware captioning, sign-language avatars, Augmentative and Alternative Communication (AAC)-friendly workflows, and blended touch-and-sound systems. Design exemplars, Braille-integrated graphics, BERT-guided sonification, Optical Character Recognition (OCR) with reasoning for chemistry notation, and Large Language Model (LLM)-supported molecular assembly are paired with reliability notes.

Chapter 5 proposes an inclusion-first blueprint that combines GenAI with the metaverse/XR, digital twin lab equipment, and teleoperated IoT/robotics to deliver rigorous, personalized distance STEM education. A case study (SLTC MechaLab Robotics Virtual Lab) demonstrates a virtual robotic arm synchronized with a physical twin, yielding significant usability/learning gains in a 100-student evaluation. This evidence suggests that such ecosystems can transform remote learning from accommodation to excellence.

This book is written for a global community of scholars, educators, technologists, and policymakers who seek to integrate AI into inclusive STEM education in a responsible manner. It serves as both a conceptual roadmap and a practical guide, combining evidence-based insights with implementation-ready models. Beyond technical guidance, it aspires to foster a new ethos: one in which the diversity of learners is not a constraint to be managed but a strength to be intentionally designed for.

H.M.K.K.M.B. Herath
S.L.P. Yasakethu
B.G.D.A. Madhusanka
Chaminda Hewage

1 The Evolution of Inclusive Education

From Integration to Universal Design in a Digital Age

1.1 THE EVOLUTION OF INCLUSIVE EDUCATION

1.1.1 WHAT "INCLUSIVE" REALLY MEANS

The concept of inclusive education has undergone a significant and complex evolution, progressing from a focus on physical placement to a profound emphasis on psychological well-being and a sense of belonging. At the earliest stage lies exclusion, characterized by the denial of the right or capacity of children with disabilities to access education in any form, resulting in their marginalization and complete lack of recognition within the educational system. The trajectory began with segregation, a historical practice of educating students with disabilities in separate classes or institutions, isolated from children without disabilities. This was followed by mainstreaming, which involved placing students with disabilities into general classrooms, but without substantial changes to curriculum or pedagogy to meet their specific needs [1, 2]. From there, the movement advanced to integration, a deliberate effort to physically place all students together. This stage often maintained a distinction between "special education" and "general education" and did not fully address the systemic or pedagogical changes needed for true inclusion [3]. The shift to inclusion marked a significant paradigm change. Inclusion is understood as providing all students with access to learning opportunities within the same educational environment, irrespective of their academic needs, through the deliberate adoption of practices and pedagogies that are inherently inclusive [4] (see Figure 1.1).

The most advanced and nuanced stage of this evolution is the concept of belonging. This concept goes beyond mere physical presence or access. Belonging is a multidimensional feeling of attachment, safety, and community, where students feel cared for by their peers and adults [6]. This sense of affiliation is crucial for psychological well-being and is positively associated with better academic and social outcomes, ultimately leading to improved life outcomes. A comprehensive understanding of inclusive education must acknowledge that simply placing students in a general classroom (inclusion) does not guarantee they will feel a sense of psychological safety, value, or connectedness. Data from the Organisation for Economic Cooperation and Development (OECD) indicates a concerning global trend where a sense of

DOI: 10.1201/9781003641490-1

FIGURE 1.1 Progression from exclusion to inclusion: conceptual representation of exclusion, segregation, integration, and full inclusion of people with disabilities in society.

Source: Adapted from The World Bank [5].

belonging is declining, despite a widespread push for inclusion. This suggests that focusing on physical presence alone is insufficient and that true inclusion must be measured by the relational and cultural factors that foster belonging [7, 8].

A critical dimension of this evolution is the distinction between equality, equity, and justice. Equality involves providing everyone with the same resources or opportunities. While well-intentioned, this approach can overlook existing disparities and fail to meet the unique needs of diverse learners. Equity is a more sophisticated approach that recognizes existing barriers and allocates resources fairly to ensure a level playing field, ensuring that different people receive what they need to succeed [5, 9]. The most progressive and comprehensive concept is justice. Justice goes beyond simply responding to existing barriers; it proactively identifies and dismantles the systemic and institutional roots of inequity, creating a system where everyone has fair opportunities and access to education from the outset. This represents a foundational shift from a reactive to a proactive mindset in educational reform.

1.1.2 Models of Disability

The philosophical underpinnings of inclusive education are deeply intertwined with prevailing models of disability. The traditional medical model views disability as an abnormal defect or pathology residing within the individual. Under this perspective, the person is the problem, and the solution is to "fix" or "cure" them through medical interventions or rehabilitation to make them appear "less disabled" and more "regular" so they can fit into a non-inclusive world. This model focuses on what a person cannot do, often leading to pity and a sense of tragedy [10]. In contrast, the social model of disability presents a fundamental shift in perspective. This model argues that disability is not an individual attribute but a result of the interaction between a person's impairment and a society filled with physical, attitudinal, and communication barriers [11]. The focus of intervention shifts from the individual to society, and the solution is to remove these external barriers, enabling full participation [12].

A common misinterpretation is that the medical and social models are mutually exclusive and jointly exhaustive. However, recent research indicates that they can be complementary. A practical approach requires synthesizing the medical understanding of a person's impairment with the social model's focus on environmental barriers. A more advanced and proactive approach, conceptually embodied by Universal Design for Learning (UDL) principles, can be considered a design model. This model is not explicitly named as a "model of disability" in the research, but its principles align perfectly with the concept. The design model is proactive and anticipatory, designing environments, curricula, and materials to be inherently accessible to all from the very beginning, preventing barriers from being created in the first place. The design model transcends the reactive nature of both the medical and social models by embedding inclusivity at the system's core. For instance, while a screen reader is a medical model tool, creating a screen-reader-friendly digital document from the outset is a proactive solution aligned with the design model. The most expert-level approach to disability in education, therefore, does not choose one model over another but demonstrates how they work in concert to create a holistic approach to inclusive education [13, 14].

Building on the philosophical models of disability, inclusive education is implemented through various dominant models that differ in approach, extent of inclusion, and structural organization. These models reflect the complexity of mainstreaming diverse learners, balancing individual needs with systemic capacities, and the evolving goals of equity and participation. Table 1.1 summarizes key inclusive education models, their characteristics, examples, strengths, and challenges as documented in recent literature.

1.2 SYSTEMS THAT ENABLE INCLUSION

1.2.1 Policy Levers, Funding, and Accountability

The transition to inclusive education is not linear but requires a profound cultural shift and a holistic, whole-of-government approach that extends beyond the education system. This requires active engagement from governments, civil society, and academia, as well as collaboration across various ministries, including health, finance, and social protection [23]. A key policy model for achieving this is the "twin-track approach." This framework involves two simultaneous efforts: the first is to make the general education system at all levels more inclusive for all learners through broad legislation and policy interventions, and the second is to specify targeted actions to support those with specific disadvantages [5]. For instance, this could mean ensuring sign language learners receive the accommodations and resources needed to succeed [23]. This twin-track approach represents a formal, policy-level solution to a central ideological debate: the tension between universal access and the need for specialized supports. Institutionalizing both principles provides a clear, actionable blueprint for countries at any stage of their inclusive journey. Effective implementation of these policies depends on robust accountability mechanisms. This requires the systemic collection and accessibility of reliable, disaggregated data about all learners. This data is crucial for measuring progress, informing decision-making, and strengthening the evidence base for effective interventions.

TABLE 1.1
Comparative Overview of Inclusive Education Models

Model	Description	Example Countries	Strengths/Outcomes	Challenges/Limitations
Complete Inclusion Model [15, 16]	Educates all students in general education classrooms with integrated support services, based on the belief that inclusive settings improve outcomes for all.	Italy and Portugal	Improved student well-being, parental satisfaction, and teacher collaboration.	Resource constraints, maintaining individualized support.
Partial Inclusion/Pull-Out Model [17, 18]	Students spend part of their time in general classrooms and part in specialized environments; individualized education programs (IEPs) determine the level of inclusion.	United States and parts of Asia	Allows tailored instruction; balances mainstreaming with specialist support.	Risk of fragmented student experience, potential stigmatization.
Integrated/Mainstreaming Model [19, 20]	Students are physically placed with peers without changing the curriculum or pedagogy; it focuses on presence rather than meaningful participation.	South Asia, Latin America	Transitional model; physical integration.	Limited teacher training and differentiation; restricted sense of belonging.
Special Schools with Inclusive Practices [21]	Special schools coexist with mainstream institutions and collaborate for inclusive activities or partial integration.	Germany	Centers of expertise supporting inclusive practices, pragmatic for some contexts.	Criticized for segregation; dual-track risks.
Inclusive Cluster/Resource Center Model [22]	Clusters of schools with inclusive expertise provide centralized services and support to local mainstream schools.	Uganda and Bangladesh	Scalable, cost-effective, improved access, and reduced dropouts.	Sustainability is contingent on funding and policy commitment.

1.2.2 School Culture, Scheduling, and Leadership

While high-level policies are essential, successful inclusion is fundamentally dependent on the culture and practices at the school level. A significant barrier to implementation is a clear gap between teachers' theoretical support for inclusive education and the practical challenges they face in the classroom. Recent studies reveal that while many teachers are willing to implement inclusive practices, they feel unprepared and lack sufficient institutional support. This feeling of isolation is a primary factor in their reluctance to adopt new methods [24].

This highlights the critical role of school leadership. Teachers feel that inclusion is nearly impossible to accomplish alone and emphasize the need for a collaborative, school-wide approach. Leadership is the central bridge between broad policy goals and the daily, lived reality of the classroom. The role of school leaders is to foster a culture of collaboration and provide the practical support necessary for teachers to feel competent and successful. This useful support can include things as fundamental as flexible scheduling to accommodate co-teaching or other collaborative efforts. National policies are insufficient without local, grassroots leadership that empowers and supports teachers on the ground [25]. Figure 1.2 illustrates that achieving successful inclusion requires school leadership to bridge high-level policies and classroom realities, fostering a culture of collaboration through support such as flexible scheduling and co-teaching.

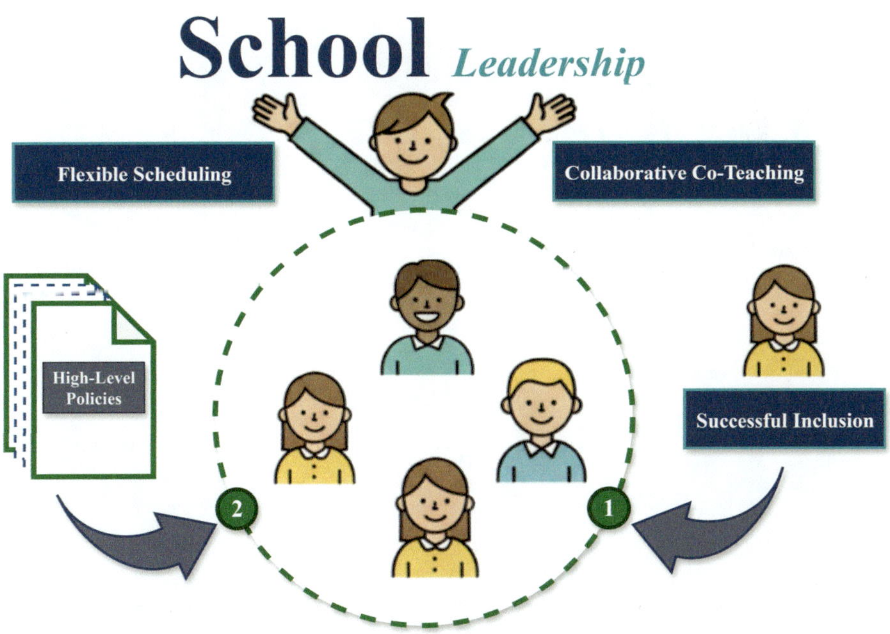

FIGURE 1.2 Successful inclusion and school leadership to bridge high-level policies.

1.2.3 Teacher Preparation, Co-teaching, and Family–Community Partnerships

Bridging the gap between inclusive education policy and classroom practice hinges fundamentally on targeted efforts in teacher preparation, co-teaching models, and cultivating strong family–community partnerships. Despite the global policy emphasis, only about one-third of countries offer teachers comprehensive, practical training in inclusive education, leaving many educators feeling underprepared to meet the diverse needs of learners. Teacher self-efficacy, teachers' belief in their capacity to effectively implement inclusive practices, plays a pivotal role in their adoption and sustained use of such methods. Professional development programs that are ongoing, collaborative, and embedded within teachers' work improve this sense of competence and willingness to engage fully in inclusive classrooms [26, 27].

Co-teaching is a highly effective pedagogical strategy addressing the dual challenges of limited teacher training and the need for robust institutional support. By pairing general education teachers and special education teachers (SETs) within the same classroom, co-teaching facilitates shared planning, instruction, and assessment, thus fostering professional growth through peer collaboration and reducing isolation. The range of co-teaching models described in the literature exemplifies varying levels of cooperation and shared responsibility [4, 28] (see Figure 1.3):

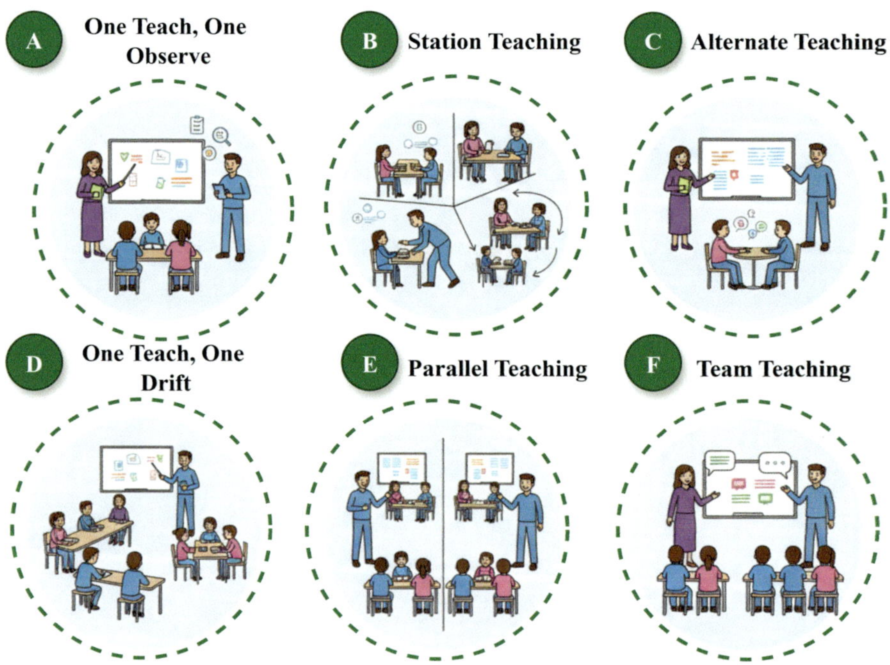

FIGURE 1.3 Co-teaching models in inclusive education: (A) One Teach, One Observe, (B) Station Teaching, (C) Alternate Teaching, (D) One Teach, One Drift, (E) Parallel Teaching, and (F) Team Teaching.

- **One Teach, One Observe**: One teacher instructs while the other collects data on student performance.
- **One Teach, One Drift**: One teacher instructs while the other provides additional assistance and support to students as needed.
- **Station Teaching**: The lesson is divided into segments, and teachers instruct at separate stations, with students rotating between groups.
- **Parallel Teaching**: The class is divided into two groups, and both teachers instruct the duplicate content to their respective smaller groups simultaneously.
- **Alternate Teaching**: One teacher works with a larger group while the other provides specialized attention and support to a small group of students.
- **Team Teaching**: The most collaborative model, where both teachers share responsibility and deliver instruction simultaneously as a "tag team."

Studies from Canada and Italy reveal that co-teaching improves student outcomes, enhances teacher confidence, and reduces feelings of isolation among both special and general educators [29]. However, effective co-teaching requires institutional support, regular planning time, and clear role definitions. Without these, co-teaching can become hierarchical or tokenistic, undermining its value in promoting professional development.

Beyond instructional strategies, family–community partnerships remain a cornerstone of inclusive education's success. Epstein's widely adopted framework conceptualizes these partnerships as overlapping spheres of influence where schools, families, and communities collectively contribute to the child's academic and social achievement. This model outlines six types of involvement: parenting, communicating, volunteering, learning at home, decision-making, and collaborating with the community, each reinforcing the shared commitment to student success and moving beyond older paradigms that positioned schools and families as isolated entities. Such partnerships strengthen support networks, enhance communication, and align goals across stakeholders to foster inclusive and equitable educational environments [27, 30].

1.3 STEM AND STEM IN INCLUSIVE EDUCATION

1.3.1 Introduction to STEM

STEM (Science, Technology, Engineering, and Mathematics) is a tightly linked toolkit for understanding the world and designing reliable solutions. Science generates testable explanations; technology turns knowledge into tools; engineering builds and optimizes systems under constraints; mathematics supplies the language, models, and proofs. In practice, these strands interweave through an iterative loop of observing, modeling, prototyping, testing, and refining. The point isn't memorizing formulas; it's developing a habit of framing problems, working with evidence, and reasoning quantitatively so that ideas become things that work, whether a climate model, a medical sensor, or a safer bridge.

In classrooms and teams, STEM often takes the form of projects, such as purifying water, coding a microcontroller, analyzing public health data, or mapping local air quality. These experiences develop transferable skills, including systems thinking, problem decomposition, data literacy, collaboration, and clear communication, and they treat failure as a valuable source of feedback. Context matters, so reasonable solutions also consider budgets, regulations, environmental impacts, and community needs. STEM's boundaries are porous (often referred to as "STEAM"), with design, storytelling, and ethics enhancing outcomes. Inclusive programs pair rigorous content with mentorship and culturally responsive teaching, thereby broadening participation and improving the quality and fairness of outcomes [31–33].

Why it matters: societies face challenges that require evidence-based trade-offs, such as decarbonizing the energy sector, safeguarding patient privacy in healthcare, and adapting cities to extreme weather conditions. A STEM-literate public can interpret uncertainty, ask sharper questions, and spot claims that outpace the data. STEM opens diverse paths for individuals, including software, civil and mechanical engineering, biotech, data science, human–computer interaction (HCI), and roles blending technical depth with policy or design. Getting started can be as small and local as automating a tedious task, logging and analyzing your sleep, prototyping a self-watering planter, or building a simple data dashboard. Keep a notebook, seek feedback, and iterate. Tools will change, but the core practice, coupling imagination with evidence and revising your model when reality disagrees, endures [31, 33].

Artificial intelligence (AI) is increasingly described as an enabling layer for STEM learning, powering personalization, formative feedback, and intelligent tutoring, while demanding human-centered, equitable, and ethical implementation (see Figure 1.4). Global guidance emphasizes these opportunities and cautions for policy and practice, including support for teachers and attention to governance and inclusion. Evidence from systematic reviews in STEM contexts documents AI's roles (e.g., adaptive tutoring, diagnostics, and data-informed instruction) across the disciplines.

1.3.2 STEM in Inclusive Education

Inclusive STEM education benefits from inclusive pedagogical practices and serves as a powerful instrument for advancing social justice, equipping students for an interconnected global society. The foundational importance of STEM lies in its capacity to drive economic growth and civic engagement, as STEM-related occupations typically offer above-average wages and are projected to expand more than twice as rapidly as non-STEM fields. However, persistent underrepresentation of women, racial and ethnic minorities, and individuals with disabilities continues to perpetuate structural socioeconomic disparities [31, 32].

By deliberately fostering inclusivity within STEM education, these fields can become catalysts for social justice, promoting equity by expanding opportunities to historically marginalized groups and by counterbalancing entrenched societal biases [32]. Research reveals that culturally relevant teaching methods and differentiated instructional strategies effectively address these disparities, helping bridge gaps in participation and achievement for underrepresented students. There is growing recognition that transforming STEM education requires systemic change encompassing

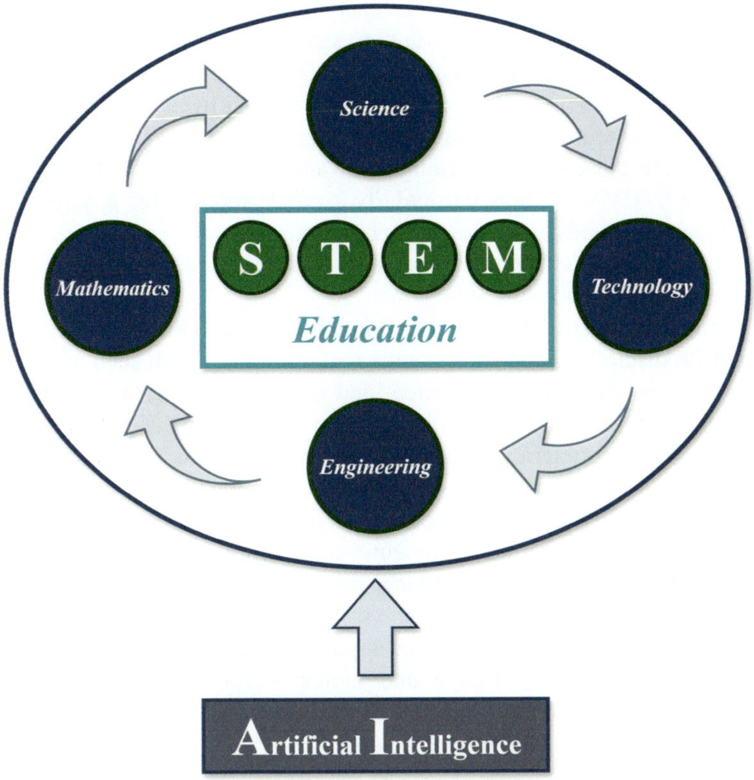

FIGURE 1.4 Conceptual map of STEM education showing the four strands, Science, Technology, Engineering, and Mathematics, with AI support for STEM Education.

curriculum content, pedagogy, teacher training, and institutional support to create genuinely inclusive learning environments [33]. Engagement in inclusive STEM education empowers marginalized youth by enhancing critical thinking, fostering a sense of belonging, and enabling them to participate actively in economic and civic life. Studies recommend sustained professional development, equitable resource allocation, and policy reforms that emphasize social justice as a foundational principle in STEM curricula [31].

STEM education naturally provides multiple entry points for diverse learners through its various instructional modalities. Unlike traditional instruction that may rely heavily on text-based learning, STEM labs and projects offer hands-on, visual, tactile, and computational pathways, allowing learners to engage with complex concepts in more accessible and meaningful ways. Authentic, project-based learning (PBL) rooted in real-world problems increases students' sense of purpose and agency. For instance, elementary math classrooms often employ routines such as "math talk," which utilizes visuals and manipulatives to facilitate students' use of physical objects to model mathematical thinking and enhance peer communication. At the secondary level, choice-based science investigations encourage students to explore community-relevant issues, such as water quality, and present their findings through multimodal formats, including whiteboards, datasets, or oral presentations. Such approaches empower students to connect academic content with their lived experiences and community contexts, thereby supporting deeper engagement and inclusivity [34, 35]. Research suggests these diverse learning pathways are essential for closing persistent equity gaps in STEM education, particularly for underrepresented groups, by honoring varied learning styles and cultural backgrounds. Equally, actively including students' voices and choice within STEM fosters motivation, identity development, and persistence in STEM pathways [35].

The pursuit of inclusive STEM education offers powerful transfer effects beyond the immediate discipline. Core skills cultivated through STEM, such as quantitative reasoning, critical thinking, persistence, and design thinking, have been demonstrated to enhance learning across all academic subjects. Inclusive STEM environments also actively counteract stereotypes by presenting students with diverse role model stories and images of successful STEM professionals who share their identities, thereby nurturing a sense of belonging and self-efficacy in historically marginalized groups [33, 36]. Furthermore, authentic collaboration in labs and project-based learning models promotes interdependence and community, as students leverage one another's diverse skills and perspectives to solve complex challenges. This collective problem-solving process fosters the development of essential social and cognitive skills necessary to build equitable and inclusive societies. Such collaboration enhances academic outcomes and strengthens students' capacities as agents of change in their fields and communities.

1.4 DESIGNING FOR DIVERSITY IN DAILY PRACTICE

1.4.1 Universal Design for Learning (UDL) Across Subjects

UDL is a proactive framework that is conceptually linked to the architectural movement of Universal Design [13]. Rooted in neuroscience, UDL is designed to improve and optimize teaching and learning for all people by anticipating learner variability from the outset of curriculum design. The framework aims to eliminate barriers before they are created, reducing the need for retroactive accommodations [14].

UDL provides the theoretical foundation for this review, emphasizing creating learning environments accessible to all students from the outset [37, 38]. In the context of digital STEM education, UDL principles guide the development of technology-enhanced curricula that provide multiple means of representation (how information is presented), engagement (how students are motivated), and expression (how students demonstrate learning) [39, 40]. The integration of UDL with digital technologies in STEM education offers particular advantages. Digital platforms can automatically provide alternative formats for content (text-to-speech, visual representations, multilingual support), enable personalized pacing and difficulty adjustment, and offer diverse assessment modalities [41]. However, the effectiveness of these features depends on intentional design and implementation guided by UDL principles.

1.4.2 Technology Acceptance and Digital Divide Theory

Understanding the adoption and effective use of digital technologies in inclusive STEM education requires considering both technology acceptance factors and theories related to the digital divide. The Technology Acceptance Model (TAM), initially developed by Davis, has been extensively applied to educational contexts and provides a framework for understanding why some technologies succeed while others fail to gain adoption [4, 28]. In inclusive STEM education, the acceptance of technology is influenced by perceived usefulness, perceived ease of use, and additional factors such as accessibility, cultural relevance, and institutional support.

The digital divide theory (DDT) provides a complementary lens for understanding educational technological inequities. Lythreatis et al. [42] conceptualize the digital divide as a multifaceted phenomenon beyond simple access issues. Table 1.2 shows the three levels of digital divide in STEM education.

Compound effects in STEM education are particularly pronounced due to several factors identified in the literature, which exacerbate these digital divides. First, the specialized nature of many STEM digital tools means they often require more

TABLE 1.2
Three Levels of the Digital Divide in STEM Education, with Emphasis on Challenges Faced by Students from Lower Socioeconomic Backgrounds and Those with Disabilities [42–44]

Level of Digital Divide	Description	Educational Context (STEM & Disabilities)
First-Level: Access Divide	Focuses on the availability of devices, internet connectivity, and technological infrastructure.	Students from lower socioeconomic backgrounds lack reliable access to high-speed internet and capable devices. Students with disabilities may also lack access to specialized assistive technologies, which are often expensive and not widely provided.
Second-Level: Usage and Skills Divide	Concerned with digital literacy, confidence, and the ability to effectively use available technologies.	Despite access, disparities remain in navigating software, troubleshooting, and adapting to new tools. Students with disabilities may face further challenges due to inaccessible platforms or insufficient training in assistive technologies.
Third-Level: Quality and Outcomes Divide	Encompasses the cultural relevance, inclusivity, and educational value of digital content.	STEM resources may fail to represent diverse perspectives or learning needs. For students with disabilities, accessibility features often meet technical compliance but lack inclusivity in practice.

sophisticated devices and higher bandwidth than general educational applications [45]. Second, the abstract nature of many STEM concepts means that digital representations become crucial for understanding, making the quality of digital content especially important for diverse learners. Research by Sama and Gul [46] demonstrates that students with disabilities face compounded challenges across all three levels of the digital divide. They often have limited access to appropriate assistive technologies, lack practical training in using these tools, and encounter STEM educational content not designed with their needs in mind. Similarly, students from rural or economically disadvantaged backgrounds may have access to basic internet connectivity but lack the bandwidth necessary for interactive STEM simulations or virtual laboratory experiences.

Technology Acceptance in Inclusive Contexts: the application of TAM to inclusive STEM education reveals additional complexity beyond traditional TAM factors. Paliwal and Singh [25] found that in educational contexts, technology acceptance is significantly influenced by institutional support, peer networks, and the alignment between technological tools and pedagogical goals. For students with disabilities, acceptance factors also include the compatibility of educational technologies with assistive devices, the availability of alternative formats and interaction methods, and the degree to which technologies support rather than hinder academic participation. Furthermore, Okoye et al. [47] identify cultural factors as crucial determinants of technology acceptance in educational contexts. In STEM education, this includes whether digital tools reflect diverse problem-solving approaches, incorporate multicultural examples and applications, and provide interfaces that accommodate different linguistic and cultural preferences. Recent research by Afzal et al. [43] suggest that addressing digital divides in inclusive education requires comprehensive approaches tackling access, skills, and quality issues while attending to the specific acceptance factors that influence different student populations. In STEM education contexts, this means ensuring that students have access to appropriate technologies and that these technologies are designed and implemented to support meaningful engagement and learning outcomes (LOs) for all students. Table 1.3 outlines the three key theoretical frameworks, UDL, DDT, and the TAM, that guide the design, analysis, and implementation of inclusive STEM education with technology.

1.4.3 MTSS Without Tracking: Tiers as Supports, Not Labels

A Multi-Tiered System of Support (MTSS) is a proactive and preventive framework that empowers schools to meet the academic and nonacademic needs of all learners, including those with skills below, at, and above grade level. This framework is not a standalone referral process but an integrated system encompassing various other supports, such as Positive Behavioral Interventions and Supports (PBIS) and school mental health initiatives [48, 49].

A core principle of MTSS is that tiers are a continuum of supports, not permanent labels for students. The framework is designed to be fluid and responsive to a student's progress, with movement between tiers driven by data and guided by assessments and progress monitoring. The system emphasizes that students do not need to "fail" at a lower tier before receiving more intensive support; instead, they should

TABLE 1.3
Key Theoretical Frameworks Guiding Inclusive STEM Education and Technology Integration

Theoretical Framework	Primary Focus	Application for Inclusive STEM Education
UDL	Proactive design for accessibility and equity [37, 38].	It guides the development of technology-enhanced curricula through multiple means of representation, engagement, and expression [39, 40]. Digital platforms provide alternative formats, personalized pacing, and diverse assessment modalities [41].
DDT	Multilayered technological inequality [42].	Analyzed across three levels: Access (devices, connectivity) [43, 45], Usage (literacy, skills) [23], and Quality (relevance, cultural responsiveness) [42]. Compound effects are particularly pronounced in STEM due to specialized tool requirements [45, 46].
TAM	Understanding user adoption of technology [42, 43].	Inclusive STEM is influenced by perceived usefulness, ease of use, accessibility, cultural relevance, and institutional support [25, 47]. Extended beyond traditional factors to include compatibility with assistive devices and cultural alignment.

receive the right type and intensity of support as soon as a need is identified. This approach places the onus on the system to proactively ensure that all students receive what they need, rather than on the student for achievement declines [50].

The foundation of MTSS is Tier 1, which provides universal, evidence-based, high-quality instruction and support for all students. Tier 2 offers evidence-based, targeted intervention to address specific skill gaps, typically delivered in small groups. Tier 3 involves intensive, individualized intervention for fewer students with significant and persistent needs. Tier 2 and Tier 3 supports must be designed to complement, reinforce, and supplement Tier 1, not replace it. The structure of MTSS serves as a practical, pedagogical mechanism for implementing the twin-track policy approach to inclusion. The framework operationalizes the policy goal of strengthening the universal system (Tier 1) and providing targeted support for those with specific needs (Tiers 2 and 3). This demonstrates a clear conceptual link between high-level policy and a functional school-based framework for ensuring all students thrive [50].

1.4.4 Assessment for Inclusion

Traditional approaches to inclusive assessment have often focused on providing reactive accommodation, such as extra time on a test, for students with documented disabilities. While these accommodations are undoubtedly essential and necessary, this approach can create an unintended dichotomy, segregating "normal" learning procedures from "alternative" ones and potentially perpetuating the very exclusion it is meant to address [51]. Assessment for inclusion represents a progressive and equitable approach to designing assessment methods that enable all students to demonstrate their knowledge and skills to their fullest potential. Unlike reactive accommodations, this paradigm emphasizes proactively creating fair and transparent assessments grounded in equity, fairness, and justice for all learners [52, 53].

- **Transparency**: Clearly articulate the purpose of the assessment and provide explicit, well-defined criteria and rubrics so all students have an equal opportunity to succeed [52].
- **Scaffolding**: Using formative, low-stakes assessments to support student learning and allow for practice and "feed-forward" before a final grade [53].
- **Multimodality**: Offering multiple modes of assessment so students can demonstrate their understanding in different ways, such as through a written response, an oral presentation, or a creative project [52].

The most advanced principle is "authenticity," where assessments mirror real-world problems and challenges. Students can apply their knowledge meaningfully by framing assessments around authentic problems such as social justice or environmental issues. This approach increases engagement and motivation, fosters critical thinking and creativity, and cultivates a sense of active citizenship [54]. The shift from accommodations to authentic assessment reflects the broader evolution from a medical to a design model of disability. Accommodation aligns with the medical model's focus on a person's deficit. At the same time, authentic assessment offers multiple, flexible, real-world-connected pathways to demonstrate knowledge, a core tenet of UDL and the design model. It proactively designs an environment where students may not need specific accommodation, as the primary assessment is already flexible enough to accommodate their needs [55].

1.5 TECHNOLOGY AND ACCESS

1.5.1 Assistive Tech and Accessible Design

A crucial distinction in the modern inclusion landscape is the difference between assistive technology (AT) and accessible design. AT is any item, equipment, or system used to increase, maintain, or improve the functional capabilities of an individual with a disability. AT is reactive and individual-focused, designed to help individuals compensate for environmental barriers [56]. AT encompasses various devices and software designed to enable functional access for individuals with disabilities [57]. AT plays a crucial role in dismantling long-standing barriers to participation in STEM education. For students with visual impairments or learning disabilities, tools like screen readers, voice-to-text software, and specialized applications are essential.

Modern AT has become increasingly sophisticated, integrating machine learning (ML) and cloud-based data to adapt in real time to user needs. For instance, apps like Proloquo2Go provide customizable communication interfaces for nonverbal students, while platforms such as Ghotit assist learners with dyslexia by offering context-aware spelling correction [57]. A key trend is the mainstreaming of AT into everyday devices. Many smartphones and tablets now include built-in accessibility features, such as screen magnifiers, voice commands, and haptic feedback, making assistive functions more affordable and less stigmatizing. The convergence of AT with general-use EdTech has broadened the reach and acceptance of inclusive tools.

A key insight into the effectiveness of AT is that it is not solely a function of the technology itself, but of the entire digital ecosystem in which it operates. A powerful AT tool is rendered useless if digital content is not created with accessibility standards in mind from the outset. For instance, while a tool may read mathematical equations aloud, it can only do so if the content is published in a compatible format, such as HTML or MS Word, rather than in standard but inaccessible formats like LaTeX or PDF [58]. This highlights a crucial pedagogical relationship: the design of a learning environment (e.g., creating accessible content with alternative text and long descriptions) is a direct prerequisite for the success of assistive technologies [59]. The goal is to move from ad-hoc, retrofitted solutions to a system where AT is an integrated and seamless part of the educational experience.

Immersive technologies, such as Virtual Reality (VR) and Augmented Reality (AR), have begun to influence inclusive education by creating multisensory, engaging learning environments. These tools can be particularly transformative in STEM by making complex, abstract concepts tangible and experiential. For example, a VR application can allow a student to virtually explore the human anatomy or a far-flung ecosystem virtually, overcoming physical or cognitive barriers to access. This can be especially beneficial for students who struggle with abstract thinking or are kinesthetic learners, thereby unlocking new pathways to understanding [60].

Accessible design represents a proactive, systemic approach to creating products and environments that are usable by the broadest possible range of people, regardless of ability. Also known as Universal Design, this philosophy seeks to prevent the creation of barriers from the outset rather than reacting to them later. A classic example is the curb cut: initially designed for wheelchair users, curb cuts have proven universally beneficial to parents with strollers, travelers with luggage, cyclists, and many others [61]. In the digital realm, accessible design means crafting websites that are compatible with screen readers and ensuring videos provide closed captions from the outset of development. Such designs not only ease use for people with disabilities but also enhance the user experience. The synergy between AT and accessible design is critical; accessible products and platforms make AT more effective and seamless. As in Figure 1.5, conceptually, this relationship mirrors the evolution of disability models: AT aligns with the medical model's focus on individual impairment and remediation, while accessible design embodies the social and design models by removing environmental and systemic barriers [62, 63].

1.5.2 Artificial Intelligence, Data, and Ethics

The rapid integration of AI into education presents tremendous opportunities and significant ethical challenges. AI promises to deliver personalized learning experiences

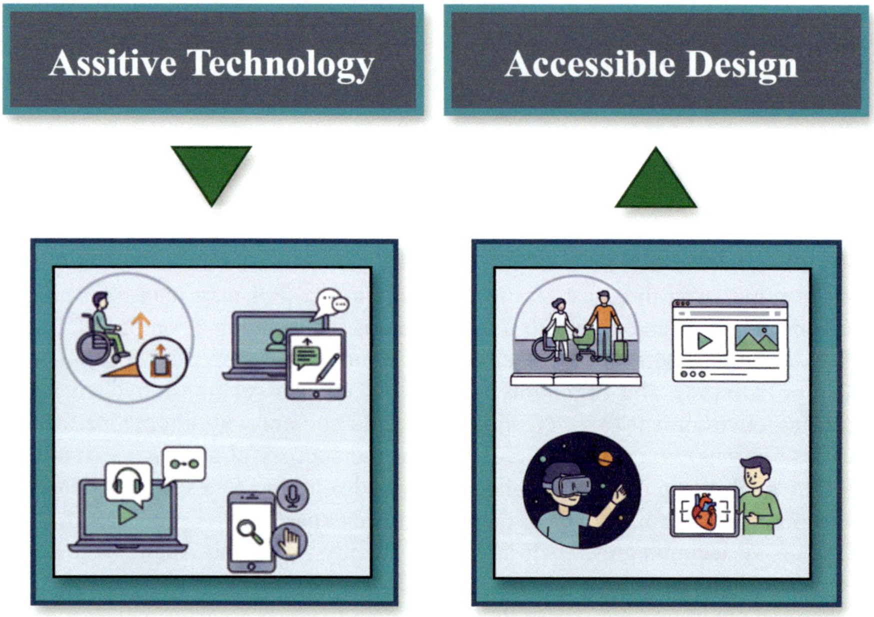

FIGURE 1.5 Assistive Technology and Accessible Design in fostering seamless inclusion within educational and digital environments.

tailored to individual student needs and enhance accessibility through tools that support diverse learners. For example, AI-powered applications can bridge language barriers via real-time translation, enabling multilingual student populations to engage more fully in educational content. Accessibility is further enhanced by assistive technologies, such as AI-driven writing assistants like Copilot, which have been shown to improve written communication and support productivity for neurodivergent individuals [64].

Nonetheless, the deployment of AI in educational settings raises critical ethical concerns. Issues surrounding data privacy, algorithmic bias, and the potential exacerbation of educational inequities demand careful attention and robust regulatory frameworks. As García-López and Trujillo-Liñán [64] noted, the integration of ethical AI requires transparency, fairness, and human oversight to prevent misuse and ensure inclusivity. Furthermore, institutions like the University of Toronto have pioneered regulated AI use models, deploying generative AI (GenAI) as a complementary support tool while safeguarding human judgment in evaluation processes.

To harness the benefits of AI while mitigating risks, educators and policymakers must emphasize digital literacy and ethical training, equipping students and teachers to critically engage with AI-generated content and understand its societal impact. This comprehensive, ethically aligned approach ensures AI enhances educational accessibility and equity without compromising students' rights and learning autonomy [65].

1.6 MEASURING WHAT MATTERS AND MOVING FORWARD

1.6.1 Metrics for Success

Evaluating the success of inclusive education necessitates moving beyond conventional outcome metrics such as graduation rates or standardized test scores. Instead, a more nuanced and holistic approach is required that captures the quality of the entire student experience. The "4Ps" framework serves as a valuable tool in this context. It provides a comprehensive lens to assess inclusive education practices by focusing on four critical dimensions: Presencc, Participation, Progress, and Placement.

"Presence" refers to students' physical and psychological attendance in the learning environment, emphasizing that students must be meaningfully present beyond mere enrollment. "Participation" highlights the importance of active engagement in classroom and school activities, ensuring all students have equitable opportunities to contribute and interact within inclusive settings. "Progress" focuses on learning growth, recognizing that success is not solely about reaching uniform benchmarks but individual academic and social development over time. Finally, "Placement" captures the affective domain, assessing how students feel included, valued, and respected within their educational communities. This dimension acknowledges that inclusion entails social and emotional integration, in addition to academic achievement [5, 66].

The 4Ps framework encourages educators and policymakers to adopt a systemic view of inclusion, embedding reflective practices, ongoing assessment, and continuous improvement strategies into educational programs to foster genuine inclusivity. By measuring these interconnected aspects, schools can better identify barriers, tailor supports, and create environments where all learners thrive.

1.6.2 Equity Audits and Continuous Improvement Cycles

Schools and districts can utilize equity audits to ensure that inclusive policies are implemented effectively and equitably. An equity audit provides an unbiased assessment of how a school meets the needs of all students by capturing "snapshots" of key areas, including classrooms, systems, public spaces, and print materials. The purpose of the audit is not to pass judgment but to serve as an observational tool for self-assessment [67]. The information gathered from an equity audit will be integrated into a school's continuous improvement plan. Applying an "equity lens" to this process means reframing the inquiry from a focus on student deficits to one that emphasizes systemic barriers. This approach requires a reflective process where teams examine their belief systems and challenge assumptions about the root causes of inequity. Focusing on "opportunity gaps" rather than "achievement gaps" aims to foster a long-term, systemic commitment to transformation, rather than a one-time conversation. This shift in mindset is critical for designing and implementing sustainable, just solutions for all learners [68].

1.7 CONCLUSION

This chapter reveals that inclusive education in the digital age represents a multifaceted and rapidly evolving discipline, marked most significantly by a philosophical shift from traditional integration models focused on physical presence to frameworks that emphasize authentic participation and belonging. This transformation is underpinned by a paradigmatic evolution from medical models seeking to remediate individual deficits to proactive design models systematically dismantling systemic barriers. To operationalize this new paradigm effectively, the field must embrace strategic implementation through four key classroom-ready approaches: reimagining assessment practices to prioritize authenticity through multimodal, project-based demonstrations of learning rooted in UDL principles; proactively designing instruction with UDL's three core principles of representation, action and expression, and engagement from the outset rather than reactively accommodating individual needs; leveraging technology as a foundational accessibility support through comprehensive captioning, screen-reader compatibility, and AI-assisted language translation; and fostering collaborative, data-driven mindsets that emphasize professional development, co-teaching models, continuous self-reflection, and fluid adjustment of supports within MTSS frameworks. These evidence-based strategies collectively represent a pathway toward truly inclusive educational environments that honor learner variability while maintaining high expectations for all students.

REFERENCES

1. Hornby, G., & Kauffman, J. M. (2024). Inclusive education, intellectual disabilities, and the demise of full inclusion. *Journal of Intelligence*, 12(2), 20–20. https://doi.org/10.3390/jintelligence12020020
2. Ainscow, M. (2020). Promoting inclusion and equity in education: Lessons from international experiences. *Nordic Journal of Studies in Educational Policy*, 6(1), 7–16. https://doi.org/10.1080/20020317.2020.1729587
3. Page, A., Anderson, J., & Charteris, J. (2024). Innovative learning environments and spaces of belonging for students with disability in mainstream settings. *Cambridge Journal of Education*, 54(5), 1–20. https://doi.org/10.1080/0305764x.2024.2397398
4. Rapp, A. C., & Corral-Granados, A. (2021). Understanding inclusive education: A theoretical contribution from system theory and the constructionist perspective. *International Journal of Inclusive Education*, 28(4), 1–17.
5. Inclusive Education Pathways to Inclusion and Equity: Disability Inclusion in Education, The World Bank, (2024). https://documents1.worldbank.org/curated/en/099120224164032400/pdf/P1775501b437210b1192fa1a44228402297.pdf
6. Long, T., & Guo, J. (2023). Moving beyond inclusion to belonging. *International Journal of Environmental Research and Public Health*, 20(20), 6907–6907. https://doi.org/10.3390/ijerph20206907
7. Alesech, J., & Nayar, S. (2020). Acceptance and belonging in New Zealand: Understanding inclusion for children with special education needs. *International Journal of Whole Schooling*, 16(1), 84–116. https://files.eric.ed.gov/fulltext/EJ1258467.pdf
8. Jardinez, M. J., & Natividad, L. R. (2024). The advantages and challenges of inclusive education: Striving for equity in the classroom. *Shanlax International Journal of Education*, 12(2), 57–65. https://doi.org/10.34293/education.v12i2.7182
9. Building Equity Through MICIP: A Toolkit to Support Continuous Improvement Leaders, Facilitators, and Team Members. (2022). https://www.michigan.gov/mde/-/media/Project/Websites/mde/MICIP/Resources/MICIP_Equity_Toolkit.pdf?rev=32030bce29ec4816b1cc5b08a546ae3f&hash=B67C6C5CA837AD6D9439563FA3CE3A9E

10. Jain, N. R., & Alwazzan, L. (2024). What's your experience?: A duoethnographic dialogue to advance disability inclusion in medical education. *Medical Education*. https://doi.org/10.1111/medu.15450
11. Adam, S., & Koutsoklenis, A. (2023). Who needs the social model of disability? *Frontiers in Sociology*, 8, 1305301. https://doi.org/10.3389/fsoc.2023.1305301
12. Lawson, A., & Beckett, A. E. (2020). The social and human rights models of disability: Towards a complementarity thesis. *The International Journal of Human Rights*, 25(2), 348–379. https://doi.org/10.1080/13642987.2020.1783533
13. Catama, B. V. (2025). Universal design for learning in action: Exploring strategies, outcomes, and challenges in inclusive education. *International Journal of Rehabilitation and Special Education (IJRSE)*, 5(2), 6–12.
14. Almeqdad, Q. I., Alodat, A. M., Alquraan, M. F., Mohaidat, M. A., & Al-Makhzoomy, A. K. (2023). The effectiveness of universal design for learning: A systematic review of the literature and meta-analysis. *Cogent Education*, 10(1). https://doi.org/10.1080/2331186x.2023.2218191
15. TSI - Shaping Inclusive Education: Combatting Disparities in Italy, Portugal, and Spain|Inclusive Education Initiative. (2025, May 21). Inclusive-Education-Initiative.org. https://www.inclusive-education-initiative.org/index.php/knowledge-repository/tsi-shaping-inclusive-education-combatting-disparities-italy-portugal-and
16. Edström, K., Gardelli, V., & Backman, Y. (2022). Inclusion as participation: Mapping the participation model with four different levels of inclusive education. *International Journal of Inclusive Education*, 28(12), 1–18. https://doi.org/10.1080/13603116.2022.2136773
17. Wang, L., Luedtke, L., Malet, R., & Malinen, O.-P. (2025). Can separate special education settings still be perceived as inclusive? A critical examination of Finnish primary teachers' attitudes. *Teaching and Teacher Education*, 155, 104914. https://doi.org/10.1016/j.tate.2024.104914
18. Logee, K., & Blais, C. (2023). The pull-out model in special education: The social and emotional effect on students. https://annamaria.edu/wp-content/uploads/2024/02/Katie-Logee-Spring-2023.pdf
19. Qu, X. (2020). A critical realist model of inclusive education for children with special educational needs and/or disabilities. *International Journal of Inclusive Education*, 26(10), 1–15. https://doi.org/10.1080/13603116.2020.1760366
20. Mainstreaming report 2025. (2025). University of Dundee. https://www.dundee.ac.uk/corporate-information/mainstreaming-report-2025
21. Ahrbeck, B., & Felder, M. (2020). Analysis of barriers to inclusive schools in Germany: Why special education is necessary and not evil. *Education Sciences*, 10(12), 358.
22. Organisation for Economic Co-operation and Development. (2023). *Equity and inclusion in education: Finding strength through diversity*. Paris: OECD Publishing. https://www.oecd-ilibrary.org/education/equity-and-inclusion-in-education_e9072e21-en
23. World Bank. (2025, March 31). Inclusive Education. World Bank. https://www.worldbank.org/en/topic/education/brief/inclusive-education
24. Gal, C., Ryder, C. H., Amsalem, S. R., & On, O. (2025). Shaping inclusive classrooms: Key factors influencing teachers' attitudes toward inclusion of students with special needs. *Education Sciences*, 15(5), 541–541. https://doi.org/10.3390/educsci15050541
25. Paliwal, M., & Singh, A. (2021). Teacher readiness for online teaching-learning during COVID–19 outbreak: A study of Indian higher education institutions. *Interactive Technology and Smart Education*, 18(3), 403–421. https://doi.org/10.1108/itse-07-2020-0118

26. Kleinlein, E. (2025). Conceptualising inclusive assessment: A critical literature review at the nexus of education, inclusion, and assessment. *European Journal of Special Needs Education*, 1–20. https://doi.org/10.1080/08856257.2025.2500137
27. Phelan, D., Maguire, H., & Finnegan, C. (2025). Scoping review of universal design for learning principles embedded in subjects in secondary education. *European Journal of Education*, 60(1). https://doi.org/10.1111/ejed.70016
28. Navas-Bonilla, C., Guerra-Arango, J. A., Oviedo-Guado, D. A., & Murillo-Noriega, D. E. (2025). Inclusive education through technology: A systematic review of types, tools and characteristics. *Frontiers in Education*, 10. https://doi.org/10.3389/feduc.2025.1527851
29. Buckingham, L. R., López-Hernández, A., & Strotmann, B. (2021, December). Learning by comparison: The benefits of co-teaching for university professors' professional development. In *Frontiers in education* (Vol. 6, p. 776991). Frontiers Media SA.
30. Dunajeva, J. (n.d.). Comparative study of inclusive education practices: the cases of Uzbekistan, Tajikistan, Moldova, Kyrgyzstan and Georgia. https://www.gpekix.org/sites/default/files/2025-02/kix-emap-comparative-study-on-inclusive-education-practices-the-cases-of-uzbekistan-tajikistan-moldova-kyrgyzstan-and-georgia.pdf
31. Vance-Chalcraft, H. D., Smith, K. C., Allen, J., Bowser, G., Cooper, C. B., Jelks, N. T. O., Karl, C., Kodner, R., & Laslo, M. (2024). Social justice, community engagement, and undergraduate STEM education: Participatory science as a teaching tool. *CBE Life Sciences Education*, 23(2). https://doi.org/10.1187/cbe.23-06-0123
32. Dawson, E., Bista, R., Colborne, A., McCubbin, B., Godec, S., Patel, U., Archer, L., & Mau, A. (2024). Inclusion for STEM, the institution, or minoritized youth? Exploring how educators navigate the discourses that shape social justice in informal science learning practices. *Science Education*, 108(3). https://doi.org/10.1002/sce.21856
33. Duncan, V. L., Holt, E. A., & Keenan, S. M. (2023). Creating an equitable and inclusive STEM classroom: A qualitative meta-synthesis of approaches and practices in higher education. *Frontiers in Education*, 8. https://doi.org/10.3389/feduc.2023.1154652
34. Galvez, G., Killilea, D. W., Berry, S., Narayanaswami, V., & Fung, E. B. (2024). Increasing STEM skills, knowledge and interest among diverse students: Results from an intensive summer research program at the University of California, San Francisco. *Innovative Higher Education*, 49(4), 645–664. https://doi.org/10.1007/s10755-024-09701-z
35. Coleman, A. (2020). D-STEM equity model: Diversifying the STEM education to career pathway. *Athens Journal of Education*, 7(3), 273–296. https://doi.org/10.30958/aje.7-3-3
36. Sansing-Helton, B., Coover, G., & Benton, C. E. (2021). Increasing STEM transfer readiness among underrepresented minoritized two-year college students: Examining course-taking patterns, experiences, and interventions. *Frontiers in Education*, 6. https://doi.org/10.3389/feduc.2021.667091
37. Kunwar, R., & Adhikari, S. (2023). An exploration of the conceptualization, guiding principles, and theoretical perspectives of inclusive curriculum. *Journal of Contemporary Research in Social Sciences*, 5(1), 1–13. https://doi.org/10.55214/26410249.v5i1.217
38. Han, C., & Lei, J. (2024). Teachers' and students' beliefs towards universal design for learning framework: A scoping review. *SAGE Open*, 14(3). https://doi.org/10.1177/21582440241272032
39. Ayeni, O. O., Hamad, N. M. A., Chisom, O. N., Osawaru, B., & Adewusi, O. E. (2024). AI in education: A review of personalized learning and educational technology. *GSC Advanced Research and Reviews*, 18(2), 261–271. https://doi.org/10.30574/gscarr.2024.18.2.0062
40. Yang, C., Wang, T., & Xiu, Q. (2025). Towards a sustainable future in education: A systematic review and framework for inclusive education. *Sustainability*, 17(9), 3837. https://doi.org/10.3390/su17093837

41. Ingavélez-Guerra, P., Robles-Bykbaev, V. E., Pérez-Muñoz, A., Hilera-González, J., & Otón-Tortosa, S. (2022). Automatic adaptation of open educational resources: An approach from a multilevel methodology based on students' preferences, educational special needs, artificial intelligence, and accessibility metadata. *IEEE Access*, 10, 9703–9716. https://doi.org/10.1109/ACCESS.2021.3139537
42. Lythreatis, S., El-Kassar, A.-N., & Singh, S. K. (2022). The digital divide: A review and future research Agenda. *Technological Forecasting and Social Change*, 175(121359), 121359. https://doi.org/10.1016/j.techfore.2021.121359
43. Afzal, A., Khan, S., Daud, S., Ahmad, Z., & Butt, A. (2023). Addressing the digital divide: Access and use of technology in education. *Journal of Social Sciences Review*, 3(2), 883–895. https://doi.org/10.54183/jssr.v3i2.326
44. Hollimon, L. A., Taylor, K. V., Fiegenbaum, R., Carrasco, M., Gomez, L. G., Chung, D., & Seixas, A. A. (2025). Redefining and solving the digital divide and exclusion to improve healthcare: Going beyond access to include availability, adequacy, acceptability, and affordability. *Frontiers in Digital Health*, 7. https://doi.org/10.3389/fdgth.2025.1508686
45. Vianney, H., & Olivier, M. (2022). Teaching and learning barriers in inclusive education for physically impaired students and their academic performance in selected secondary schools in Rwanda: a case in Bugesera District. *Journal of Education*, 5(1), 97–129. https://doi.org/10.53819/81018102t6008
46. Sama, A., & Gul, H. (2024). Inclusion of students with disabilities in mainstream classrooms: Challenges and strategies post COVID-19. *Al-Aijaz Research Journal of Islamic Studies & Humanities*, 8(3), 40–44.
47. Okoye, K., Hussein, H., Arrona-Palacios, A., Quintero, H. N., Ortega, L. O. P., Sanchez, A. L., Ortiz, E. A., Escamilla, J., & Hosseini, S. (2022). Impact of digital technologies upon teaching and learning in higher education in Latin America: An outlook on the reach, barriers, and bottlenecks. *Education and Information Technologies*, 28. https://doi.org/10.1007/s10639-022-11214-1
48. Kearney, C. A., Fensken, M., & Dupont, R. (2025). Implementing multi-tiered systems of support in rural schools: A practice perspective for improving mental health care for underserved youths. *Frontiers in Education*, 10. https://doi.org/10.3389/feduc.2025.1553528
49. Collins, A. B. (2025). Evaluating the effectiveness of Multi-Tiered System of Supports (MTSS) Tier 2 reading intervention in a middle school setting. *Western CEDAR*. https://cedar.wwu.edu/wwuet/1371/
50. Nitz, J., Brack, F., Hertel, S., Krull, J., Stephan, H., Hennemann, T., & Hanisch, C. (2023). Multi-tiered systems of support with focus on behavioral modification in elementary schools: A systematic review. *Heliyon*, 9(6). https://doi.org/10.1016/j.heliyon.2023.e17506
51. Bain, K. (2023). Inclusive assessment in higher education: What does the literature tells us on how to define and design inclusive assessments? *Journal of Learning Development in Higher Education*, 27. https://doi.org/10.47408/jldhe.vi27.1014
52. UCD Assessment for Inclusion Framework. (2019). www.ucd.ie. https://www.ucd.ie/teaching/resources/inclusiveandinterculturallearning/ucdassessmentforinclusionframework/
53. University of Oxford. (2024). IncludED: A guide to designing inclusive assessments. www.ctl.ox.ac.uk. https://www.ctl.ox.ac.uk/included-designing-inclusive-assessments
54. Vlachopoulos, D., & Makri, A. (2024). A systematic literature review on authentic assessment in higher education: Best practices for the development of 21st century skills, and policy considerations. *Studies in Educational Evaluation*, 83(101425), 101425–101425. https://doi.org/10.1016/j.stueduc.2024.101425

55. Archer, M., Morley, D. A., & Souppez, J.-B. R. G. (2020). Real world learning and authentic assessment. *Applied Pedagogies for Higher Education*, 323–341. https://doi.org/10.1007/978-3-030-46951-1_14
56. Quintero, C. (2020). A review: Accessible technology through participatory design. *Disability and Rehabilitation: Assistive Technology*, 17(4), 1–7. https://doi.org/10.1080/17483107.2020.1785564
57. Oyedokun, T. T. (2024). Assistive technology and accessibility tools in enhancing adaptive education. *Advances in Educational Technologies and Instructional Design Book Series*, 125–162. https://doi.org/10.4018/979-8-3693-8227-1.ch006
58. Mukhtarkyzy, K., Smagulova, L., Tokzhigitova, A., Serikbayeva, N., Sayakov, O., Turkmenbayev, A., & Assilbayeva, R. (2025). A systematic review of the utility of assistive technologies for SEND students in schools. *Frontiers in Education*, 10. https://doi.org/10.3389/feduc.2025.1523797
59. Haleem, A., Javaid, M., Qadri, M. A., & Suman, R. (2022). Understanding the role of digital technologies in education: A review. *Sustainable Operations and Computers*, 3(1), 275–285. https://doi.org/10.1016/j.susoc.2022.05.004
60. Chițu, I. B., Tecău, A. S., Constantin, C. P., Tescaşiu, B., Brătucu, T.-O., Brătucu, G., & Purcaru, I.-M. (2023). Exploring the opportunity to use virtual reality for the education of children with disabilities. *Children*, 10(3), 436. https://doi.org/10.3390/children10030436
61. AlRawi, J. M., & AlKahtani, M. A. (2021). Universal design for learning for educating students with intellectual disabilities: A systematic review. *International Journal of Developmental Disabilities*, 68(6), 1–9. https://doi.org/10.1080/20473869.2021.1900505
62. O'Neill, J. L. (2021). Accessibility for all abilities: How universal design, universal design for learning, and inclusive design combat inaccessibility and ableism. *Journal of Open Access to Law*, 9(1), 15–15. https://ojs.law.cornell.edu/index.php/joal/article/view/107
63. Nielsen, A. F., & Landa-Mata, I. (2025). Expanding the understanding of universal design beyond technical solutions and physical environment: 8 policy intervention areas. *Transport Policy*, 167, 157–177. https://doi.org/10.1016/j.tranpol.2025.03.028
64. García-López, I. M., & Trujillo-Liñán, L. (2025). Ethical and regulatory challenges of Generative AI in education: A systematic review. *Frontiers in Education*, 10. https://doi.org/10.3389/feduc.2025.1565938
65. Wiese, L. J., Patil, I., Schiff, D. S., & Magana, A. J. (2025). AI ethics education: A systematic literature review. *Computers and Education Artificial Intelligence*, 8, 100405–100405. https://doi.org/10.1016/j.caeai.2025.100405
66. Niall, M., McCormack, O., & O'Flaherty, J. (2024). The 4 P's of enactment: Purpose, praxis, problems, and policy lessons from a framework on ethos. *Leadership and Policy in Schools*, 1–17. https://doi.org/10.1080/15700763.2024.2405964
67. Butera, B. J. (2025). Equity audits as catalysts for change: A case study on racial disparities in a university Spanish language program. *Journal of Language Identity & Education*, 1–19. https://doi.org/10.1080/15348458.2025.2546403
68. Jones Roberson, J. (2023). Beyond evaluation: Using equity audits for advanced-level programs. *Gifted Child Today*, 46(2), 119–127. https://doi.org/10.1177/10762175221149442

2 Artificial Intelligence for Inclusive STEM Education

2.1 INTRODUCTION

According to the latest United Nations Conference on Trade and Development (UNCTAD) report (2025), the global AI market will expand 25-fold within a decade (from 189 billion USD in 2023 to 4.8 trillion USD by 2033) [1]. Therefore, trustworthy, transparent, and responsible AI solutions will penetrate the entire population, society, and economy. One of the key domains that AI is expected to impact is the education sector. AI will support policymakers in creating better education platforms for teachers, learners, and parents. This intervention can significantly change the landscape of education and research.

Inclusive education aims to provide equal and fair access to learning resources, ensuring that all learners have equal opportunities to fulfill their educational needs. Learners have diverse needs and varying physical and cognitive abilities. Furthermore, learners can come from different socioeconomic backgrounds. Therefore, catering to a diverse learning community in education is a significant challenge. This requires considerable investments in humans and other physical resources, which is not always possible in certain situations. The advancement in ML and AI technologies could provide inclusive education opportunities for learners by identifying their needs and giving adaptive solutions. This chapter elaborates on such opportunities as discussed in this section. STEM education stands to gain immensely from advancements in AI, particularly GenAI and Large Language Models (LLMs). Figure 2.1 illustrates potential opportunities for achieving inclusive education through AI- and ML-based solutions and applications.

As illustrated in Figure 2.1, AI and ML can immensely support inclusive education by providing personalized learning experiences. For instance, this can be in the form of personalized learning platforms or intelligent tutoring systems. Since students' abilities and needs are diverse, personalized education platforms supported by AI and ML will provide learners with adaptive or customized learning opportunities.

AI-powered ATs can play a significant role in inclusive education. For instance, simple tools such as speech-to-text (STT) and text-to-speech (TTS) can help learners in mainstream education and special educational settings that support Special Educational Needs (SENs). Furthermore, this is useful for learners who require Augmentative and Alternative Communication (AAC). AAC refers to various methods of communication that can supplement or compensate (either temporarily or permanently) for the impairments and disabilities associated with individuals with severe expressive communication disorders [2].

DOI: 10.1201/9781003641490-2

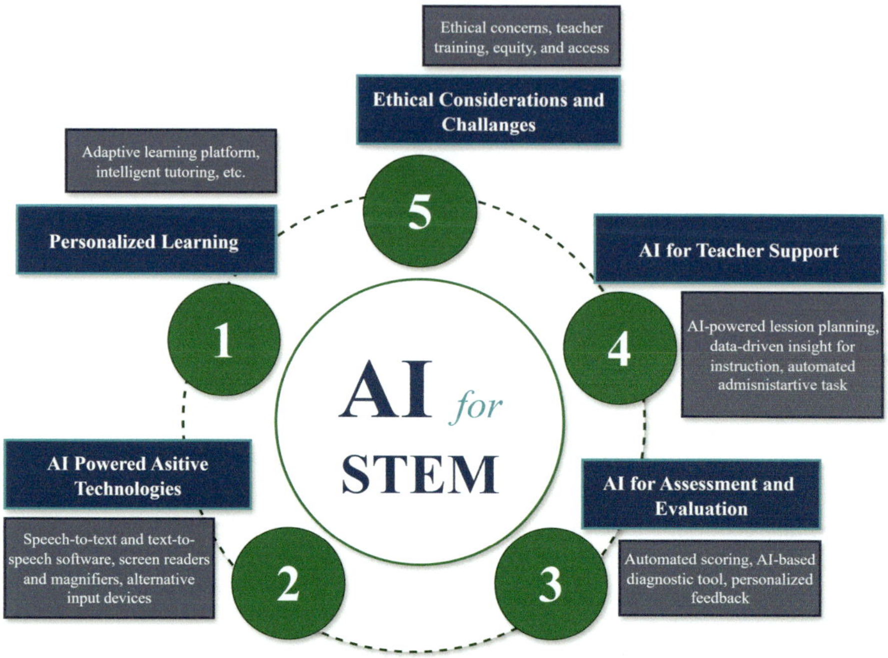

FIGURE 2.1 The AI methodologies for inclusive education.

AI for assessment and feedback is another key usage of AI in inclusive education. This provides the required support for teachers to use their valuable time on critical aspects rather than marking students' exams and assignments. Furthermore, this can help identify knowledge and skills gaps in students, allowing teachers to make the necessary interventions. This is particularly useful when learners have a disability or SENs background. Providing personalized feedback on assessments to individuals consumes a significant amount of time. Therefore, feedback often tends to be more general and not specific to an individual's performance. AI and ML can support this case by providing personalized feedback to improve performance. Personalized feedback is a key aspect of student-centered learning. Therefore, improvements to accurate, timely, customized feedback would be instrumental in the education ecosystem.

AI-powered teacher support is another crucial aspect of AI-supported inclusive education practices. This includes AI-driven lesson planning, administrative tasks, and data-driven insights to make crucial decisions. These applications and tools will significantly reduce the administrative workload of teachers while also enabling data-informed decision-making on student performance, attendance, and achievements. These AI systems can flag student behaviors and achievements to make timely interventions.

Although AI methodologies can significantly support inclusive education, several challenges must be overcome. The first is the accessibility of AI tools for learners; for example, learners should have the required hardware, software, Internet connection, and digital literacy. Therefore, when deploying AI-enabled processes, decision-makers should ensure that learners have sufficient resources to utilize the AI tools and applications fully. For example, special care should be taken when deploying AI interventions in areas of digital poverty and low digital literacy. Then the required outcomes would not be able to achieve the set objectives of AI-enabled educational and learning tools [3].

Another key concern is the use of Blackbox AI models and tools.[1] To avoid bias and minimize any violation of personal rights related to AI, deployed solutions should be transparent, trustworthy, and responsible. The new demand for responsible AI solutions would pave the way for more transparent AI solutions in inclusive education. This is paramount when dealing with learners from disabled and SEN backgrounds. Special care should be taken to minimize any impact on learners, carers, and parents. For instance, a Data Protection Impact Assessment (DPIA) can be carried out when processing learners' personal data to provide personalized support.

2.2 GENERATIVE ARTIFICIAL INTELLIGENCE FOR STEM

GenAI is the broad effort to build systems that perform tasks requiring human-like perception, reasoning, and decision-making. ML within AI focuses on algorithms that learn patterns from data, rather than following handcrafted rules. GenAI is a rapidly evolving subset of ML that produces text, images, code, and audio. Today's GenAI systems are typically foundation models: huge, pre-trained models that can be adapted to many downstream uses with minimal additional data. LLMs are the text-centric branch of this family, optimized for reading, writing, and reasoning over language. Most leading LLMs use transformer architectures, which excel at representing long-range relationships and can be scaled efficiently across massive datasets [3]. As shown in Figure 2.2, GenAI is best understood as a nested subset within the broader AI landscape. The diagram depicts AI as the widest umbrella, within which ML resides; GenAI is then presented as a further specialization of ML focused on creating new content (e.g., text, code, images, molecular structures). Within GenAI, the figure highlights foundation models as large, general-purpose models trained on broad data, and identifies LLMs as a prominent class of foundation models tailored for language-based tasks. At the core, transformers are shown as a key model architecture underpinning many modern LLMs, emphasizing how contemporary GenAI capabilities used across STEM applications commonly build from transformer-based foundation-model approaches.

GenAI for STEM sits at the intersection of language, vision, code, and speech, so an effective methodology begins by choosing among complementary model families and then composing them into reliable classroom workflows. General-purpose LLMs, such as GPT-4o, Claude 3.5 Sonnet, Gemini 1.5 Pro, and strong open models like Llama 3, Mistral Large/Mixtral, Qwen2, and Phi-3, form the backbone for explanation, hinting, and formative dialogue because they support stepwise reasoning, Socratic questioning, and rubric-aligned feedback. Multimodal LLMs extend this to text-vision (and sometimes audio), allowing students and teachers to interrogate a free-body diagram, a geometry proof sketch, or a residual plot from a regression; the model can describe what it "sees," flag missing forces or mislabeled axes, and

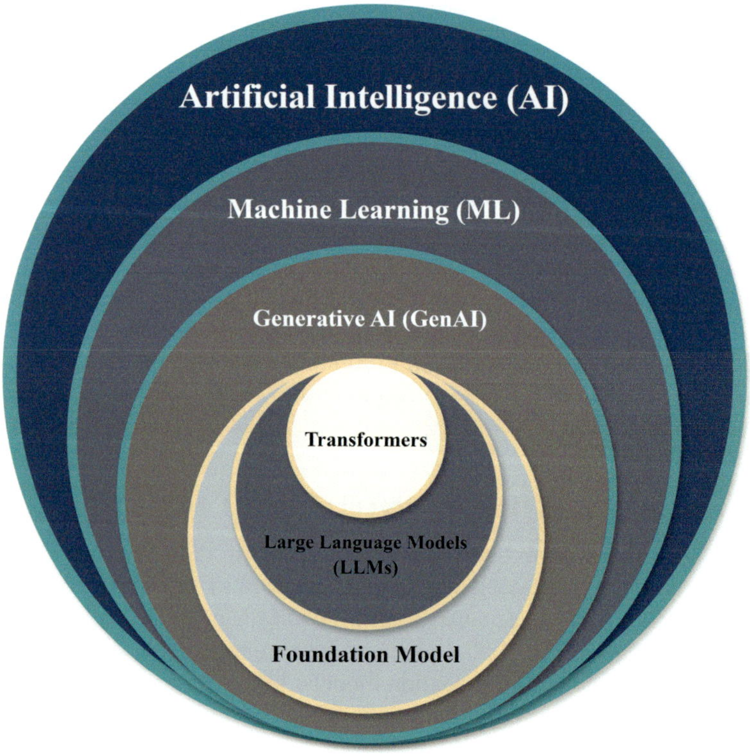

FIGURE 2.2 Concentric relationship among AI, ML, GenAI, foundation models, LLMs, and transformers.

Source: user-provided diagram.

connect visual evidence to symbolic manipulations. Code-specialized LLMs, Code Llama, StarCoder2, DeepSeek-Coder, Codestral, shine whenever practice becomes computation: they draft starter simulations, write testable helper functions, scaffold notebooks, and debug student code while narrating fixes. Vision and diffusion models (Stable Diffusion XL, DALL·E 3, Midjourney), paired with grounding models like CLIP or BLIP-2, generate or interpret visuals that make abstractions concrete, such as clean apparatus diagrams, consistent molecule renderings, or alternative representations aligned with the principles of UDL. Speech models round out the toolkit: Whisper for transcription, modern TTS for accessible read-aloud and multilingual delivery, and speech-to-speech systems such as SeamlessM4T for mixed-language classrooms [4, 5]. For mathematically sensitive tasks, such as math-aware or tool-augmented setups, Minerva-style training, or LLMs wired to a circuits and systems (CAS), units library, or high-precision calculator, preserving exactness is crucial. With these families in view, map tasks to capabilities: use text LLMs for explanations and feedback; multimodal LLMs for diagram critique and data-plot reading; code LLMs for autograding and simulation; diffusion/vision models for STEM visuals; and speech models for accessibility and multilingual equity.

2.2.1 Model Families and When to Use Them

General-purpose LLMs are the backbone for explanation, hinting, and formative dialogue. They handle step-wise reasoning, Socratic questioning, and rubric-aligned feedback across various STEM topics. Multimodal LLMs extend this to text-vision (and sometimes audio) tasks, allowing questions about free-body diagrams, geometry proof sketches, or statistical plots. The model can describe what it "sees," point out missing forces or mislabeled axes, and connect visual evidence to symbolic manipulations.

Code-specialized LLMs, such as Code Llama, StarCoder2, DeepSeek-Coder, and Codestral, become central whenever STEM practice becomes computation. They generate starter simulations, write testable helper functions, scaffold notebooks, and debug student programs while narrating the fix. Vision and diffusion models (Stable Diffusion XL, DALL·E 3, Midjourney), paired with grounding models like CLIP or BLIP-2, create or interpret visuals that make abstract content concrete: crisp apparatus diagrams, molecule renderings with consistent conventions, or alternative representations of the same concept for UDL [3, 4]. Speech models complete the toolset: Whisper for transcription, modern TTS for accessible read-aloud and multilingual delivery, and speech-to-speech translators such as SeamlessM4T for mixed-language classrooms. For mathematically sensitive tasks, math-aware or tool-augmented approaches, Minerva-style training, or LLMs wired to a CAS, units library, or high-precision calculator, help enforce exactness.

2.2.2 Core Usage Patterns in STEM

Across the curriculum, several usage patterns recur. Retrieval-augmented generation (RAG) grounds responses in your syllabus, lab manuals, and policy documents. Hence, the model cites the exact lab safety clause or the specific rubric language, rather than inventing a generic rule. Tool use and lightweight "agents" enable an LLM to call an application programming interface (API): evaluate an integral with a CAS, run a quick Python snippet against teacher-provided tests, generate a plot, or verify units; the LLM remains the orchestrator, while external tools deliver correctness.

Item and dataset generation scales practice without repetition; the model can produce isomorphic problems at controlled difficulty, vary parameters to promote transfer, or synthesize clean, labeled datasets for statistics labs, always paired with worked solutions that model sound reasoning. Feedback co-pilots draft rubric-aligned comments that a teacher approves ("human-in-the-loop"), so turnaround is faster, but instructional judgment stays with the educator. Simulation scaffolding is a high-leverage pattern: a code LLM emits a skeleton with docstrings and "TODO"s, then explains failing tests so that students learn by iterating. Similarly, for data analysis, the model proposes hypotheses, plots, and checks, but students run and critique them.

2.2.3 STEM-Specific Evolution and Reliability

Reliable classroom use depends on evaluation, risk management, and concrete subject-level patterns that show what "good" looks like. For technical quality, consider benchmarks that stress STEM reasoning and code, such as MMLU-STEM for broad knowledge, GSM8K and MATH for stepwise arithmetic and proof-style reasoning, GPQA for graduate-level science and philosophy questions, HumanEval/MBPP for code generation, and software engineering (SWE)-bench for repository-level software tasks. Benchmarks are only a starting line; your instructional evaluation should measure didactic quality and safety at once: does the model's explanation align with your rubric (clarity, correctness, scaffolding, and misconception detection)? Are diagrams described accurately with units and uncertainty noted? Do code suggestions compile, pass the provided tests, and adhere to the course style guides?

Build small, renewable test sets from past assignments and lab prompts; require structured outputs (e.g., JSON with fields for "Claim," "Evidence citations," "Units check," "Next-step hint") so you can auto-score aspects like citation presence and unit consistency. Guard against hallucinations by forcing retrieval with inline citations, adding solver checks (CAS, unit libraries, numerical verifiers), and rejecting outputs that fail validation ("self-consistency" or majority voting can help). For fairness and accessibility, audit across student subgroups: are hints equally specific, language similarly plain, and reading levels adjustable? Log refusals and edge cases to improve prompts and content filters.

2.2.4 Subject-Specific Cases

This section explores how AI-enhanced tools integrate with disciplinary practices in physics, chemistry, mathematics, and computer science.

- **Physics**: In a forces unit, students upload a photo of a lab setup; a multimodal LLM identifies masses, pulleys, and angles, sketches a free-body diagram, and uses a CAS tool to derive tensions with uncertainty from measured lengths, then generates targeted hints if a student's work omits friction.
- **Chemistry**: Diffusion/vision tools render standardized glassware arrangements and hazard icons; an LLM reads a lab protocol from your RAG index and produces a pre-lab checklist with PPE, waste disposal, and error-reduction tips; during lab, Whisper transcribes observations and the model converts them into balanced equations and qualitative versus quantitative notes.
- **Mathematics**: A code LLM emits unit-tested functions for sampling distributions; when tests fail, the model explains the mismatch, prompting students to reason about variance and bias; the text LLM offers layered hints for proofs ("consider contrapositive"), always requiring explicit justification for each step.
- **Computer Science**: An autograder wraps a code LLM with a fixed test suite; the model proposes feedback tied to the rubric, but release requires teacher approval for fairness; students can query the model with error messages, and the system refuses to hand over complete solutions when the assignment is still open.

2.3 OPERATIONALIZING ARTIFICIAL INTELLIGENCE IN STEM

2.3.1 Artificial Intelligence–Powered Assistive Technologies

AI-powered ATs are one of AI's key developments and successes in inclusive education. AT is an umbrella term encompassing assistive products, their related systems, and services. AT is of fundamental importance for people with permanent or temporary functional difficulties as it improves their functional ability and enables and enhances their participation and inclusion in all domains of life. Assistive products may be digital, in the form of software and apps that support interpersonal communication, access to information, daily time management, rehabilitation, education, and training. ATs, whether in software or hardware, are widely used in education and training. This includes technologies for those in mainstream education and special educational setups supporting SENs. Tools and applications such as STT or TTS are standard AI-enabled educational tools. These tools are widely used in accessibility, voice assistants, and dictation software. Some standard STT tools include Apple Dictation, Windows Speech Recognition, Google Docs Voice Typing, and Dragon by Nuance, which are used for dictation, transcription of audio and video content, accessibility features, and voice commands. Most of these tools are freely available and effective for longer texts. The background noise and accents can affect the accuracy of these tools, and some may require longer training times. On the other hand, TTS technologies are helpful for learners with visual impairments and learning difficulties. This is also beneficial for creating audio versions of documents and websites for educational purposes. Some widely used TTS tools include NaturalReader, Speechify, and Amazon Polly. The quality of synthesized voices can vary and often sound robotic and unnatural. On the other hand, these tools make content more accessible and can improve reading comprehension and focus. These are also useful in creating audiobooks and podcasts.

ATs are helpful for learners who require AAC.[2] AAC describes multiple ways to communicate that can supplement or compensate (either temporarily or permanently) for the impairment and disability patterns of individuals with severe expressive communication disorders. A recent report by the United Nations Educational, Scientific, and Cultural Organization (UNESCO) titled "*Innovative Technologies for Inclusive Education-A Review of Best Practices from Global Resource Centers*" highlights the use of new technologies such as AI and information communication technology (ICT) to improve access to education for children, youth, and adults from SEN and disability backgrounds [12]. This report presents several case studies that demonstrate how the joint efforts of researchers, professionals, educators, teachers, learners with disabilities, and parents are working together to improve educational accessibility and create inclusive learning environments. New technologies, such as AI, have enabled practitioners to break down barriers and create personalized learning experiences by providing a more accessible, equitable, and customizable learning environment. This study also highlights the challenges for inclusive education, including accessibility, affordability, and digital literacy. The case studies presented in this report demonstrate how AAC systems (e.g., specialized communication software) improve engagement and social participation for learners with severe disabilities. Furthermore, this emphasizes the importance of personalized and adaptable learning environments, guided by frameworks such as UDL and Student, Environment, Tasks, and Tools (SETT) [12]. One of the key case studies highlighted in this report discusses the use of technology for AAC systems by an organization (i.e., Asociación en Defensa del Infante Neurológico [AEDIN]) in Argentina. The primary beneficiaries of AEDIN are children and adolescents aged 3–21, their parents, and carers. The center engages learners with a wide range of disabilities and SEN, including physical and intellectual disability, Autism Spectrum Disorder (ASD),[3] specific language impairment (SLI), genetic syndromes, and cortical visual impairments.

AEDIN deploys the UDL framework and the SETT framework as pedagogic strategies to integrate AI and ICT into learning and teaching in mainstream schools. Furthermore, to provide better access for differently able learners, AEDIN uses a variety of AT and AAC hardware and software, including special/adapted keyboards, eye-gaze systems, AAC software, and simple communication devices such as AbleNet speech devices. According to the report, these tools help the assessment process to understand students' needs and capabilities effectively. Furthermore, AEDIN has utilized HelpKidzLearn, a software suite designed for young children and students with learning difficulties. These tools have helped the teachers understand whether a child knows cause-and-effect relationships between two events (a fundamental skill for using AT) when playing a simple game with eye tracking.

According to a World Health Organization (WHO) report published in [13], globally, at least 2.2 billion people have near or distance vision impairment, with 43 million being blind. Learners with visual impairment will struggle with conventional education support and technologies. For example, accessing printed material for them will be a significant challenge. Integrating AI and ML technologies has significantly increased accessibility for visually impaired learners. AI-enhanced screen readers and magnifiers enhance the functionality of these tools, making digital STEM content more accessible to students with visual impairments. Furthermore, AI can improve the accuracy of screen readers by recognizing and interpreting complex STEM notations and diagrams. Authors in [14] presented an AI-enabled smart reader as an assistive tool for visually impaired learners. This smart reader application integrates OCR and TTS technologies to convert printed documents into spoken language. The results of this study demonstrate that the proposed approach significantly enhances access to written information, thereby improving the quality of life for individuals with visual impairments. The web-based image-to-text-to-speech tool proposed in [15] utilizes OCR and TTS technologies to convert images in printed materials into speech. The results in this study show improved accessibility for visually impaired learners through the proposed intervention.

AI-enabled alternative input devices, such as eye trackers or voice recognition systems, can help students with physical disabilities interact with STEM software and tools. Eye tracking can be effectively used to support learners with special needs. The studies show that eye tracking can significantly improve mathematics skills, social communication, motor learning, language development, and eyesight improvement, among other benefits [16]. Therefore, using eye trackers integrated with AI can be utilized as an AT for learning platforms and setups supporting learners with SEN.

Like eye-tracking devices, voice recognition systems (e.g., voice instructions) can play a significant role in inclusive education, especially for visually impaired students. The study presented in [17] demonstrates that accessibility for information and instructions can be significantly increased using voice instructions, as was experimented with 50 learners. The challenges, such as counting instruction, social life, mental well-being, physical well-being, relaxation exercises, and career chances for visually impaired learners, can be overcome through AT underpinned by voice recognition systems. This study also highlights the requirement of these tools in different native languages for them to be widely used.

2.3.2 Artificial Intelligence for Assessment and Evaluation

Assessment is the key to measuring the achievement of LOs. AI methodologies can be applied in various areas of inclusive education, including the creation of authentic assessments, automated assessment and grading, the diagnosis of learners' misconceptions and knowledge gaps, and the provision of personalized feedback. In summary, *Automated Assessment, Diagnostic Tools, and Personalized Feedback* are the wider usages that can be realized through AI methodologies.

Creating authentic and inclusive assessments is crucial for providing a platform that enables learners to demonstrate their understanding of the subject's knowledge and skills, regardless of their cognitive and physical abilities. Designing inclusive assessments aims to proactively reduce the likelihood of students being excluded, overlooked, and disaffected through the approaches used for assessment [18]. These can include a range of assessment tasks (e.g., exams, assignments, presentations), the conditions in which the assessments are conducted (e.g., invigilated), and the timings of the assessments. The original driving force behind inclusive assessments was to meet the requirements of individual or group students, such as students with disabilities. However, it went beyond this need to create inclusive assessments to provide an equal opportunity for all learners to demonstrate their learning and reduce the need for individual adjustments to assessment. AI can create authentic assessments by creating new ideas through LLMs and summarizing the latest developments in the subject area [19]. Then, students would get motivated by applying their knowledge and skills in real-world scenarios created using next-generation AI technologies.

Similarly, AI can be deployed to create inclusive assessments. Creating inclusive assessments to capture the diverse requirements and needs of learners is not trivial. Therefore, AI-based tools can support educators in creating inclusive assessments, including various assessments spread over the study period [20]. These AI tools can take one more step by designing inclusive assessments for the entire program, rather than creating an assessment for a single module. This way, students will have a good opportunity to demonstrate program outcomes while achieving the LOs of individual modules. A fully integrated AI tool for inclusive assessment would avoid assessment overload and overlapping assessments, and recommend a mix of assessments for the entire program of study. This would further reduce the workload of teachers and administrators in managing assessments for individual modules and program levels. Such assessments would avoid the need to adjust to individual and group needs.

In England, Standard Assessment Tests (SATs) are taken by primary school pupils at the end of Key Stage 1 (Year 2) and Key Stage 2 (Year 6). These tests are part of the national curriculum assessment used to gauge a child's progress and inform teaching. SATs use adaptive assessments catered to individual abilities and needs to evaluate the LOs at different Key Stage levels. These provide valuable insights to learners, teachers, and parents. Furthermore, the education inspection bodies such as Ofsted in England and Estyn in Wales, UK, use these results to inform the quality and standards of education practices in different regions of the United Kingdom.

Another use of AI in inclusive education assessment is the automated grading of exams, essays, assignments, and other coursework. AI is being wisely utilized for marking exam questions, including those in mathematics. The KEATH.ai (Key Evaluation and Assessment Tools Hub) has been used by higher education institutions in the United Kingdom to evaluate and provide feedback to students against the assessment criteria set for the assignment [21]. Tools like KEITH.ai can potentially enhance student LOs while freeing up academic time for teaching and research. These AI-enabled automated assessment tools can be utilized for both formative and summative assessments, providing timely and valuable feedback to enhance student learning. The time saved through automated evaluations can be used for personalized instructions and mentoring in schools. To rely on automated grading tools, the accuracy and efficiency of such tools should be significantly improved. And developing a subject-agnostic, automated grading application based on AI will be challenging, given the diverse marking criteria for each subject. Due to the training involved, subject or module-specific automated marking tools may perform better than a more general tool and provide valuable feedback. Due to the advancement in understanding natural language and text using AI methodologies, the automation of scoring essays and other written assignments is becoming increasingly widespread. The study by Tamara [22] compares human grading with ChatGPT scores of secondary student essays. It has been found that there is no significant statistical difference between these two gradings. However, it highlights the importance of human-graded essays in training such AI models for improved accuracy.

This has been the case for other STEM subjects, such as the grading of programming codes in computer science. The studies reported in [23, 24] highlight the potential for using automated grading tools to evaluate code-based assignments. They are not only assessing the code's functionality but also the code's quality. Such approaches are beneficial in reducing the time spent grading programming assignments in STEM education. Additional insights provided by these tools will enable teachers to offer individualized support to learners and groups that require extra attention to reach their full potential.

While automated grading tools offer numerous advantages, they must be carefully evaluated to understand their strengths and limitations. Pilot studies involving learners would help them improve the effectiveness of these tools. Tackling bias in such applications is crucial to prevent any unfair marking of individuals or groups. Therefore, comprehensive user studies should be conducted to understand the requirements of individuals and the impact on their learning journey. A carefully designed and validated grading tool can revolutionize education by identifying knowledge and skill gaps and providing personalized feedback to students.

AI-based diagnostic tools, when integrated with assessment tools, can help identify students' misconceptions and learning gaps. This allows teachers to provide customized and targeted support and interventions. Furthermore, the information from such tools can be used to provide personalized instructions that enhance LOs and the student experience. In a traditional classroom setting, it is not always possible to accurately understand the strengths and weaknesses of learners using conventional assessment methods. Therefore, AI-driven diagnostic tools can be deployed to understand students' learning patterns, strengths, and weaknesses in a particular subject. These tools and platforms can provide detailed diagnostic information about students and their LOs. The use of such tools for formative assessment is essential, as it enables the early identification of students who are excelling as well as those who are struggling. This information can provide opportunities and support to achieve the best student outcomes tailored to each student's ability.

Feedback for students' work is the key to learning from their strengths and weaknesses. This provides a valuable opportunity for students to correct themselves and achieve greater success in subsequent assessments, ultimately meeting the set LOs for the subjects. However, providing feedback for individual student assessment is not easy in a traditional school classroom setting with 30 students or in a university lecture where more than 300 students take a core module. Feedback in these situations will be more general, rather than inclusive or personalized. Without personalized feedback, students would be unable to understand their strengths and weaknesses, and thus they would be unable to improve their learning throughout the rest of their studies. Due to the importance of feedback for student work, student satisfaction surveys such as the National Student Survey (NSS) in UK universities consider feedback as one of the key elements in students' learning. According to these surveys, universities often struggle to provide timely and effective student feedback. Human interventions to provide personalized feedback in current educational settings are not feasible due to resource limitations. AI-based assessment and feedback tools can provide detailed, timely, and customized feedback on student work. These tools can highlight areas of strength and weakness and suggest ways to improve. Some of the feedback will be instant after grading via an AI-based tool. Then, there will be enough time for learners to respond and act on that feedback. Most of these tools will provide personalized feedback and recommendations to help individual learners achieve their full potential in their learning journey. Furthermore, teachers and parents can use this customized feedback to develop intervention strategies that maximize learning and establish supportive and reinforcing mechanisms. Moreover, these tools will help teachers focus more on supporting students rather than spending time providing detailed and personalized feedback.

2.3.3 Artificial Intelligence for Teacher Support

In current education practice, teachers play a crucial role. However, when addressing the requirements for inclusive education, the time and resources of teachers can be exhausted due to the need for individual attention and support for students who are disabled or from a SEN background. Therefore, AI can support teachers in diverse ways to reduce their routine workload and free them for more personalized teaching and support based on data insights. These can range from:

- AI-powered lesson planning: AI can assist teachers in creating engaging and effective STEM lessons by suggesting relevant resources, activities, and assessments.
- Automated grading and feedback: AI can automate the grading of routine assignments, freeing up teachers' time to focus on providing personalized feedback and support to students.
- Data-driven insights for instruction: AI can analyze student data to provide teachers with insights into student progress, identifying areas where students are struggling, and suggesting interventions.

There is a shortage of SETs due to significant workload expectations. SETs are expected to adapt and modify the mainstream curriculum to meet the diverse needs of learners, as well as communicate and manage the expectations of learners and their parents. Studies highlight that SETs spend over half of their time on non-teaching tasks [25–27]. Some studies suggest that additional stress and burnout may result from the demand for administrative paperwork [28, 29]. Emerging AI and ML methodologies can help SETs reduce the workload of non-teaching tasks. For example, predictive texts, adaptive learning platforms, and digital assistants can help them to achieve their full potential as SETs. This study demonstrates how SETs can use advanced AI tools to automate and streamline tasks such as collaboration and progress monitoring assessments [25]. In the analysis presented in [25], ChatGPT is the primary tool used in the proposed approach. The proposed approach will be limited by the limitations of AI technology and a lack of transparency. Therefore, responsible and transparent AI solutions help ensure that the outcomes and support received through these solutions are acceptable and usable. The freed-up time through these AI tools can be used to develop an individualized education program (IEP) for the learner, which serves as the foundation for providing special education services to children with disabilities.

2.4 PERSONALIZED LEARNING

Learners have diverse educational needs, and their cognitive and physical abilities to capture learning content differ. If we deliver duplicate content to each learner, differentiation won't be achieved, and some learners will not meet the required LOs. Therefore, differentiation or personalization is widely applied in education to ensure we cater to diverse needs and abilities. This is a key requirement in inclusive education to ensure every learner has acquired the required knowledge and skills, regardless of their abilities.

Classroom differentiation is crucial for meeting the diverse needs of a student population. However, the resources regarding teachers' attention, time, and support are limited. Therefore, this resource decision affects students' LOs and is considered an

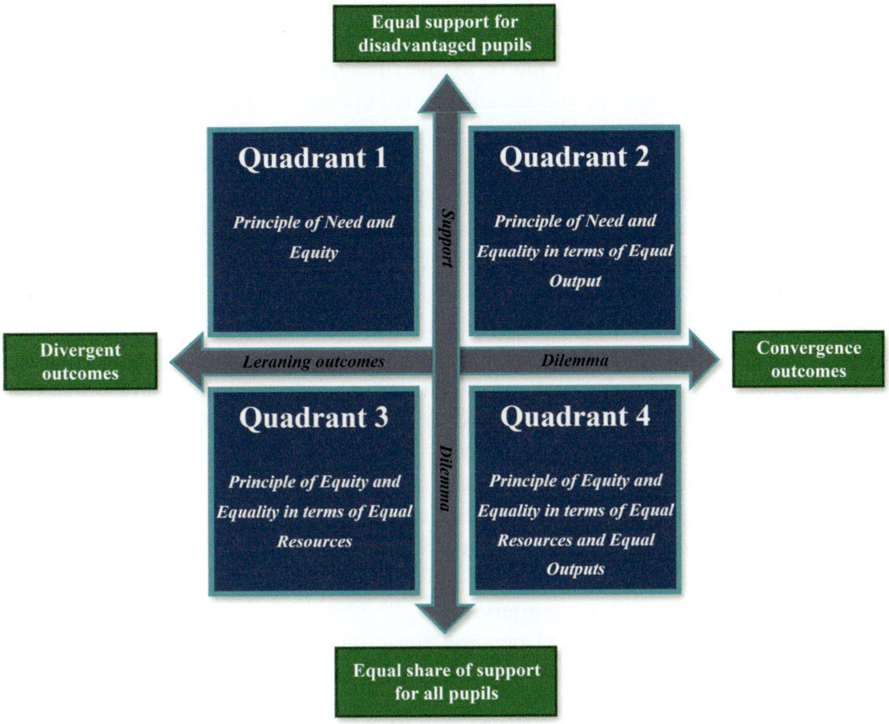

FIGURE 2.3 Conceptual framework on support and learning outcomes dilemmas [6].

ethical dilemma. The study by van Vijfeijken et al. [6] categorizes these decisions within a conceptual framework, as illustrated in Figure 2.3, based on two dilemmas: the support dilemma (the amount of extra support provided to disadvantaged students) and the LOs dilemma (divergent vs convergent outcomes). The support dilemma (*Y-axis)* can range from giving equal support to offering extra support for disadvantaged students. On the other hand, the LO dilemma can range from achieving divergent LOs for each student in the classroom to convergent outcomes for all students.

Educators are responsible for meeting the academic, social, and emotional needs of every child, including those from gifted or high-achieving backgrounds. For talented students to thrive in the differentiated classroom, teachers can consider how they establish and promote positive affective, physical, and digital learning environments. AI technologies can be an effective tool for achieving differentiation in these situations. The study presented by Gilson et al. [7] introduces the Reciprocal Learning Environments Model, in which we describe four teacher actions based on research and recommended best practices from the field of gifted education to cultivate a more positive classroom culture conducive to differentiation.

AI and ML methodologies can be utilized to provide classroom differentiation, as well as personalized or adaptive learning opportunities for learners. AI can analyze a student's strengths, weaknesses, and learning style (e.g., learning pace) to adjust the difficulty and content of learning materials dynamically. This ensures students are neither bored nor overwhelmed, maximizing their learning potential. Furthermore, this enables students to reach their maximum potential. For example, through an AI-driven personalized learning platform, the strengths and weaknesses of a particular subject can be identified, and recommended content and study programs can be provided to learners. Moreover, AI can support students in following the content at their own pace, tailored to their cognitive and physical abilities. This will also ensure that each student receives the appropriate level of challenge and support.

In the current context, delivering personalized learning experiences to learners in a traditional classroom is challenging. For example, assessing individual needs and capabilities in a mixed classroom takes time, resources, and effort. In a traditional classroom in the United Kingdom, one teacher looks after about 30 students at a time. A teacher may not have enough time to meet the individual needs and demands of each student. Many educational establishments operate with limited resources and budgets. Hence, recruiting additional staff members to manage a single classroom is a significant challenge for many academic institutions, local authorities (LAs), and regional/national governments. Therefore, if AI tools and applications can support teachers in profiling student needs, identifying knowledge and skill gaps, and recommending appropriate and authentic interventions, students can achieve LOs at their own pace. Teachers can also be freed up to more critical tasks, including direct engagement and mentoring of learners.

Intelligent tutoring systems: AI-powered tutors can provide personalized feedback, guidance, and hints to students as they work through STEM problems, adapting their approach based on the students' responses and understanding. Furthermore, AI-powered tutors can provide personalized feedback and guidance, resulting in a more tailored learning experience. They can identify knowledge gaps and tailor explanations and exercises accordingly. Personalized Content Generation using GenAI can create customized learning materials, such as practice problems, quizzes, and explanations of complex concepts, tailored to a student's needs and learning style.

AI-enabled tutoring or personalized tutoring systems are becoming widely available as a supportive tool for schoolteachers, a tool for additional learning, and a reinforcement tool for learners. Table 2.1 summarizes a range of AI-driven platforms designed to support educators and learners across diverse contexts. Tools like Khanmigo and Magic School AI emphasize comprehensive teaching and tutoring assistance, while solutions like Diffit and Eduaide.Ai focus on lesson creation and differentiated instruction. Platforms, including Cognispark AI Tutor, TutorOcean AI Tutor, and Third Space Learning's Skye, offer personalized tutoring, each tailoring content to meet the needs of individual students. Meanwhile, Quizizz, Curipod, and Canva Magic Write highlight the role of interactivity and creativity in learning by providing adaptive assessments, lesson interactivity, and brainstorming support. These tools collectively demonstrate how AI is reshaping education by enhancing personalization, efficiency, and engagement in the teaching and learning processes.

These tools can provide automated assessment, learning recommendations, and real-time feedback. These tools are developed through AI models trained on learners' needs, input, and required LOs. These tools often use Optical Character Recognition

TABLE 2.1
Overview of AI-Powered Educational Tools for Teaching and Learning

Tools	Description
Khanmigo	A tool from Khan Academy that serves as both a personal tutor and a classroom assistant, offering interactive lessons and progress tracking.
Magic School AI	A platform that provides comprehensive teaching support, including lesson planning, assessment creation, and interactive presentations.
Diffit	An AI tool that simplifies differentiation for reading materials, allowing teachers to create leveled texts and activities.
Cognispark AI Tutor	Offers personalized learning experiences through interactive content and real-time feedback, adjusting lesson difficulty based on student progress.
Third Space Learning's Skye	A voice-based AI maths tutor designed for personalized, interactive support in mathematics.
TutorOcean AI Tutor	Provides personalized support for homework help, test preparation, and language learning through instant chat, practice tests, and lesson plans.
HyperWrite AI Tutor	Offers comprehensive overviews of subjects, explains complex concepts, and generates practice exercises tailored to individual learning styles.
Quizizz	A platform that uses AI to create personalized learning paths based on student responses.
Canva Magic Write	An AI text-to-image generator that provides ideas, helps with brainstorming, and supports lesson planning.
Curipod	Helps teachers create interactive lessons and offers AI functionality for personalized instruction.
Eduaide.Ai	An AI-assisted lesson development tool with over 100 resource types for creating high-quality instructional materials.

(OCR) to read learners' character and numerical inputs. Then, the AI tool will perform the specified classification or recommendation tasks.

Several AI models have been proposed in the literature for AI tutoring. The model proposed by Gan et al. [8] is based on cognitive diagnostic assessment to generate remedial questions and answers. The schematic diagram of the proposed AI tutoring framework is shown in Figure 2.4.

The AI-tutoring model proposed by Hernández et al. [9] is a general affective behavior model that integrates information from the student's pedagogical state, affective state, and tutorial situation to determine the best tutorial action, considering the tutor's preferences from both pedagogical and affective perspectives. The proposed framework is shown in Figure 2.5.

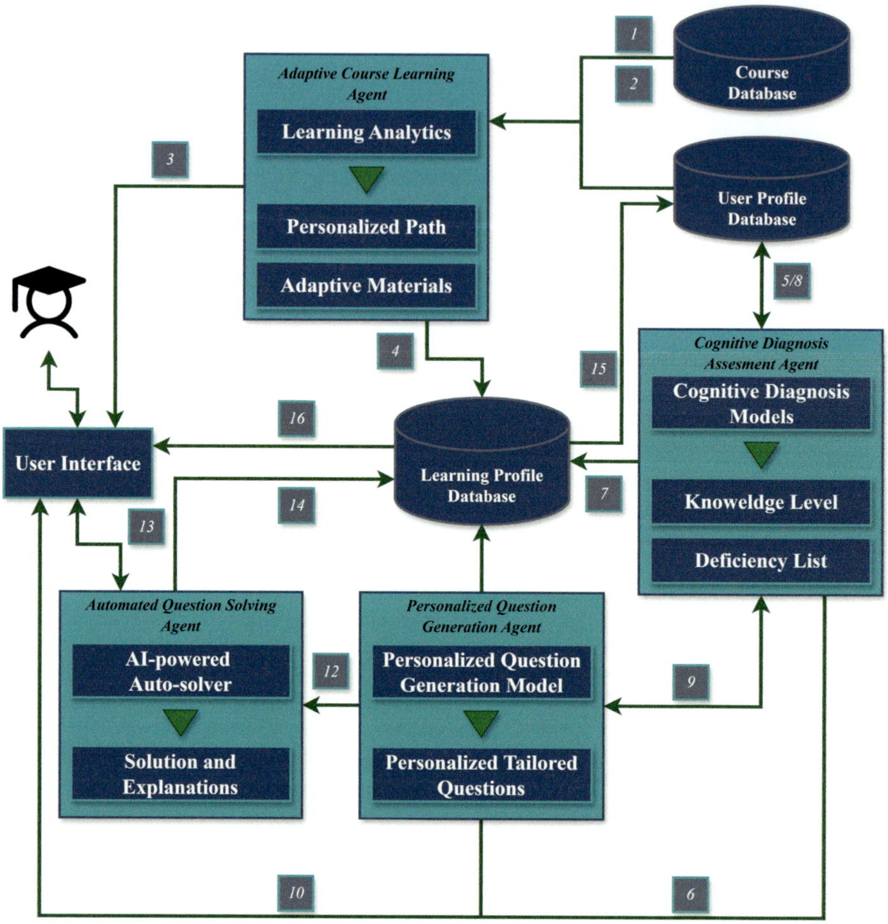

FIGURE 2.4 The proposed AI tutoring framework based on cognitive diagnostic assessment [8].

The design of an Intelligence Tutoring System (ITS) for programming is discussed by Sharma and Harkishan [10]. This ITS (see Figure 2.6) was designed using intelligent algorithms, such as an optimized ant colony, to support the online tutoring system, which can facilitate the application of complex learning principles in computer science courses.

An ITS designed for STEM education (specifically, the learning of Electronics) is presented in Graesser et al. [11]. The model structure and the parameters are shown in Figure 2.7. This integrated system was developed using several intelligent learning resources, including AutoTutor, Dragoon, LearnForm, ASSISTments, and BEETLE-II. This system incorporates a student model, as well as student and teaching contexts, which feed into the recommender system. In this system, model, student, and curriculum weights are calculated to determine top learner recommendations.

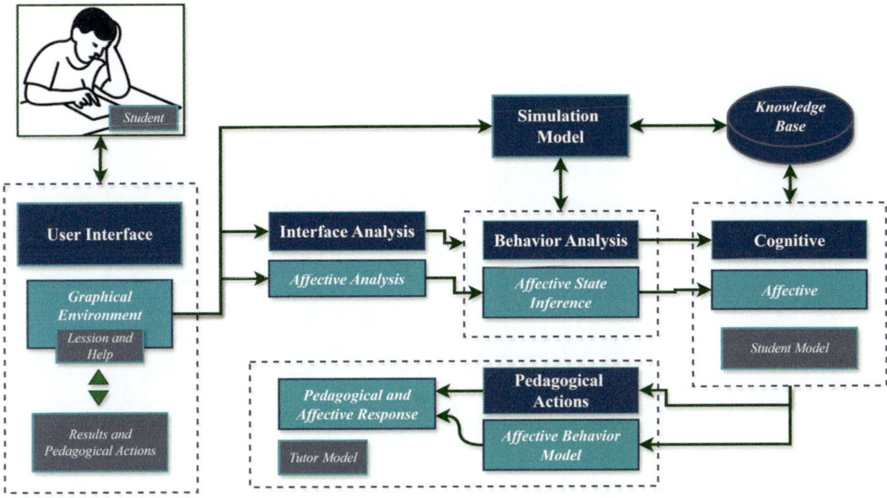

FIGURE 2.5 Architecture of the affective intelligent tutoring system for mobile robotics [9].

Future research and innovation are needed in this space to design next-generation AI-based, personalized, and intelligent learning platforms. The existing approaches are limited in scope and have targeted specific disciplines. More general models would increase wider adaptation. Codesign approaches are required to involve learners, teachers, and parents in developing personalized AI learning and teaching solutions. This will increase buy-in, utility, effectiveness, and wider adaptation. The accuracy, performance, and transparency of AI models hinder their wider adoption by educators and policymakers. Personalized learning tools based on responsible, trustworthy, or transparent AI would increase the acceptability and adaptability of these tools, thereby providing inclusive education for a broader range of learners in both formal and informal settings.

The following are some key research directions for the future.

- Integration of AI performance predictions with learning analytics feedback to enhance student LOs.
- Experiment with the effectiveness of AI-enabled personalized learning platforms.
- Device best practice guidelines on integrating AI into personalized learning to avoid any ethical and legal consequences.
- Use GenAI to create adaptive learning resources to suit individual learner needs.

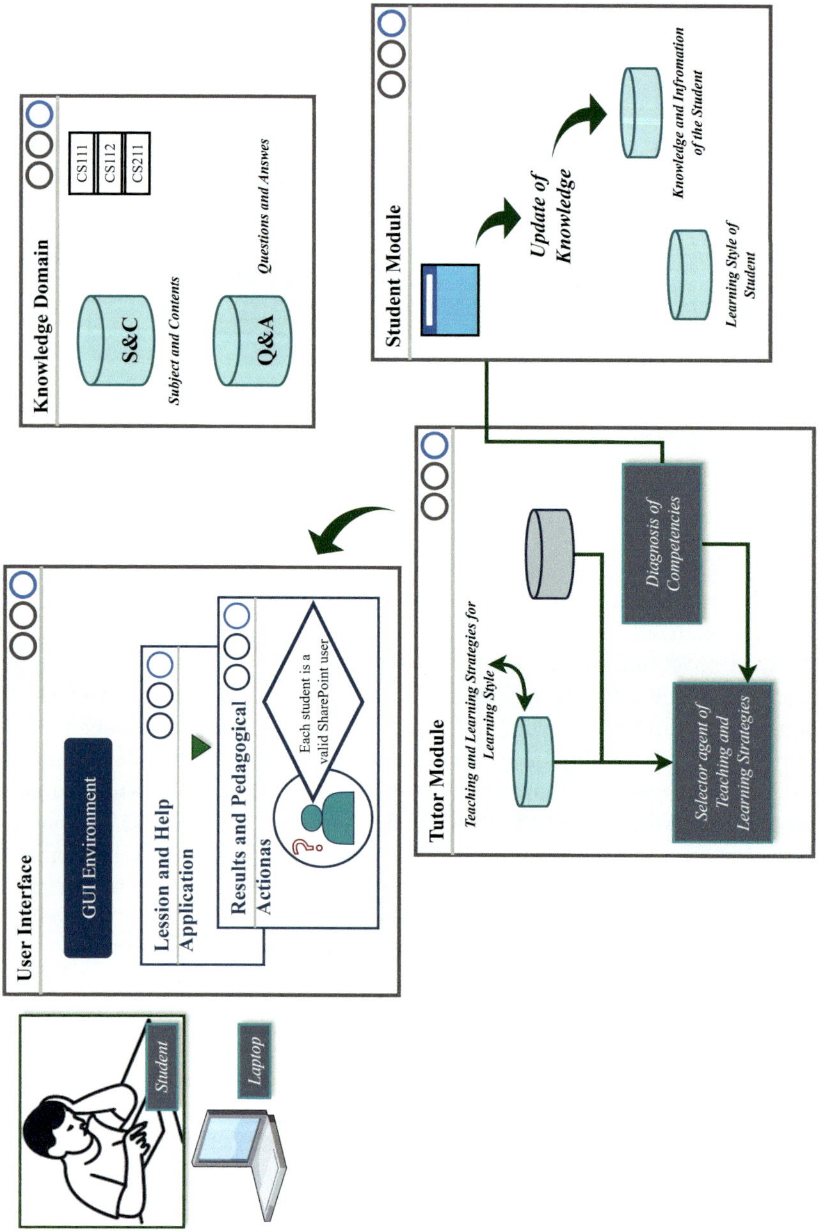

FIGURE 2.6 Intelligent tutoring system for computer programming [10].

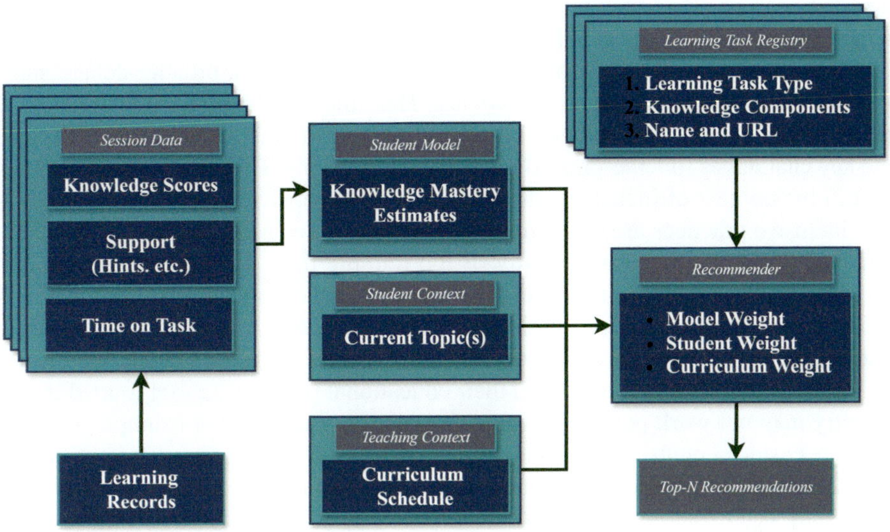

FIGURE 2.7 ElectronixTutor: An intelligent tutoring system (ITS) with multiple learning resources for electronics (STEM Education) [11].

2.5 CHALLENGES AND DATA PROTECTION

By leveraging the power of AI, we can create a more inclusive and equitable education system that provides all students with an equal opportunity to succeed. While there are vast opportunities to use AI effectively in education, there are far greater challenges. The primary concerns include bias in AI algorithms and concerns regarding data protection. Furthermore, accessibility to AI technology is a key aspect that needs to be addressed by all involved. Otherwise, the full potential of educational opportunities enabled by AI will not be realized. Therefore, training on AI technologies, digital literacy, addressing digital poverty, and ensuring Internet access are key challenges to be addressed to enable AI in inclusive education.

Most of the AI tools that can be beneficial for education are Blackbox AI tools or licensed software. Therefore, there is hesitation among learners, teachers, parents, and policymakers regarding the use of existing AI tools, such as ChatGPT. There are also ethical considerations and concerns regarding data protection. According to the 2024 Literacy Trust survey, caution is a primary barrier for AI adoption in the classroom [30]. According to this survey, nearly 40% of UK teachers are concerned about their pupils using GenAI technologies [30]. Since the possibilities are endless with GenAI, the caution is understandable. This has also made teachers curious about AI tools and learn how to use them effectively in the classroom. According to the Educator Confidence Report, 2023 [28], 58% of teachers in the United States expressed interest in developing their AI skills and using GenAI in the classroom. This is a positive development where AI impacts our lives like never before in many domains, including education. A good understanding of how AI technologies work, how they can be effectively utilized, and how to assess their impact would pave the way for the broader adoption of AI tools in the education sector.

The ethical considerations of AI technologies have been a broader debate since the inception of AI and ML technologies. This impacts the wider adoption of AI technologies in many fields, including education. Ensuring fairness and avoiding bias are key challenges for emerging AI tools and applications. This is particularly important in the context of inclusive education, where personalized learning experiences and inclusive practices are of the utmost importance. The accuracy of AI algorithms depends on the quality and quantity of the training data. Therefore, accurate and large-scale datasets are necessary to minimize bias and enhance fairness when developing educational technology with AI. More field trials, testing, and validation in various sectors and regions are needed to ensure that the developed technology meets its intended purpose. Depending on their educational practices, a tool trained in one country may not work perfectly in another country or region. For example, in some Middle Eastern countries, educational establishments are separated into male and female schools. The needs and requirements can differ in these situations, and the AI tools may need training on specific datasets. This is also a barrier to the broader adoption of an AI tool globally. A customizable AI solution (e.g., Transfer Learning (TL)) would help apply to different scenarios and regions in these situations.

There are two main types of AI technologies: black box and white box. While Blackbox AI technologies do not provide information on the algorithm and its operating boundaries, Whitebox AI technologies offer visibility into the algorithm's operating conditions and operational boundaries. One of the causes of reluctance to use AI tools in education is a lack of understanding of the underlying AI algorithms, which impacts privacy, well-being, and accuracy of its predictions. To this end, responsible, trustworthy, and transparent AI technologies would make them more believable and reduce anxiety for learners, teachers, and educators. The article in [31] elaborates on the use of responsible AI technologies, their relationship, and their impact on education. Neurosymbolic AI solutions are widely predicted to be a frontrunner in providing explainability and trust to AI applications. Neurosymbolic AI is considered the third wave of AI evolution. It combines neural networks with symbolic representations, making them more versatile, explainable, and dependable. Moreover, Neurosymbolic AI combines the powers of neural network-based deep learning with Symbolic AI, which deploys explicit rules and logic for reasoning. This can address the Blackbox nature of traditional deep learning AI models by integrating symbolic reasoning to improve accountability and transparency. Several studies in the literature discuss the pros and cons of neuromyotonic AI and its applications in different sectors, including the education sector [32–35]. Neurosymbolic AI can support adaptive and personalized learning experiences. The paper presented in [36] discusses and proposes the integration of Knowledge Graphs (KGs) with LLMs to advance personalized instruction via neurosymbolic educational agents. The proposed approach leverages structured knowledge through symbolic AI, providing individualized learning experiences aligned with specific learner preferences and desired learning paths, while mitigating the biases inherent in traditional AI systems [36]. The results of this study demonstrate that the proposed neurosymbolic approach enhances learning by making it more accessible, equitable, and aligned with real-world skills. Therefore, neurosymbolic-enabled education systems have the potential to interpret complex human concepts and contexts while employing advanced problem-solving strategies based on established pedagogical frameworks. The work presented in [37] also highlights the use of neurosymbolic AI in various educational settings, demonstrating how it can provide reliable decision-making support through symbolic reasoning and rules, even with sparse and/or heterogeneous data.

Bennett and Schuett in [38, 39] argue that current legal definitions are vague and do not cover the current status of technology development. Furthermore, several other studies highlight the Artificial General Intelligence (AGI) systems that exceed human cognitive abilities [40, 41]. To tackle out-of-control AI algorithms and avoid them negatively impacting users, regulators worldwide are enacting laws to support transparent and responsible AI technologies [42, 43].

Many countries are adopting AI laws and regulations to avoid AI tools going out of control or negatively impacting users. These laws and regulations promote a risk-based governance approach to AI technologies. The EU AI Act categorizes AI systems into four risk levels [44], as shown in Table 2.2.

Similar to regulations and laws, best practice guidelines for organizations using AI technology are also emerging. For example, ISO 42001:2023 [45], the AI Management System, is considered the first global standard for AI. This standard supports organizations managing risks and opportunities with AI [45]. Furthermore, this standard wants organizations to develop and use AI technologies more responsibly. The key areas covered in this standard include ethical considerations, transparency, and continuous learning. Enabling responsible AI practices, building trust and confidence, and compliance are key benefits for organizations that follow best practices recommended by the ISO 42001:2023 AI standard. Unlike AI laws and regulations, ISO standards on AI are applicable universally, and best practice guidelines can be shared among all users and organizations. It would be a good approach to implement and adhere to international best practice guidelines, such as ISO42001:2023 AI Management System, by educational establishments that extensively use AI technologies in inclusive education. This will reduce the risks and help comply with related laws, such as the EU AI Act.

2.5.1 Data Protection Concerns

In the wake of the rapid proliferation of AI and ML technologies, data protection has emerged as a pressing concern [46]. The author's book in [46] discusses this issue in detail. AI methodologies heavily rely on vast amounts of data to train and refine their models, often encompassing personal and sensitive information. In the case of personalized learning practices powered by AI, the AI models must be trained on personal data, behaviors, and traits. Therefore, ensuring the privacy of this data (i.e., data protection) has become a complex challenge, necessitating robust frameworks to balance AI's transformative potential with individuals' fundamental rights. Privacy protection concepts such as anonymization, which involves removing personally identifiable information, and differential privacy, which adds noise to data to protect individual identities, are being integrated into AI pipelines to safeguard against data

TABLE 2.2
Categories of AI Risks under the EU AI Act and Their Implications for Inclusive Education

Risk Category	Description	Examples of AI Applications	Implications for Inclusive Education
Unacceptable Risk	AI applications are considered incompatible with EU values and fundamental rights.	• Subliminal manipulation. • Exploiting vulnerabilities (age, disability, economic situation, etc.). • Biometric categorization based on sensitive traits. • General-purpose social scoring. • Real-time remote biometric identification in public spaces. • Emotion recognition. • Predictive policing. • Scraping facial images.	Any AI that exploits learners' vulnerabilities (e.g., SEN students, socioeconomic status) is prohibited. AI in education must either avoid or mitigate these risks.
High-Risk	Most regulated AI systems are allowed but heavily controlled. Must not negatively affect health, safety, rights, or the environment. Require strong safeguards.	• Non-banned biometrics. • Critical infrastructure. • Education and vocational training. • Employment and workforce management. • Access to essential services. • Law enforcement. • Migration, asylum, and border control. • Justice and democratic processes.	Includes AI for admissions, access, evaluating learning outcomes, supporting teachers, and monitoring learning/ behavior. Must consist of risk management, data governance, documentation, human oversight, accuracy, robustness, and cybersecurity.
Limited Risk	Risk of manipulation or deceit. Transparency and trustworthiness are required.	• Chatbots • Generative AI systems	Transparency should be ensured when used in education, especially in learner interactions.
Minimal Risk	AI systems with negligible risk. No mandatory obligations, but ethical principles are encouraged.	• Spam filters	Minimal concern, but should still follow principles like fairness, non-discrimination, and human oversight.

Source: Adapted from [44].

breaches. Additionally, federated learning techniques enable model training across decentralized end-nodes/devices, minimizing the need for centralized data repositories and reducing the risk of unauthorized access to sensitive information.

Another critical dimension of AI and ML models, as well as emerging technologies, is that they should take necessary steps to protect individual rights when using sensitive personal data, such as biometrics. Most of the emerging technologies and innovations are venturing into areas such as:

- Location tracking
- Behavior tracking
- Systematic monitoring of a publicly accessible place
- Processing of sensitive data (racial or ethnic origin, sexual orientation, political opinions, religious or philosophical beliefs, or trade union membership), as well as the processing of genetic and biometric data.
- Automated decision-making/Automated profiling
- Processing of data of minors

The processing of personal data using emerging AI and ML technologies could have an adverse impact or harm to individuals. A few such example scenarios are listed below:

- A CV filtering tool based on AI/ML may block a learner by error or bias who had an opportunity to be shortlisted.
- A GNOME-based sequencing tool that identifies kids at a young age who have the potential to be high performing at mathematics tasks in the future.
- A face recognition software that fails to identify people of color.
- Monitoring of behaviors of individuals or groups without consent (e.g., knife crime tackling tools, within educational establishments).
- Social scoring systems by governments.
- Profiling social media accounts/individuals based on interests and behaviors using AI/ML.
- Recommendation systems based on AI/ML (Educational or health recommendations).

The above types of processing may have a significant impact or pose a "high risk" to the learners' privacy and rights if we do not take appropriate measures to mitigate the severity of the effect. The data protection regulations, such as the EU GDPR, advise data controllers and processors to conduct a DPIA to assess the impact and devise mitigation measures to minimize the effect [47]. These regulations also impose penalties for those not carrying out DPIA when launching new applications like AI and ML (including a fine of up to £8.7 million, or 2% global annual turnover if higher – Data Protection Act (DPA) – 2018 UK).

2.5.2 LLMs versus Data Protection

The LLM-based applications (e.g., ChatGPT) have significantly impacted society, including education, and have instigated a considerable debate on ethics and fair usage. Currently, these models are being trained on publicly available data, and to date, personal data has not been utilized. However, this situation can change rapidly if these models are trained using personal data, which would start providing recommendations for individuals and groups. For example, to provide a personalized learning experience in inclusive education practices, AI models may need to be trained on personal data. Therefore, content owners, controllers, and processors handling learners' personal data should handle data carefully and not share it with any other party that could use it to train LLM models on personal data. If such models come into existence, they will violate individual rights and could cause lasting harm to individuals mentally and physically.

2.5.3 Deepfake Generation versus Data Protection

Increasingly, learners share personal images and features on social media and other educational platforms. GenAI algorithms could use these widely available images to create face swaps and deepfake videos. Therefore, educators, learners, and parents should be vigilant when personal photos and videos are shared on educational platforms. Users need to be extra vigilant when using AI apps integrated with Facebook, TikTok, or other emerging social media platforms, and they should carefully read their privacy notices to understand how their data is used for further processing. The acquired face data may not necessarily be used to create deepfakes, but as training data for their AI models. Either way, these categories of apps should enforce explicit consent to avoid privacy and security infringements.

AI-generated content also creates havoc in the creative arts sector [48]. Many AI tools can create songs, poems, music, and animations [49]. These technologies may harm the creativity of future learners as they will generate copyright issues with original creators [48].

2.5.4 Challenges and Considerations

Teacher Training: Teachers need to be trained on effectively using AI tools and integrating them into their teaching practices. Furthermore, teachers should understand how AI and ML models work, their performance, and limitations. They can then oversee the deployment of AI tools in various educational settings and evaluate the effectiveness of these tools in student learning. Furthermore, with appropriate knowledge, extra care can be taken to ensure the AI models perform within the specified parameters and achieve the set objectives. AI technologies do evolve rapidly. Therefore, continuous professional development (CPD) opportunities should be run regularly to upskill teachers and educators in emerging AI technologies. This will help teachers and educators stay up-to-date with the new technologies that align with the needs of learners and society. For instance, there was resistance from the education sector to ChatGPT-like LLMs. However, learners adapted well to the new technologies, and teachers subsequently provided guidelines for their effective use in learning and teaching.

To effectively deploy AI-powered learning tools in inclusive education, learners should have equal, fair, and uninterrupted access. This is essential for promoting equity in inclusive education. The resources required for AI-powered learning tools can range from access to PCs, tablets, and AACs to Internet access and the necessary skills to utilize these resources. This is widely known as digital poverty as an umbrella term. The key aspects of digital poverty include lack of access (access to devices and internet), affordability (cost of equipment and internet services, leading to digital exclusion), digital skills, motivation, and confidence, and socioeconomic factors (poverty and low educational attainment). This leads to education disparities and social isolation. Individuals experiencing digital poverty will struggle with equal access to learning materials and may face challenges in achieving expected LOs. Therefore, when deploying AI-powered inclusive educational practices, special care should be taken to address digital poverty among learners and the community.

Another critical aspect of digital poverty is digital literacy. Teachers, students, parents, and other stakeholders should be digitally literate, confident, and motivated to deploy inclusive education practices successfully. Otherwise, they would fall behind in the use of digital technology. Therefore, adequate training and support are needed to upskill or enhance their knowledge of new technologies, including AI. Community education ventures, such as the Digital Technology Learning Support Network (DTLSN) at the community level, should be deployed to increase awareness of the latest digital technologies [50]. This will increase the support received from other stakeholders for learners. Without digital literacy, the full potential of AI-powered educational tools will not be achieved.

2.5.5 Future Directions and Opportunities

Further research and development should occur using AI and GenAI technologies in inclusive education. Special attention should be given to its use with learners with disabilities and SENs. Joint research based on action research should be undertaken to evaluate the use of AI technologies in inclusive education. These collaborative studies, involving AI technology developers and educators, would enable the design of practical educational tools that can be widely used. Further research would make these AI tools explainable, transparent, and trustworthy. Responsible AI Education tools will avoid Blackbox AI tools and provide reliable solutions to stakeholders. Furthermore, policies and guidelines should be developed for the use of AI in inclusive education. This will enable more standard education practices and policies to be used as best practice guidelines.

- Further research should take place to foster creativity and problem-solving using AI educational technologies. For instance, for open-ended problem-solving, LLMs can provide students with open-ended problems and challenges, encouraging them to think creatively and develop their problem-solving skills.
- AI can facilitate student collaboration, providing tools for communication, project management, and knowledge sharing. This will enable students to communicate effectively, understand lessons and activities, and ultimately achieve LOs.
- AI can help learners to explore cutting-edge concepts. For instance, LLMs can provide students access to the latest research and advancements in STEM, allowing them to explore cutting-edge concepts and technologies.

- AI can also support accessibility, inclusion, and engagement. For example, AI can support multimodal learning by integrating different modalities, such as text, images, audio, and video, to make STEM content accessible and engaging for all students. AI-powered gamification, as well as VR and AR, can also enhance accessibility, inclusion, and engagement. AI can be used to create gamified STEM learning experiences that are more engaging and motivating for students. Furthermore, AI can enhance VR and AR experiences, making STEM concepts more interactive and immersive. AI can power immersive learning environments where students can conduct virtual experiments, explore complex systems, and visualize abstract concepts, making STEM more engaging and accessible. AI-powered tools can also provide real-time translation, transcription, and other ATs, making STEM education more accessible to students with disabilities and SENs.

2.6 CONCLUSION

AI methodologies hold significant potential for advancing inclusive education by offering personalized learning platforms, ATs, automated assessments, and teacher support. These tools help educators evaluate student performance, identify learning gaps, set individualized goals, and implement classroom differentiation. By automating routine tasks, AI allows teachers to concentrate on personalized instruction and tailored lesson planning.

For learners with SENs and those who are differently abled, AI-enabled ATs provide crucial support in accessing, engaging with, and achieving LOs. Without such tools, significant investments would be required to meet these students' needs. AI can therefore make education more accessible and equitable by offering insights and support for learners outside mainstream classrooms. However, concerns about ethics, bias, and privacy limit widespread adoption. AI systems must become explainable, transparent, responsible, and trustworthy to gain trust among educators, learners, parents, and policymakers. Digital poverty further complicates implementation, as access to devices, Internet connectivity, digital skills, and confidence is often lacking. Overcoming these barriers is essential to realize the full benefits of AI-powered education.

AI tools can become reliable and widely used with sustained research, innovation, pilots, and case studies. Once these challenges are addressed, AI will make education more personalized, engaging, and effective, while preparing learners for the future workforce. Ultimately, education will be one of the key sectors most influenced by AI advancements.

NOTES

1 The term "Blackbox AI models and tools" refers to artificial intelligence systems whose internal workings are not transparent or easily understood, even by their creators or users.
2 Augmentative and Alternative Communication (AAC) is an umbrella term for any method that helps people communicate when speech is hard or not possible.
3 Autism Spectrum Disorder (ASD) is a neurodevelopmental condition that affects how a person communicates, interacts socially, and experiences the world.

REFERENCES

1. Technology and Innovation Report 2025. (2025). United Nations Conference on Trade and Development (UNCTAD) Technology and Innovation Report (TIR). https://doi.org/10.18356/9789211068016
2. Elsahar, Y., Hu, S., Bouazza-Marouf, K., Kerr, D., & Mansor, A. (2019). Augmentative and Alternative Communication (AAC) advances: A review of configurations for individuals with a speech disability. *Sensors*, 19(8), 1911–1911. https://doi.org/10.3390/s19081911
3. Lv, Z. (2023). Generative artificial intelligence in the metaverse era. *Cognitive Robotics*, 3, 208–217. https://doi.org/10.1016/j.cogr.2023.06.001
4. Feuerriegel, S., Hartmann, J., Janiesch, C., & Zschech, P. (2023). Generative AI. *Business & Information Systems Engineering*, 66(1), 111–126. https://doi.org/10.1007/s12599-023-00834-7
5. Generative AI and ChatGPT: Applications, challenges, and AI-human collaboration. (2023). *Journal of Information Technology Case and Application Research.* https://doi.org/10.1080/15228053.2023.2233814
6. van Vijfeijken, M., van Schilt-Mol, T., van den Bergh, L., Scholte, R. H. J., & Denessen, E. (2023). How teachers handle differentiation dilemmas in the context of a school's vision: A case study. *Cogent Education*, 10(1). https://doi.org/10.1080/2331186X.2023.2165006
7. Gilson, C. M., & Lee, L. E. (2023). Cultivating a learning environment to support diverse gifted students. *Gifted Child Today Magazine*, 46(4), 235–249
8. Gan, W., Sun, Y., Ye, S., Fan, Y., & Sun, Y. (2019). AI-Tutor: Generating tailored remedial questions and answers based on cognitive diagnostic assessment, *2019 6th international conference on behavioral, economic and socio-cultural computing (BESC)*, Oct. 2019. https://doi.org/10.1109/besc48373.2019.8963236
9. Hernández, Y., Noguez, J., Sucar, E., & Arroyo-Figueroa, G. (2006). Incorporating an affective model to an intelligent tutor for mobile robotics. Oct. 2006. https://doi.org/10.1109/fie.2006.322407
10. Sharma, P. & Harkishan, M. (2022). Designing an intelligent tutoring system for computer programming in the Pacific. *Education and Information Technologies*, Jan. https://doi.org/10.1007/s10639-021-10882-9
11. Graesser, A. C. et al. (2018). ElectronixTutor: an intelligent tutoring system with multiple learning resources for electronics. *International Journal of STEM Education*, 5(1), Apr. https://doi.org/10.1186/s40594-018-0110-y
12. Innovative Technologies for Inclusive Education: A Review of Best Practices from Global Resource Centers – UNESCO IITE. (2025). UNESCO IITE, Jan. 10, 2025. https://iite.unesco.org/publications/technologies-for-inclusive-education-a-review-of-best-practices/
13. World Health Organization, "Blindness and vision impairment," World Health Organization, Aug. 10, (2023). https://www.who.int/news-room/fact-sheets/detail/blindness-and-visual-impairment
14. Palarimath, S., Radhakrishnan, V., Veerasamy, D., Valsalan, P., Viswan, V., & Thumu, M. B. (2025). Artificial Intelligence and Machine Learning for Accessibility: Smart Reader as an Assistive Tool for the Visually Impaired. 424–430, Mar. 2025. https://doi.org/10.1109/icmlas64557.2025.10968797
15. Gupta, A. K., Kaur, S., Kaur, P., & Kumari Sharma, T. (2024). Image to text to speech: A web-based application using optical character recognition and speech synthesis. In edited by Ramakant Bhardwaj, Pushan Kumar Dutta, Pethuru Raj, Abhishek Kumar,

Kavita Saini, Alfonso González Briones and Mohammed K.A. Kaabar, *Hybrid information systems: Non-linear optimization strategies with artificial intelligence*, (pp.329–342). De Gruyter. https://doi.org/10.1515/9783111331133-016

16. Donmez, M. (2022). A systematic literature review for the use of eye-tracking in special education. *Education and Information Technologies*, Nov. 2022. https://doi.org/10.1007/s10639-022-11456-z
17. Khasawneh, Y. J. A., & Khasawneh, Y. J. A. (2023). Availability of voice-recognition devices to support visually impaired students in Saudi Arabian Universities. *Journal of Wireless Mobile Networks, Ubiquitous Computing, and Dependable Applications*, 14(3), 186–193, Sep. 2023. https://doi.org/10.58346/jowua.2023.i3.014
18. University of Oxford (2024). IncludED: A Guide to Designing Inclusive Assessments. www.ctl.ox.ac.uk. https://www.ctl.ox.ac.uk/included-designing-inclusive-assessments
19. The Assessment Network. (2024). Authentic assessment and AI: Making the grade in HE. Cambridgeassessment.org.uk, Jul. 18, 2024. https://www.cambridgeassessment.org.uk/blogs/authentic-assessment-and-ai-making-the-grade-in-he/ (accessed Jul. 20, 2025).
20. Nayak, R., Yassin, H., Ramesh, G., & Godishala, A.. (2024). Inclusive learning and assessment in the era of AI. *SN Computer Science*, 5(8), Oct. 2024. https://doi.org/10.1007/s42979-024-03346-7
21. AI-driven academic marking tool unveiled – offering potential to enhance student learning outcomes and free up academic time for teaching and research|University of Surrey. (2023). www.surrey.ac.uk, Nov. 30, 2023. https://www.surrey.ac.uk/news/ai-driven-academic-marking-tool-unveiled-offering-potential-enhance-student-learning-outcomes-and
22. Tamara, P. (2024). Tate, Jacob Steiss, Drew Bailey, Steve Graham, Youngsun Moon, Daniel Ritchie, Waverly Tseng, Mark Warschauer, Can AI provide useful holistic essay scoring? *Computers and Education: Artificial Intelligence*, 7, 100255, ISSN 2666-920X. https://doi.org/10.1016/j.caeai.2024.100255
23. Chen, H. M., Nguyen, B. A., Yan, Y. X., & Dow, C. R. (2020). Analysis of learning behavior in an automated programming assessment environment: A code quality perspective. *IEEE Access*, 8, 167341–167354. https://doi.org/10.1109/ACCESS.2020.3024102
24. Conejo, R., Barros, B., & Bertoa, M. F.. (2019). Automated assessment of complex programming tasks using SIETTE. *IEEE Transactions on Learning Technologies*, 12(4), 470–484, 1 Oct.–Dec. https://doi.org/10.1109/TLT.2018.2876249
25. Goldman, S. R., Taylor, J., Carreon, A., & Smith, S. J. (2024). Using AI to support special education teacher workload. *Journal of Special Education Technology*, 39(3), May. https://doi.org/10.1177/01626434241257240
26. Perks, S. AI could reduce teacher workload. *Physics World*, 33(8), 11–11, Aug. 2020. https://doi.org/10.1088/2058-7058/33/8/15
27. Hashem, R., et al. (2024). AI to the rescue: Exploring the potential of ChatGPT as a teacher ally for workload relief and burnout prevention. *Research & Practice in Technology Enhanced Learning*, 19, 1–26.
28. Jones, N. D., Camburn, E. M., Kelcey, B., & Quintero, E. (2022). Teachers' Time Use and Affect Before and After COVID-19 School Closures. *AERA Open*, 8, 233285842110680, Jan. 2022. https://doi.org/10.1177/23328584211068068
29. Kartika, A., et al. (2017). *Individual Education Program (IEP) paperwork: A narrative review*, 1–14.
30. National Literacy Trust. (2024). Children, young people and teachers' use of Generative AI to support literacy in 2024. *National Literacy Trust*, Jun. 25, 2024. https://literacytrust.org.uk/research-services/research-reports/children-young-people-and-teachers-use-of-generative-ai-to-support-literacy-in-2024/

31. 2023 Educator Confidence Report|Annual Teacher Survey|Houghton Mifflin Harcourt. (2025). www.hmhco.com; https://www.hmhco.com/educator-confidence-report
32. Dignum, V. (2021). The role and challenges of education for responsible AI. *London Review of Education*, 19(1), 1–11.
33. Colelough, B. C., & Regli, W. (2025). Neuro-symbolic AI in 2024: A systematic review. arXiv preprint arXiv:2501.05435.
34. Di Maio, P. (2020). Neurosymbolic knowledge representation for explainable and trustworthy AI. *Preprints* 2020, 2020010163.
35. Renkhoff, J., Feng, K., Meier-Doernberg, M., Velasquez, A., & Song, H. H. (2024). A survey on verification and validation, testing and evaluations of neurosymbolic artificial intelligence. *IEEE Transactions on Artificial Intelligence*, 5(8), 3765–3779, Aug. 2024. https://doi.org/10.1109/TAI.2024.3351798
36. Jaldi, C. D., et al. (2025). Education in the era of Neurosymbolic AI. *Journal of Web Semantics*, 85, 100857
37. The Impact of Neuro-Symbolic AI on Cognitive Linguistics. (2025). *ACADEMIA International Journal for Social Sciences*, [S.l.], 4(3), 455–466. https://doi.org/10.63056/ACAD.004.03.0386
38. Bennett Moses, L. (2007), Recurring dilemmas: The law's race to keep up with technological change. *SSRN Electronic Journal*. https://doi.org/10.2139/ssrn.979861
39. Schuett, J. (2023). Defining the scope of AI regulations. *Law, Innovation and Technology*, 15(1), 1–23, Mar. https://doi.org/10.1080/17579961.2023.2184135
40. Cichocki, A., & Kuleshov, A. P. (2021). Future trends for Human-AI collaboration: A comprehensive taxonomy of AI/AGI using multiple intelligences and learning styles. *Computational Intelligence and Neuroscience*, 2021(1), 1–21, Feb. 2021. https://doi.org/10.1155/2021/8893795
41. Korteling, J. E., van de Boer-Visschedijk, G. C., Blankendaal, R. A. M., Boonekamp, R. C., & Eikelboom, A. R. (2021). Human- versus artificial intelligence. *Frontiers in Artificial Intelligence*, 4, Mar. https://doi.org/10.3389/frai.2021.622364
42. Global AI Legislation Tracker. IAPP. https://iapp.org/resources/article/global-ai-legislation-tracker/
43. Sheehan, M. (2023). China's AI regulations and how they get made. *Carnegie Endowment for International Peace*. https://carnegieendowment.org/research/2023/07/chinas-ai-regulations-and-how-they-get-made?lang=en
44. EU Artificial Intelligence Act (2024). High-level Summary of the AI Act. EU Artificial Intelligence Act, Feb. 27, 2024. https://artificialintelligenceact.eu/high-level-summary/
45. ISO. Information technology — Artificial intelligence — Management system for, "ISO/IEC 42001:2023, ISO. (2023). https://www.iso.org/standard/42001
46. Hewage, C., Yasakethu, L., & Jayakody, D. N. K. (2024). *Data protection*. Springer Nature.
47. European Union. (2018). General Data Protection Regulation (GDPR). *GDPR*. https://gdpr-info.eu/
48. Abbott, R., & Rothman, E. (2023). Disrupting creativity: Copyright law in the age of generative artificial intelligence. *Florida Law Review*, 75, 1141.
49. Gupta, P., Ding, B., Guan, C., & Ding, D. (2024). Generative AI: A systematic review using topic modelling techniques. *Data and Information Management*, 8(2), 100066, Feb. 2024. https://doi.org/10.1016/j.dim.2024.100066
50. Carroll, F., Faruque, R., Hewage, C., Bentotahewa, V., & Meace, S. (2023). The journey to making 'Digital Technology' education a community learning venture. *Education Sciences*, 13(5), 428–428, Apr. 2023. https://doi.org/10.3390/educsci13050428

3 Generative AI for Emotional and Behavioral Analysis in STEM Education

3.1 EMOTIONAL AND BEHAVIORAL ANALYSIS IN STEM EDUCATION

In modern education, particularly in STEM, the need for innovative solutions that address both cognitive and emotional aspects of learning has never been more critical. As the demands of STEM disciplines continue to evolve, students must engage with complex concepts and navigate the emotional and psychological challenges accompanying such intellectual rigor [1–3]. The ability to thrive in STEM education extends beyond mastering abstract reasoning and technical problem-solving; it requires students to manage stress, persevere through failure, and effectively regulate their emotions. Despite the growing recognition of the role of emotional and behavioral factors in student success, traditional educational approaches have mainly overlooked these aspects. This gap in understanding creates a significant opportunity for technology to make a meaningful impact, especially with the rise of AI. AI's potential to analyze cognitive performance and monitor and respond to emotional and behavioral cues presents a new frontier for creating more personalized, supportive, and inclusive learning environments in STEM education.

The importance of understanding emotional states in STEM education cannot be overstated. STEM subjects are intellectually demanding, requiring students to engage in abstract reasoning and tackle problems that do not always have clear or immediate solutions. These cognitive demands can elicit various emotional responses, directly impacting students' learning experiences and outcomes [4, 5]. For example, when confronted with challenging STEM problems, students may experience feelings of confusion or frustration. On the other hand, mastering complex concepts may inspire confidence, curiosity, and a sense of achievement. However, without an accurate understanding of these emotional states, students may silently struggle with negative emotions that hinder their cognitive progress or fail to fully capitalize on positive emotions that enhance their engagement and motivation. Unfortunately, traditional educational assessments, such as quizzes and exams, typically focus on cognitive performance and overlook the emotional and behavioral aspects of learning, which are equally crucial to a student's success [4, 6]. As a result, educators may miss critical cues about student well-being, leading to missed opportunities for intervention

DOI: 10.1201/9781003641490-3

FIGURE 3.1 Visual metaphors for emotional challenges. (a) *The Scream* (1893) by Edvard Munch and (b) *The Desperate Man* (c. 1845) by Gustave Courbet serve as symbolic representations of the internal emotional states, such as anxiety, confusion, and despair, that students may silently experience in cognitively demanding STEM environments.

Image sources: Wikipedia.

and support. This is especially problematic in STEM education, where the emotional demands of the subject matter are often overlooked or ignored.

One effective way to understand and visualize these emotional struggles is to look at symbolic representations of emotional turmoil in art history. Figure 3.1 shows two iconic works vividly depicting psychological distress: Edvard Munch's *The Scream* (1893) and Gustave Courbet's *The Desperate Man* (c. 1845) [7]. Both paintings capture a profound sense of internal emotional states, such as anxiety, confusion, and despair. The anxiety portrayed in "*The Scream*" and the despair captured in "*The Desperate Man*" resonate with the silent emotional battles that many students may experience in their pursuit of STEM mastery. These works are more than just artistic expressions; they serve as visual metaphors for humans' emotional states, or those of a student, which may not always be outwardly visible but significantly impact their academic journey. Much like the figures in these paintings, students often face emotional barriers that are difficult to articulate or recognize, and these emotional challenges can go unnoticed in traditional academic environments that emphasize cognitive achievement over emotional well-being. This underscores the need for a more nuanced approach to student assessment that considers not just what students know, but also how they feel and how those feelings influence their learning experiences.

GenAI offers an innovative solution with advanced capabilities in Natural Language Processing (NLP), multimodal sensing, and real-time interaction. By analyzing data from various sources, including facial expressions, voice inflections, written reflections, and physiological signals such as heart rate and skin conductance, GenAI systems can detect emotional markers in students' behavior, such as engagement, boredom, anxiety, or distress. These emotional markers are often subtle and complex for humans to detect without the aid of advanced technology. For example, a student may look outwardly engaged in a lesson. Still, AI-powered systems can detect subtle changes in facial expression or voice tone that indicate confusion or frustration. By analyzing these cues in real time, GenAI enables a more comprehensive understanding of students' emotional and behavioral states, allowing educators to respond more effectively and promptly [8, 9]. This is particularly important in STEM education, where students may be reluctant to express frustration or confusion openly. Still, such emotions can significantly hinder their ability to learn and persist in the subject matter.

Moreover, GenAI holds the potential to create adaptive learning environments that are responsive not only to students' cognitive progress but also to their emotional well-being. In traditional learning environments, students may experience periods of emotional distress or disengagement that are not immediately addressed, leading to adverse outcomes such as academic burnout or disengagement from the subject [8–11]. However, by using AI to monitor students' emotional states, educators can intervene early, providing support when students are at risk of becoming overwhelmed or disconnected. For example, if a student's emotional markers indicate frustration or anxiety, the system could suggest personalized interventions, such as additional resources, alternative explanations, or a break from the material (see Figure 3.2). By promoting emotional regulation and resilience, GenAI can enhance students' ability to persevere through complex tasks and maintain engagement, particularly in challenging fields such as STEM. The ability to respond to students' emotional needs in real time improves LOs and fosters a more inclusive and supportive classroom environment, where students feel valued and understood [8, 10].

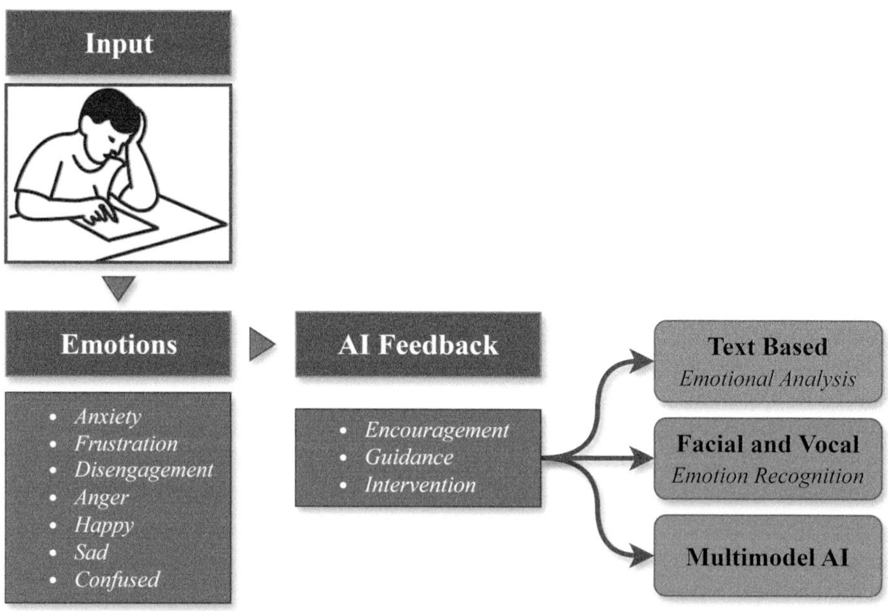

FIGURE 3.2 The use of GenAI in emotional and behavioral analysis for STEM education.

One of the most exciting aspects of GenAI is its ability to integrate multiple data sources, enabling a more comprehensive understanding of students' emotional and behavioral states. Familiar data sources used in emotional and behavioral analyses include video (such as facial expressions and body language), audio (including voice tone and speech patterns), written reflections (through text analysis), and physiological signals (such as heart rate or skin conductance). Combining these diverse data streams, GenAI systems can create a richer and more accurate picture of students' emotional responses. Traditional ML models, while effective at identifying patterns in large datasets, often struggle to generate new insights or adapt to changing conditions in real time. In contrast, GenAI can analyze past data and synthesize new responses based on current emotional states, providing more dynamic and personalized feedback. This ability to generate real-time insights and adapt to changing emotional conditions represents a significant step forward in emotional and behavioral analysis, surpassing the capabilities of traditional ML models [8, 11–15].

Integrating GenAI into STEM education holds tremendous potential to enhance students' cognitive, behavioral, and emotional outcomes. GenAI equips educators with the tools to craft more personalized and responsive learning environments by leveraging multimodal data sources to analyze students' emotional and behavioral states [16–20]. Figure 3.3 depicts a layered technical architecture for integrating GenAI into STEM Learning Platforms for emotion and behavior analysis. This architecture outlines a four-layered system designed to enhance STEM education. The four layers include (1) Data ingestion gathers multimedia and behavioral logs; (2) Emotion and Behavior Analysis interprets student engagement and actions via facial emotion recognition (FER) and LLM-based behavioral modeling; (3) Generative Feedback Engine personalizes learning through LLM-generated hints and gamification; and (4) Delivery provides interactive elements like integrated chat, voice synthesis, dashboards, and notifications to students and instructors.

These AI-driven interventions support intellectual growth and foster emotional resilience, engagement, and well-being, essential components for success in the challenging context of STEM education [17, 19]. Consequently, GenAI can redefine the educational landscape, creating more inclusive, equitable, and emotionally intelligent environments that address students' emotional hurdles while tackling complex academic material [19].

The applications of GenAI in education are broad and rapidly advancing, with several state-of-the-art models and architectures leading the charge. Text-based models, such as GPT, LLaMA, and Mistral, are transforming how we interact with educational content, enabling natural and contextually aware conversations and creating more personalized learning experiences. In image synthesis, tools like Stable Diffusion and DALL·E are making remarkable progress in simulating emotional states and behaviors through visual representations, offering new avenues to explore and engage with students' emotional and cognitive experiences [20, 21]. Additionally, audio models focused on speech emotion simulation provide deeper insights into students' emotional responses, analyzing vocal tone and speech patterns to capture nuances of engagement, frustration, or excitement. Together, these innovations are setting the stage for more adaptive and emotionally attuned educational environments that can respond in real time to the dynamic needs of students [20–22].

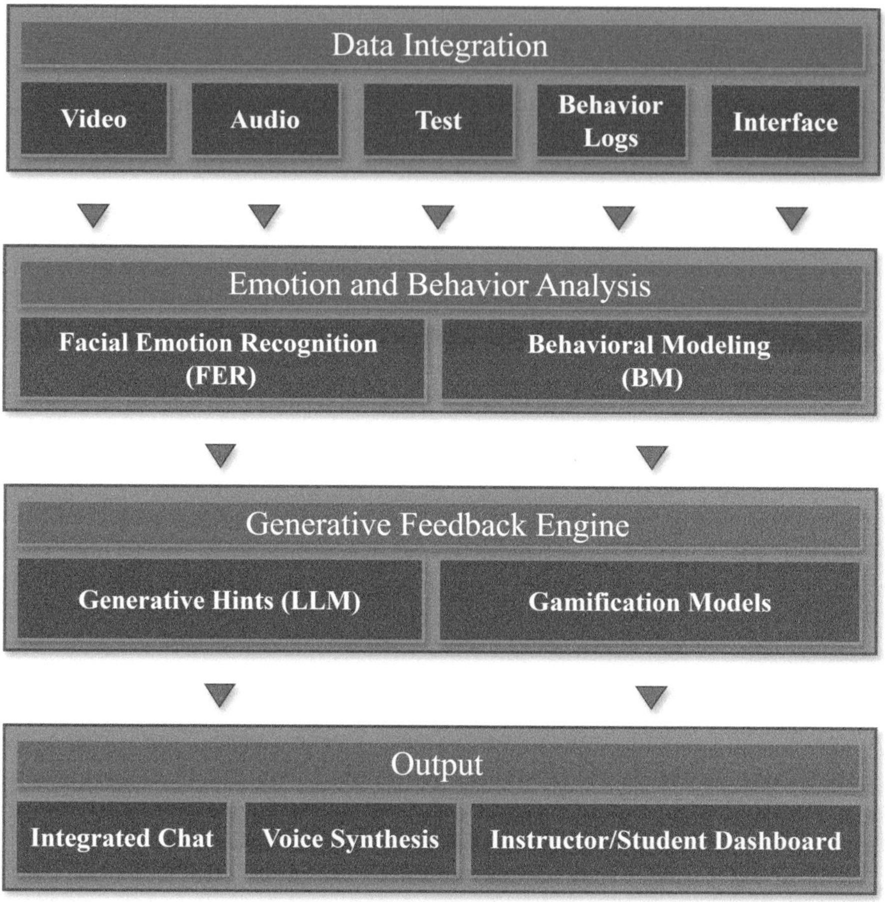

FIGURE 3.3 The layered technical architecture for integrating GenAI into STEM Learning Platforms for emotion and behavior analysis.

3.2 REAL-WORLD ENGAGEMENT OF GENERATIVE AI FOR EMOTIONAL AND BEHAVIORAL ANALYSIS

The relationship between student emotion and learning is crucial, as negative emotions can hinder cognitive processes, while positive emotions enhance engagement and academic performance. In response, STEM education researchers have focused on developing "*affect-aware*" learning technologies capable of detecting and adapting to students' emotional and behavioral states [23]. Early work in this area included intelligent tutoring systems, such as Carnegie Mellon University's Project LISTEN, which integrated human-simulated emotional support [24]. In this system, a human operator monitored student frustration and provided real-time encouragement or simplified tasks as needed to alleviate it. The intervention significantly increased student persistence, particularly among boys, demonstrating the motivational benefits of affective scaffolding. Although the system relied on human input, it set a precedent for fully automated emotion-responsive educational technologies. It highlighted two core technical challenges: accurately sensing student affect and generating appropriate responses.

Fast-forward to the era of deep learning and GenAI, and the field has gained powerful new tools to analyze and respond to students' affective states. Modern multimodal LLMs and Visual Language Models can process complex combinations of inputs, from text responses to facial expressions, to gauge student engagement. For instance, Marquez-Carpintero et al. [25] report that multimodal generative models can reliably track student attention in real time by analyzing videos of posture and gaze. In their experiments, a Vision Language Model fine-tuned with a few-shot learning approach outperformed traditional ML baselines in detecting nuanced visual cues of attentiveness (e.g., eye focus, head movement) in a science class. Such advances hint at classroom AI assistants that monitor who's confused or disengaged and generate instant feedback to re-engage them. Indeed, recent studies on LLM-based tutoring agents show promise for boosting student motivation.

A systematic mini-review by Ortega-Ochoa et al. [26] examined GenAI tools, such as ChatGPT, in the context of education. These systems often increased student engagement and helped with emotional regulation during learning tasks. For example, an interactive coding tutor that chats with students in natural language can offer encouraging feedback or hints when it "notices" a student's struggle, thereby reducing frustration. Immediate, dialogic feedback is a strength of GenAI; students feel heard and supported, which can buffer negative emotions. However, the same review cautions that current generative tutors have apparent limitations: they sometimes give incorrect or overly generic help (undermining trust). They cannot effectively tailor their responses to each learner's unique emotional needs.

In other words, a ChatGPT-based math tutor might cheerily respond to a wrong answer with *"Not quite, try reviewing the earlier steps!"* which may encourage one student but annoy another. Truly sensitive adaptation, the kind a human teacher intuitively does by reading the room, remains an open challenge. Real-world case studies from diverse educational settings illustrate the potential and pitfalls of GenAI in sensing and responding to learner emotions. In an industry-leading effort, International Business Machines Corporation's (IBM) Watson AI has been applied to build empathetic student support systems. Ralston et al. [27] developed a multilingual student chatbot using the IBM Watson Assistant and its Tone Analyzer to detect affect in students' voices and text. One use case was helping university students cope with exam anxiety: the AI would ask how a student feels about an upcoming exam, analyze the tone of their response (e.g., detecting stress or confusion), and then generate a supportive reply or study tip. In evaluations at the University of Rwanda, 76.5% of students reported that the Watson-powered chatbot accurately responded to their feelings about exam stress, a strong validation that GenAI can parse a learner's emotional state and respond in a way the learner finds appropriate.

One focus is on ability-diverse learners: Prof. Yun Huang at the University of Illinois at Urbana–Champaign (UIUC) is designing emotion-AI tools for deaf and hard-of-hearing (D/HH) students, exploring how GenAI can interpret nonverbal cues (like facial expressions or sign language dynamics) to gauge understanding and frustration in STEM learning contexts [28]. The goal is to create an AI that can adapt explanations or modalities (text, sign, and visual) in response to the learner's affect, ensuring that no student is left behind due to unrecognized confusion. Such projects highlight that emotional analytics in education must consider diversity; AI should not assume a one-size-fits-all model of "engagement," but instead learn the varied expressions of emotion across different cultures and learner profiles. Similarly, the University of Leeds contributes to the global discourse on ethical AI tutoring. Leeds scholars [29] have critically examined the trend of giving chatbots an "empathetic" persona. They argue that simulated empathy by current generative models can be "deeply morally problematic" because, without genuine understanding, an AI might manipulate emotions in undesirable ways. For example, a conversational AI might consistently cheer up a student who is justifiably frustrated at poor instruction, thereby "soothing" an emotion that signals a need for change in reality. The Leeds team warns that by blunting certain negative emotions (which, in humans, serve as important feedback mechanisms), AI tutors could induce a one-dimensional positivity that is ultimately counterproductive. This perspective urges caution: emotional AI should support healthy emotional processing, not simply try to erase discomfort to keep the student happy. It also calls for accountability; unlike a human teacher, an AI cannot truly be held responsible for the consequences of emotional intervention, so designers must tread carefully in determining the extent of authority such systems have over learners' emotional trajectories.

The implications and outcomes of these case studies are multifaceted. On one hand, GenAI clearly promises to improve STEM education by making it more responsive and personalized. Research conducted by Carnegie Mellon and the University of British Columbia (UBC) found that when a tutor recognizes a student is frustrated or bored and adapts accordingly, students benefit through greater persistence and possibly better LOs [30, 31]. Newer systems with LLMs and vision models can scalably detect these states and even produce natural language encouragement or hints, which could be a game-changer in large classes or online learning where human teachers struggle to give individualized attention. The IBM Watson chatbot case demonstrated a tangible outcome: students felt understood and supported by the AI, an outcome long sought in AI-in-education research, often referred to as "positive affective computing." There is also evidence that these systems can influence academic behavior: a well-timed empathetic hint can re-engage a student who is stuck, and reducing anxiety can improve assessment performance [27]. On the other hand, challenges abound. A consistent thread is the accuracy and appropriateness of AI's emotion detection. Misreading a student's state (e.g., falsely detecting confusion) could lead to incorrect interventions (such as over-explaining a concept the student actually grasps, which is annoying). Unlike simpler rule-based tutors, GenAI still makes such errors; its mistakes can be unpredictable. Another key implication is the effect on students' own skills. Suppose AI tutors become adept at modulating a learner's emotions (for instance, always providing motivational boosts). In that case, we must ask: *could this inadvertently make students less able to regulate their own emotions related to learning?* Some educators compare this to the concern that GPS navigation weakened people's map-reading skills. In fact, a 2025 study by Carnegie Mellon University and Microsoft Research found that individuals who heavily relied on AI tools exhibited reduced critical thinking, essentially offloading the effort to the AI [32]. By analogy, if a student comes to lean on an ever-cheerful AI tutor for inspiration, will they develop less grit or self-motivation? These are open questions. The answer likely lies in a balanced approach where AI supports and scaffolds students' metacognitive awareness (teaching them to recognize and manage their frustration or boredom).

GenAI for emotional and behavioral analysis in STEM education is rapidly transitioning from concept to classroom implementation, as validated by global case studies from institutions such as Carnegie Mellon, the UBC, IBM[1,2], and the UIUC. These deployments promise to enhance personalized learning experiences by detecting students' emotional states, addressing frustration, boredom, or excitement with targeted interventions. While AI technology has advanced significantly, enabling the multimodal detection of complex emotional states, achieving truly empathetic AI remains a challenge. Ethical considerations, including privacy, bias, and psychological impacts, necessitate interdisciplinary collaboration among educators, technologists, ethicists, and policymakers. Successful integration involves hybrid approaches where AI supports, rather than replaces, human teachers, combined with rigorous evaluation to ensure beneficial outcomes and mitigate risks. GenAI has excellent potential as a supportive tool in STEM education, provided its deployment remains careful, ethical, and human-centered [33–37].

3.3 DATA COLLECTION AND PREPROCESSING FOR EMOTIONAL AND BEHAVIORAL ANALYSIS

The effectiveness of any GenAI system for emotional and behavioral analysis depends fundamentally on the quality, diversity, and readiness of its data. In STEM education, where students' emotions, cognitive engagement, and behavioral patterns significantly impact LOs, robust data collection and preprocessing strategies are essential [38–40].

This section examines how multimodal data, encompassing text, audio, video, and sensor-based signals, can be systematically collected, annotated, and prepared for integration into GenAI models that drive adaptive and responsive learning environments.

GenAI models are susceptible to the quality of input data. Well-prepared datasets that are clean, accurately labeled, and rich in relevant features enable models to:

- Detect subtle emotional states with precision.
- Avoid overfitting to irrelevant noise or misleading patterns.
- Produce contextually appropriate and effective responses in a real educational scenario.

Conversely, poor preprocessing can compromise the reliability of AI. For example, a feedback system trained on noisy or inaccurately labeled audio might misinterpret a student's frustration as boredom, resulting in ineffective or even counterproductive responses. Careful preprocessing safeguards against such errors, ensuring accuracy, reliability, and trustworthiness of AI-driven interventions.

3.3.1 Multimodal Data Sources in STEM Education for Generative AI

Emotions and behaviors in STEM classrooms manifest in various ways, including verbal cues in written responses, vocal tone during discussions, facial expressions during problem-solving, and even physiological signals, such as changes in heart rate, under cognitive stress. GenAI models work best when fed with rich, multimodal data (text, audio, video, and sensor data) that captures these diverse channels [41–46].

3.3.1.1 Text Data

Textual data is one of the most valuable and readily available forms of input in STEM learning environments. It comes from students' problem-solving explanations, chat logs in virtual classrooms, or reflective responses in assessments.

- Learning management systems (LMS) provide text through discussion boards, assignment feedback, and peer review activities.
- Collaborative tools like Microsoft Teams, Slack, or Discord capture informal discussions, brainstorming sessions, and group project communication.
- Online assessments contribute free-response answers, clarification requests, and open-ended feedback that can reveal cognitive and emotional states.

This text often reflects confusion, curiosity, or frustration, making it a powerful source for emotional inference. GenAI can detect these states and generate supportive or clarifying responses when processed and analyzed.

3.3.1.2 Audio Data

Audio data captures the emotional nuances of speech, such as tone, pitch, and pacing, which are often lost in text alone.

- Recorded lectures and discussions from physical or virtual classrooms provide teacher–student interaction samples.
- Oral explanations of problem-solving steps offer direct insight into cognitive processing.
- Voice interactions with AI tutoring systems capture spontaneous emotional feedback during learning.

These audio streams can be analyzed using Mel-Frequency Cepstral Coefficients (MFCCs), prosody, and pitch variance to detect engagement, boredom, or excitement.

3.3.1.3 Video Data

Video provides a visual window into behavioral and emotional states through facial expressions, posture, gestures, and gaze direction.

- Classroom recordings (with consent) capture group dynamics and attention levels.
- Virtual classroom platforms such as Zoom record facial expressions and participation patterns.
- Webcam feeds during quizzes and assignments offer real-time behavioral observation.

Facial expressions (such as smiling and frowning), eye gaze, and gestures are key indicators of motivation, frustration, or focus, which GenAI can model to adjust feedback strategies.

3.3.1.4 Sensor Data

Sensor-based data expands emotional and behavioral analysis beyond visible or audible cues. Wearable devices and environmental sensors detect physiological and interaction-based signals correlating with cognitive and emotional states.

- Heart rate variability (HRV) strongly indicates stress and cognitive load during challenging STEM tasks.
- Galvanic skin response (GSR) measures emotional arousal in problem-solving situations.
- Eye-tracking technology detects focus, distraction, or cognitive engagement.
- Keyboard/mouse interaction logs reveal hesitation, speed, and confidence levels.

Combined with text, audio, and video, these modalities enable AI systems to create a comprehensive learner profile, allowing for nuanced, context-aware, and generative interventions.

Table 3.1 presents a combined multimodal summary that consolidates all four modalities (text, audio, video, and sensor) in a single view, including sources, strengths, limitations, and example GenAI use cases.

3.3.2 Data Labeling Approaches

Once collected, raw multimodal data must be labeled to be valuable for the training of emotion-aware GenAI models. Labels commonly denote either discrete or continuous emotional states, such as happy, frustrated, or neutral, or behavioral states like engaged, distracted, or struggling. This labeling process transforms unstructured data into structured input, enabling models to learn associations between observable signals and underlying states, ultimately improving prediction accuracy and enhancing human–AI interaction [47, 48].

1. **Manual Annotation**: Manual labeling involves human annotators reviewing data and assigning emotional or behavioral tags. This process can involve:

    a. Frame-by-frame video annotation for facial expressions.
    b. Transcript labeling for text emotions.
    c. Audio clip labeling for vocal emotions.

    While accurate, manual annotation is labor-intensive, expensive, and susceptible to inter-annotator variability. Multiple annotators are often used in conjunction with consensus-building methods, such as Cohen's Kappa, to measure agreement and improve reliability.

TABLE 3.1
Multimodal Data for Emotional and Behavioral Analysis in STEM Education

Modality	Typical Sources	Strengths	Limitations	GenAI Use Cases
Text	LMS discussion boards, assignment feedback, peer reviews, chat logs (Teams, Slack, Discord), online assessments.	Easily stored and processed; rich in cognitive and emotional cues; supports large-scale analysis.	Lacks tone and nuance present in speech; may contain informal or ambiguous language.	Emotional sentiment analysis, generating adaptive feedback, summarizing student questions, and auto-generating hints or explanations.
Audio	Recorded lectures, oral problem explanations, and voice interactions with AI tutors.	Captures tone, pitch, and pacing; detects emotional intensity; supplements text data.	Background noise requires a high-quality recording, as well as language/accent variability.	Speech emotion detection, generating empathetic spoken responses, and audio-based personalized coaching.
Video	Classroom recordings, Zoom/Teams video sessions, webcam feeds during quizzes.	Captures facial expressions, gestures, eye gaze; strong behavioral indicators.	Requires consent; storage-intensive; lighting and camera quality affect accuracy.	Real-time engagement monitoring, avatar-based feedback generation, and detecting frustration or confusion for adaptive interventions.
Sensor	HRV monitors, GSR devices, eye trackers, keyboard/mouse logs.	Detects physiological arousal, stress, and cognitive load; objective engagement signals.	Requires specialized hardware, privacy, and ethical concerns; interpretation can be complex.	Multimodal adaptive systems, stress-aware tutoring, workload-balanced task recommendations.

2. **AI-Assisted Labeling**: AI-assisted labeling leverages pretrained models to automatically suggest labels that a human annotator can verify or refine. This hybrid approach accelerates dataset creation while maintaining a reasonable level of accuracy. For example:
   a. Pre-trained facial emotion detectors can label thousands of frames, with humans correcting misclassifications.
   b. NLP-based emotion classifiers can pre-tag textual data for sentiment categories.
   c. Speech emotion recognition models can automatically categorize large audio datasets into arousal/valence categories.

The advantage of AI-assisted labeling is speed; however, it requires careful human oversight to prevent the propagation of model biases into the labeled dataset.

3.3.3 Preprocessing Techniques

Before being utilized in GenAI models, data must first undergo rigorous preprocessing to ensure quality and consistency. This stage involves standardizing diverse formats into uniform structures, eliminating irrelevant noise that could distort results, and extracting key features that are meaningful for analysis. Such preparation is especially critical when targeting emotional and behavioral insights, as it enhances the model's ability to detect subtle patterns and generate reliable outputs for interpretation [49].

Table 3.2 outlines the typical preprocessing pipelines applied to text, audio, and video data. For text, preprocessing ensures that raw inputs from informal sources

TABLE 3.2
Preprocessing Techniques for Text, Audio, and Video Data

Modality	Step	Description	Techniques/Tools
Text	Tokenization	Breaks text into words or subword units for model input.	Word tokenizers, subword tokenizers (BPE, SentencePiece).
	Cleaning	Removes stopwords, punctuation, special symbols, and irrelevant tags.	NLTK stopword removal, regex cleaning.
	Normalization	Converts text into a consistent form (lowercasing, stemming, lemmatization).	Porter Stemmer, WordNet Lemmatizer, spaCy.
	Embedding preparation	Transforms text into numerical vectors for ML models.	Word2Vec, GloVe, BERT, transformer embeddings.
Audio	Noise reduction	Filters out background noise for a clearer signal.	Spectral subtraction, Wiener filtering.
	Framing and windowing	Splits audio into small overlapping segments.	Hamming/Hanning windows.
	Feature extraction	Extracts features representing perceptual sound properties.	MFCCs, spectrograms, log-mel features.

(*Continued*)

TABLE 3.2 (CONTINUED)

Modality	Step	Description	Techniques/Tools
Video	Frame sampling	Selects key frames at fixed intervals to reduce redundancy.	Uniform sampling, scene change detection.
	Face detection and alignment	Identifies and aligns faces for consistent analysis and interpretation.	OpenCV [50], MediaPipe [51].
	Feature extraction	Captures visual cues like facial landmarks, gaze direction, and expression intensity.	Landmark detectors, pose estimation models.

The Table Summarizes Common Steps Used in Preparing Multimodal Data for Machine Learning and Deep Learning Applications.

such as classroom discussions or chat logs are transformed into structured representations through tokenization, cleaning, normalization, and embedding preparation. Audio data often requires noise reduction and segmentation, followed by feature extraction using MFCCs to capture perceptually relevant sound features. Video preprocessing involves sampling frames, detecting and aligning faces, and extracting features such as facial landmarks and expression intensity, using libraries like OpenCV and MediaPipe [50, 51]. Together, these steps ensure that raw multimodal inputs are standardized and optimized for downstream learning tasks.

3.4 GENERATIVE AI TECHNIQUES FOR EMOTIONAL ANALYSIS

GenAI has revolutionized the way we detect, interpret, and simulate emotional and behavioral states in educational environments, particularly in STEM education. Unlike traditional ML methods that primarily focus on classification or prediction, GenAI enables the creation of novel outputs based on patterns learned from training data. This makes it exceptionally powerful for emotional analysis, where emotions are not just static labels but dynamic, context-driven states that can influence LOs. In STEM classrooms, emotional fluctuations such as frustration, curiosity, confusion, or motivation can have a direct impact on problem-solving, engagement, and persistence [52]. GenAI models, encompassing LLMs, Generative Adversarial Networks (GANs), Variational Autoencoders (VAEs), and transformer-based architectures, can extend beyond detection to synthesize realistic scenarios, simulate emotional responses, and even adapt instructional strategies in real time [53].

3.4.1 Text-Based Emotion Synthesis and Analysis

Text remains one of the most widely available data streams in modern STEM classrooms, especially in online learning platforms where students frequently interact through chat messages, discussion forums, and written assignments [54, 55]. GenAI, particularly transformer-based LLMs, can process these text inputs to detect emotional signals embedded within linguistic cues. For example, a student writing

"*I don't think I'll ever understand this equation*" might express discouragement, while another saying *"This is taking too long; I give up"* could signal frustration or disengagement. Traditional sentiment analysis techniques often oversimplify expressions as "positive" or "negative." GenAI models, however, can perform fine-grained emotion recognition, categorizing them into emotions such as anger, sadness, confusion, or excitement.

Beyond detection, GenAI can synthesize emotional summaries from classroom transcripts. For instance, given a transcript of a physics problem-solving session, a model like GPT-4 or Bidirectional Encoder Representations from Transformers (BERT) can summarize moments of peak frustration, motivation, or confusion, providing educators with a timeline of emotional dynamics in the class. These summaries are particularly valuable in adaptive learning systems, where emotional awareness can guide interventions, such as providing hints at heightened frustration or celebrating achievements at moments of emotional uplift. Prompt engineering plays a key role here. Carefully designed prompts can instruct an LLM to analyze text (E1) for emotional content and output structured reports, such as:

> ***E1: "Between 10:15 and 10:30, several students expressed confusion about Newton's Third Law. Student A displayed persistent frustration, while Student B shifted from curiosity to excitement after solving a challenging problem."***

Such outputs can be integrated directly into teacher dashboards or automated tutoring systems. Algorithm 3.1 performs event-level emotion classification and produces an interval-level summary. It loads the DistilRoBERTa emotion classifier, predicts a label and confidence for each event, and stores results in a table. The table is filtered to a user-specified interval. If no events fall within the interval, it returns the table and the message "No events in interval." Otherwise, it counts labels within the window, selects the dominant emotion, and returns the summary and predictions.

ALGORITHM 3.1 EMOTION ANALYSIS

Require: Model ID "j-hartmann/emotion-english-distilroberta-base"; events $E = \{(s_i, t_i, \tau_i)\}$; interval $[\tau_{start}, \tau_{end}]$
Ensure: Table D of predictions; one-sentence summary S
1. **Load** classifier pipeline with given model
2. **For each** (s, t, τ) in E: predict (*label*, *score*) and **append** to D
3. **Filter** $I \leftarrow \{r \in D \mid \tau_{start} \leq r.Timestamp \leq \tau_{end}\}$
4. **if** I empty **then**
5. $S \leftarrow$ "No events in interval."; **return** (D, S)
6. **end if**
7. **Count** labels in I and **select** dominant label
8. $S \leftarrow$ "Between τ_{start}–τ_{end}, dominant emotion: *label*."
9. **return** (D, S)

Table 3.3 presents the results of the E1 analysis, highlighting the emotional states expressed by two students during a problem-solving session. Student A displayed a range of emotions, including high-confidence anger (0.986) when frustrated with a physics problem, moderate-confidence surprise (0.449) when struggling to understand Newton's Third Law, and sadness (0.844) after a prolonged session. In contrast, Student B's interactions reflected both positive and neutral affect, with strong confidence in joy (0.974) when enjoying a coding assignment and again (0.976) upon solving an equation, but also a moderate-confidence neutral state (0.607) when feeling uncertain about a problem. These results demonstrate the variability of emotional expression within short intervals and underscore the importance of capturing fine-grained emotional shifts during learning activities.

3.4.2 Image and Video Generation for Behavioral Simulation

While text provides explicit emotional indicators, nonverbal cues captured in images and videos, such as facial expressions, gestures, and body posture, offer rich, often subconscious insights into student engagement. In STEM classrooms, a student's behavior during problem-solving can indicate persistence, confusion, boredom, or enthusiasm. Traditional computer vision techniques have long been used for facial emotion detection, but GenAI now enables something far more transformative: behavioral simulation.

Using generative models such as GANs or diffusion models, we can create synthetic video data that depicts classroom scenarios under various emotional conditions. For instance, one could generate video clips showing students reacting with curiosity to a science experiment or struggling with a coding problem. These simulations can be invaluable for training AI models where labeled real-world emotional video data is scarce. By generating diverse, synthetic emotional data, we can improve

TABLE 3.3
Predicted Emotion and Confidence Level of Two Students Generated from Text E1

Timestamp	Student	Text	Predicted Emotion	Confidence
28/07/2025 10:05	Student A	I'm feeling frustrated with the physics problem.	Anger	0.986
28/07/2025 10:10	Student B	This coding assignment is actually fun!	Joy	0.974
28/07/2025 10:15	Student A	I don't understand Newton's Third Law example.	Surprise	0.449
28/07/2025 10:18	Student B	I'm stuck on this problem, and I'm not sure what to do.	Neutral	0.607
28/07/2025 10:20	Student B	Finally solved the equation! Feeling great now.	Joy	0.976
28/07/2025 10:25	Student A	I'm a bit tired after this extended session.	Sadness	0.844

model robustness while minimizing privacy concerns, since synthetic videos do not require real students' faces.

In addition, GenAI can create simulated classroom environments for teacher training. For example, a GAN-powered system could produce classroom videos where students display varying emotions, allowing trainee educators to practice recognizing and responding appropriately to emotional cues. In an AI-powered tutoring system, generated behavioral scenarios can stress-test the model's ability to adapt to emotional shifts, for example, by providing motivational feedback when the simulated "student" exhibits disengagement [15, 56].

These simulations are critical in STEM education, where certain emotions (like confusion and frustration) can be constructive if recognized and addressed quickly. For example, controlled frustration during problem-solving may drive deeper engagement, but unchecked frustration can lead to disengagement. Generative video simulations enable AI systems and teachers to distinguish between productive struggle and emotional burnout.

3.4.3 Speech Synthesis and Emotion Transfer

Speech carries an additional layer of emotional nuance through tone, pitch, pacing, and emphasis. In virtual STEM classrooms or AI tutoring systems, the ability to synthesize speech that conveys accurate information and mirrors a supportive emotional tone is essential. GenAI enables two key capabilities here: emotion-aware speech synthesis and emotion transfer.

Emotion-aware speech synthesis enables TTS models to generate spoken responses that convey a desired emotional state. For instance, when an AI tutor detects that a student is frustrated, it can respond in a calm, empathetic tone rather than a neutral or robotic voice. This emotional alignment can have a significant impact on student receptivity and engagement [57].

Emotion transfer in speech synthesis involves transferring the emotional tone from one audio source to another. For instance, suppose a teacher records a set of instructions in a neutral tone. In that case, generative models can transform it into a more encouraging or enthusiastic version without requiring the teacher to re-record. Models such as VALL-E, Tacotron, or neural voice cloning systems can perform this transformation with high fidelity [58].

In practical applications, emotion-aware TTS could allow AI-driven virtual assistants to deliver customized motivational prompts during STEM lessons. Imagine an AI tutor saying, *"You're doing great, let's try another approach"* with an upbeat and encouraging tone when the system detects a dip in the student's confidence. The emotional delivery could be as impactful as the content of the feedback itself.

3.5 GENERATIVE AI FOR BEHAVIORAL PATTERN RECOGNITION

Behavioral pattern recognition in STEM education is a complex but highly valuable process. Understanding students' cognitive and affective behaviors over time enables educators and intelligent tutoring systems to adapt instruction in real time, ensuring more effective LOs. Traditional behavioral analysis relies on manually labeled logs, structured questionnaires, and observational methods. While these methods can be insightful, they are resource-intensive, limited in scale, and often struggle to model subtle, nonlinear relationships between multiple behavioral factors.

GenAI offers a transformative approach, particularly with models such as VAEs and GANs. These models can learn latent representations of student behavior patterns from large datasets, generate synthetic yet realistic behavioral traces, and aid in clustering similar student profiles. Such capabilities enable more robust behavior modeling while addressing common data scarcity issues [59].

3.5.1 Using VAEs and GANs to Model Behavioral Patterns

VAEs are particularly effective for learning compact, meaningful representations of student behaviors. In STEM learning, behaviors can be represented as features, such as time spent on tasks, problem-solving sequences, frequency of hint requests, engagement patterns in interactive simulations, or mouse/keyboard activity in programming tasks. A VAE learns a compressed latent space that captures the essential behavioral characteristics of the data. Once trained, the VAE can generate variations of these behaviors by sampling from its latent space. For example, a VAE could model the behavioral patterns of a "persistent problem solver," versus a "fast guesser," versus a "hesitant learner." This allows educators and AI systems to simulate how different types of students might respond to instructional changes [60–62].

GANs extend this capability by producing highly realistic synthetic behavioral datasets. While VAEs focus on latent representation, GANs operate as a competitive framework between two models: a generator that produces synthetic samples and a discriminator that distinguishes between real and synthetic samples. In behavioral modeling, GANs can generate realistic learning trajectories or event logs that mimic student engagement. This is especially useful when there is a lack of balanced behavioral data (e.g., not enough data on disengaged students or high performers) [61, 62].

The advantage of using GANs in STEM education is that synthetic data generation can fill in gaps, support data balancing, and train downstream predictive models more effectively, without breaching privacy by relying solely on actual student records.

3.5.2 Generating Synthetic Behavioral Datasets for Model Training

One major challenge in behavioral modeling is data imbalance. For instance, certain behaviors (e.g., "consistent engagement") may dominate datasets, while less frequent but critical behaviors (e.g., "sudden disengagement" or "rapid switching between tasks") appear sparsely. This imbalance can cause predictive models to underperform on rare but essential behavioral patterns [61, 63].

Generative models, such as VAEs and GANs, or hybrid architectures, help synthesize balanced datasets. These synthetic datasets preserve the statistical properties of real behaviors while providing more coverage across the full spectrum of patterns. This is particularly beneficial for:

- Training engagement prediction models.
- Simulating diverse student types in adaptive learning systems.
- Testing interventions on underrepresented behaviors.

For example, a GAN trained on task-switching logs could generate synthetic behavior sequences representing students with low engagement. These synthetic logs could then be used to stress test an adaptive learning platform to ensure it responds effectively to disengagement.

From an academic standpoint, synthetic datasets also provide a privacy-preserving mechanism for sharing research. Institutions can generate behaviorally realistic, yet anonymized, datasets for publication and benchmarking without exposing student data.

3.5.3 Clustering Student Behaviors Using Embeddings from Generative Models

Once behavioral patterns are learned through a VAE or GAN, the latent embeddings can be analyzed for clustering. These embeddings capture high-level characteristics of student behavior, enabling us to identify behavioral archetypes.

Clustering methods (e.g., K-Means, DBSCAN, hierarchical clustering) applied to the latent space can group students into meaningful categories, such as:

- Consistent Strivers: Students who work steadily, request hints appropriately, and rarely disengage.
- Burst Learners: Students who alternate between intense activity and inactivity.
- High-risk Disengagers: Students whose behaviors suggest a high probability of dropout or frustration.

Such clusters are invaluable for adaptive systems, which can tailor interventions to meet specific needs and requirements. For instance:

- Consistent Strivers may face more challenging problems in sustaining engagement.
- Burst Learners may receive nudges during idle periods.
- High-risk Disengagers may receive personalized encouragement or targeted scaffolding.

The power of generative embeddings lies in their ability to capture nuanced differences that are not obvious from raw logs or basic statistical summaries. Two students may have similar engagement percentages, but embeddings might reveal that their approach to problem-solving differs drastically, placing them in distinct behavioral clusters.

3.5.3.1 Example Uses of Student Behavior Clusters

To analyze latent patterns in learner engagement, the authors clustered student activity logs using embeddings derived from generative models. Each student's behavior was summarized from system logs, capturing activity types, frequency, and quiz performance. The summaries were embedded using a transformer-based sentence embedding model and then clustered with the K-Means algorithm. Figure 3.4 illustrates the workflow for analyzing student behavior.

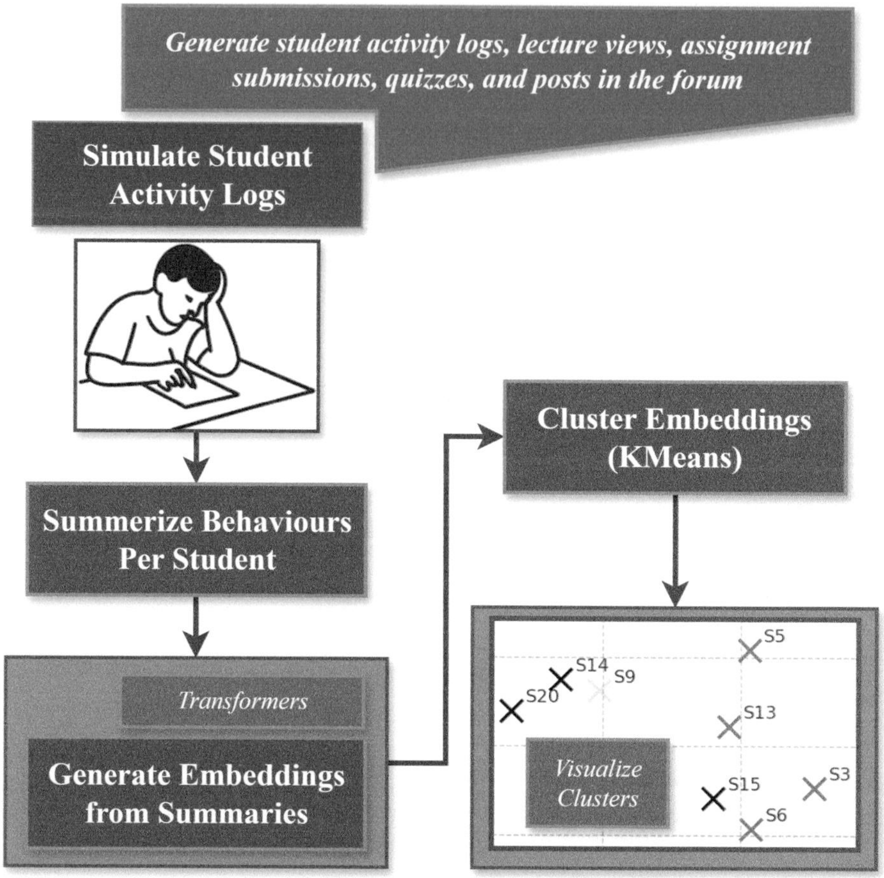

FIGURE 3.4 Workflow for student behavior analysis. The process begins with simulating student activity logs, followed by summarizing behaviors per student and generating text-based summaries.

Algorithm 3.2 discusses the integration of LLMs and transformer-based sentence encoders to enhance the interpretability of student activity data. The process begins with salience selection, where representative behavioral events are extracted for each learner. These events are then summarized through an LLM-driven text synthesis step, resulting in concise, natural-language descriptions of student engagement. Each summary is subsequently converted into a semantic embedding vector using a pre-trained sentence encoder such as Sentence-BERT or MiniLM. The embeddings are normalized and aggregated to form a feature matrix suitable for clustering. Following the clustering stage, the algorithm groups student summaries within each cluster and applies the LLM again to generate narrative-level explanations that articulate the shared behavioral patterns. This hybrid pipeline bridges structured log data and human-readable insights, leveraging GenAI capabilities for both representation learning and explanatory synthesis.

ALGORITHM 3.2 GENERATIVE AI COMPONENTS FOR BEHAVIOR CLUSTERING

1. **Inputs:** per-student event traces $\mathcal{L}$; sentence encoder M; LLM L
2. **Salience selection:** for each s, $C_s \leftarrow \texttt{SelectTopK}(\mathcal{L}_s, k)$
3. **LLM summary:** $\mathrm{BS}_s \leftarrow L(\text{"Summarize concisely"}, C_s)$
4. **Embed text:** $E_s \leftarrow M.\texttt{encode}(\mathrm{BS}_s)$
5. **Normalize:** $E_s \leftarrow \texttt{Normalize}(E_s)$
6. **Batch stack:** $E \leftarrow [E_s]_s$
7. **Cluster corpora:** given $\{\mathcal{C}_j\}$, $\mathcal{B}_j = \{\mathrm{BS}_s : s \in \mathcal{C}_j\}$
8. **LLM explain:** $\mathrm{Narrative}_j \leftarrow L(\text{"Explain common behaviors"}, \mathcal{B}_j)$

Three prominent clusters emerged: Cluster 0 (Consistent Learners) exhibited regular logins, lecture reviews, and high quiz scores; Cluster 1 (Deadline-Driven Learners) displayed irregular activity concentrated near deadlines with moderate quiz performance; and Cluster 2 (Low Engagement Learners) showed minimal participation and lower quiz averages. This clustering highlights distinct behavioral archetypes that can inform targeted interventions and personalized feedback strategies.

Table 3.4 presents the clustering results for the student behavior analysis. Each student was assigned to one of three clusters based on their activity patterns and quiz

TABLE 3.4
Clustering Results of Student Behaviors using Embeddings from Generative Models

Student	Average Quiz Score	Cluster	Behavior Description
Student 1	88.5	0	Consistent engagement with frequent lecture reviews and high quiz performance.
Student 2	76.3	1	Irregular logins, delayed assignments, and moderate quiz performance.
Student 3	91.2	0	High activity in discussions and early quiz submissions.
Student 4	65.7	2	Minimal interaction, low forum participation, average scores.
Student 5	84.4	0	Regular logins, balanced lecture review, and quiz performance.
Student 6	70.8	1	Last-minute quiz attempts and sporadic logins.
Student 20	68.5	2	Low engagement, irregular activity, and lower quiz averages.

Students are grouped into three clusters representing distinct learning archetypes: Consistent Learners (Cluster 0), Deadline-Driven Learners (Cluster 1), and Low Engagement Learners (Cluster 2). Representative students and their average quiz scores are examples of each group.

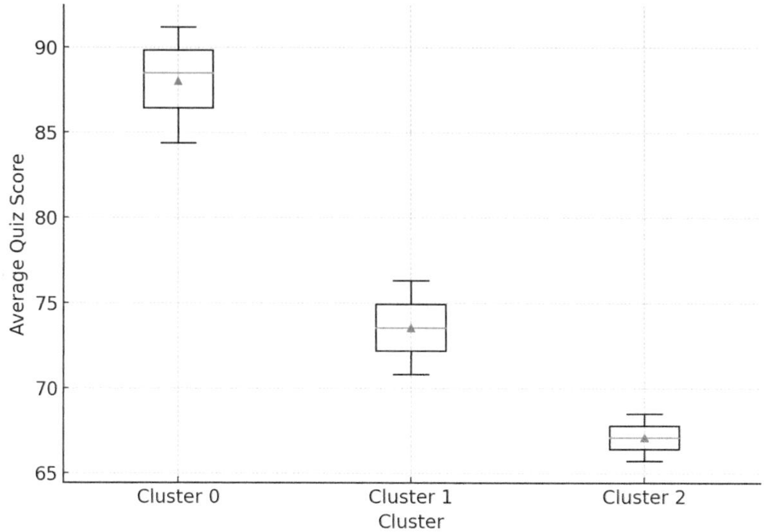

FIGURE 3.5 Visualization of the distribution of average quiz scores by cluster.

performance. Cluster 0 (Consistent Learners) consists of students who regularly log in, review lectures, and achieve consistently high quiz scores. Cluster 1 is characterized by irregular engagement, with activity spikes close to deadlines and moderate quiz outcomes. Cluster 2 comprises students who exhibit minimal platform interaction, limited discussion participation, and comparatively lower quiz performance. The table highlights representative students from each cluster, illustrating how the clustering approach captures meaningful behavioral archetypes that can guide targeted academic interventions.

As shown in Figure 3.5, the distribution of average quiz scores differs markedly by cluster. Cluster 0 exhibits the highest central tendency with relatively tight dispersion, reflecting consistently strong performance. Cluster 1 shows mid-range scores with moderate spread, while Cluster 2 has the lowest center and a narrow range. Cluster 0 shows sustained, proactive engagement; Cluster 1 exhibits irregular participation and procrastination (last-minute work); and Cluster 2 reflects minimal interaction and low overall engagement.

3.6 INTEGRATING GENERATIVE AI IN STEM LEARNING PLATFORMS

Integrating GenAI into STEM learning platforms represents a paradigm shift in how educational environments adapt to learners' emotional and behavioral states. The combination of real-time monitoring, adaptive feedback, and behavioral nudging mechanisms enables the creation of a learning ecosystem that dynamically supports students in a personalized, empathetic, and engaging manner. Unlike static, preprogrammed tutoring systems, GenAI can synthesize responses, adjust strategies, and produce content, transforming a one-size-fits-all educational experience into an evolving, student-centered learning environment.

3.6.1 Real-Time Emotion Monitoring in Virtual Classrooms

Real-time emotion monitoring is one of the most impactful applications of GenAI in online STEM learning. Virtual classrooms, enabled by platforms such as Zoom, Microsoft Teams, or WebRTC-based systems, are increasingly common in blended and remote STEM education. These platforms provide multiple streams of multimodal data, including video (facial expressions, gaze direction), audio (tone, pacing, speech hesitations), and text chat (sentiment, lexical patterns).

By integrating GenAI with these data streams, we can detect subtle emotional cues that might go unnoticed in a virtual environment. For example, persistent frowning and reduced verbal participation could indicate frustration or confusion, while frequent rapid chat messages might suggest excitement or cognitive overload. AI models, such as transformer-based text classifiers (for chat sentiment) and facial emotion recognition models (like FER or MediaPipe-based convolutional neural networks (CNNs)), process these inputs in real-time.

> **Technical Implementation**: The Zoom SDK, for example, allows developers to access video frames and chat transcripts. These can be piped into an AI inference layer where a combination of pretrained emotion classifiers and generative summarizers processes the incoming data. WebRTC provides similar hooks for peer-to-peer real-time streaming, making it feasible for custom learning platforms to integrate native emotion analysis.

The output of real-time monitoring is a continuously updated emotional profile of the class or individual students, which can be used to trigger targeted interventions. For example, if a group of students simultaneously shows rising confusion during a problem explanation, the instructor may receive a prompt to re-explain or provide hints.

3.6.2 AI Generates Personalized Hints or Encouragement

A real-time monitoring system is only as effective as the interventions it triggers. This is where GenAI-powered feedback loops excel. Rather than simply flagging an issue, the system actively engages the learner by generating personalized hints, scaffolding explanations, or encouragement messages.

Feedback loops work in three stages:

1. **Emotion Recognition**: The AI detects the learner's emotional state (e.g., frustration, boredom, confidence).
2. **Contextual Understanding**: The AI cross-references the emotional state with the current learning activity (e.g., a calculus problem, physics simulation, coding exercise).
3. **Generative Output**: The AI synthesizes a personalized response, a motivational prompt, an alternative problem-solving hint, or a simplified explanation.

This is achieved by leveraging LLMs fine-tuned on STEM-specific content. The key innovation is contextual grounding, ensuring that generated responses are directly tied to the learner's current task and emotional state.

Example Use Case: If a learner appears disengaged during a programming exercise on recursion, the AI might generate:

> Recursion can be tricky, but think of it like a set of Russian dolls. Let's try a smaller function first to see how it works.

Such responses make the feedback more human-like, empathetic, and instructional, creating an adaptive tutoring loop that adjusts in real time.

3.6.3 Gamified Behavioral Nudges Using Generative Models

Gamification has long been recognized as an effective strategy to sustain engagement in STEM learning, but GenAI takes gamification to a new level. Instead of relying on static badges or leaderboards, AI-driven gamification adapts dynamically to the learner's current motivation and engagement levels.

GenAI can:

- Create custom challenges when engagement drops.
- Adapt narrative-driven problem sets (e.g., turning a physics lesson into a space exploration quest).
- Generate meaningful rewards for each student (e.g., unlocking a custom badge or storyline when a difficult concept is mastered).
- Introduce behavioral nudges to encourage perseverance, curiosity, or collaboration.

The nudge system is particularly valuable in moments where students are at risk of disengagement. If emotion monitoring indicates a drop in attention or a plateau in performance, a generative model can create an on-the-fly challenge:

> You've unlocked a secret STEM quest: Solve this bonus coding puzzle to gain 50 exploration points.

Such nudges can be calibrated to each learner's profile, ensuring the challenge is achievable and stimulating. Over time, AI-generated nudges can be integrated into adaptive reward systems, building a sustained engagement loop.

3.6.4 Technical Integration of Generative AI in STEM Platforms

Integrating GenAI into STEM learning platforms requires a modular and scalable architecture that can process real-time multimodal inputs, perform inference on emotional and behavioral states, generate adaptive responses, and deliver them seamlessly to learners. This integration involves orchestrating several interconnected layers: data ingestion, processing, inference, generation, and delivery.

At its core, the integration relies on three foundational elements:

1. Real-time data collection pipelines.
2. AI inference engines for analysis and content generation.
3. Bidirectional feedback channels with the learning environment.

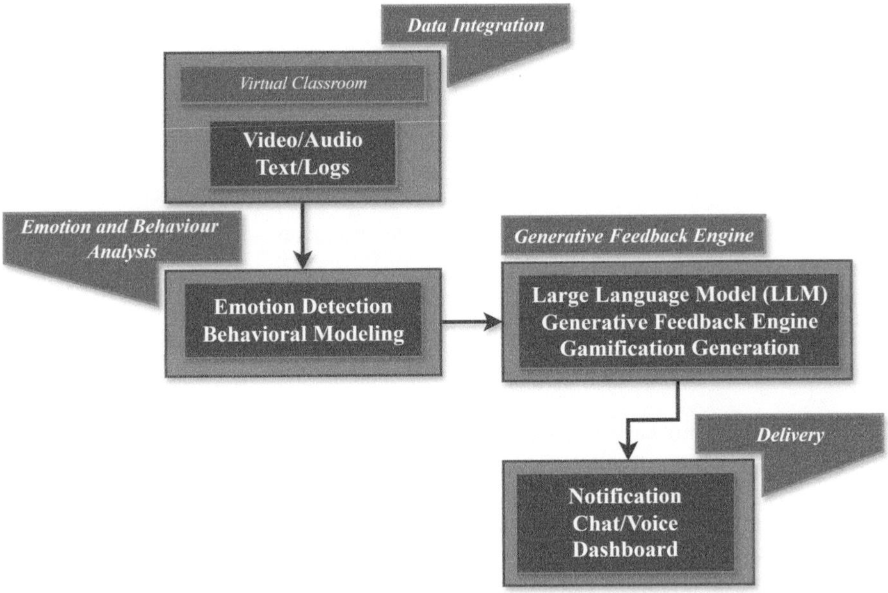

FIGURE 3.6 Layered technical architecture for integrating GenAI into STEM learning platforms, illustrating the flow from multimodal data ingestion to emotion and behavior analysis, generative feedback, and delivery of adaptive interventions.

The architecture illustrated in Figure 3.6 outlines the four-layer integration model for deploying GenAI within STEM learning platforms. At the top, the Data Ingestion layer captures multimodal input streams, including video, audio, text, and behavioral logs, through APIs such as Zoom SDK or WebRTC interfaces. These inputs feed into the Emotion and Behavior Analysis layer, where specialized models perform real-time emotion detection and behavioral modeling, generating structured affective profiles of learners. This information is then processed by the Generative Feedback Engine, which uses LLMs and gamification modules to create adaptive hints, motivational messages, and engagement challenges. Finally, the Delivery layer transmits these AI-generated interventions to the learner or instructor through integrated channels such as chat interfaces, voice synthesis, dashboards, or notification systems. This layered approach ensures modularity, scalability, and real-time responsiveness, making it a robust architecture for academic, professional, and enterprise STEM learning environments.

3.6.4.1 Data Ingestion Layer

The data ingestion layer captures all relevant multimodal inputs from the virtual learning environment. These can include:

- Video streams (captured from Zoom API, WebRTC, or proprietary platform SDKs) for facial expression and gaze analysis.
- Audio streams (microphone input during lectures or discussions) for speech-based emotion recognition and vocal engagement detection.

- Text-based interactions (chat messages, Q&A, discussion boards) for sentiment and emotional state analysis.
- Interaction logs (click behavior, problem attempts, tool usage patterns) for behavioral modeling.

The ingestion system must handle low-latency streaming for real-time emotion detection and batch processing for historical trend analysis. Technologies such as Kafka, WebSockets, or SignalR can provide scalable, event-driven ingestion.

3.6.4.2 Emotion and Behavior Analysis Engine

The analysis engine processes raw inputs into meaningful emotional and behavioral signals. This layer typically combines:

- Pretrained emotion detection models:
  - Facial emotion recognition (e.g., FER2013, MediaPipe-based CNNs).
  - Text sentiment classification (transformer-based models such as DistilRoBERTa fine-tuned for emotion detection).
  - Speech emotion analysis (prosody-based Recurrent Neural Network (RNN)/CNN models).
- Behavioral pattern detection:
  - Using embeddings from VAEs or clustering methods to detect engagement, persistence, or disengagement.

The engine produces structured emotional and behavioral metrics such as:

- Current emotional state: frustration, curiosity, confidence, and boredom.
- Engagement level: high, medium, and low.
- Risk prediction: likelihood of disengagement or error persistence.

These outputs are stored in a low-latency cache *(e.g., Redis)* for immediate retrieval by the feedback system.

3.6.4.3 Generative Feedback Engine

The generative feedback engine uses the analyzed emotional and behavioral context to create adaptive interventions. This engine has two primary subsystems:

1. LLM-based Hint and Encouragement Generator
   a. Uses models like GPT, GPT-Neo, or LLaMA to generate personalized responses.
   b. Inputs include: detected emotion, current learning activity, student history, and difficulty level.
   c. Example input prompt: *"Student is frustrated with a calculus derivative problem. Generate an empathetic hint with a step-by-step suggestion."*
   d. Example output: *"You're making good progress. Let's simplify the problem: focus on differentiating one term at a time."*

2. Gamification and Nudge Generator
   a. Uses generative models to create challenges, quizzes, or storylines dynamically.
   b. Adjusts the difficulty level to match engagement and proficiency.
   c. Example output: *"You've unlocked a bonus physics puzzle—solve it to earn 20 exploration points!"*

This layer can operate in real time (responding instantly during a live session) or asynchronous mode (providing follow-up resources after the session).

3.6.4.4 Delivery Layer

The delivery layer ensures that generated outputs are integrated into the learning platform in a nondisruptive, timely, and contextually appropriate manner. Delivery channels include:

- In-class notifications (chat messages, visual overlays).
- Voice feedback (via TTS engines such as gTTS, Tacotron, or VALL-E).
- Gamified dashboards (displaying rewards, challenges, and progress).
- Instructor alerts (summaries of student emotional trends and suggested interventions).

This layer acts as the interface between the AI system and the learning platform's user interface (UI).

3.6.4.5 Platform Integration Models

There are two primary integration models for adding GenAI into STEM learning platforms:

1. Embedded Integration (Native AI capabilities within the LMS/virtual classroom software)
   a. Suitable for proprietary platforms where the AI system is tightly integrated into the codebase.
   b. Offers low latency and better control of data flow.
   c. Example: A custom WebRTC platform with built in real-time AI modules.
2. External AI Microservices (AI as a separate service connected via API)
   a. Suitable for scalable, cross-platform integration.
   b. Uses REST/GraphQL APIs or WebSockets to exchange emotional data and receive generative responses.
   c. Allows the same AI engine to serve multiple learning platforms.

3.7 EMOTION-AWARE GEN-AI MODELS FOR ADAPTIVE SUPPORT IN STEM LEARNING

The Gen-AI-based vision model in Figure 3.7 demonstrates its capability to interpret students' emotions, including neutral, happiness, sadness, and anger, through facial

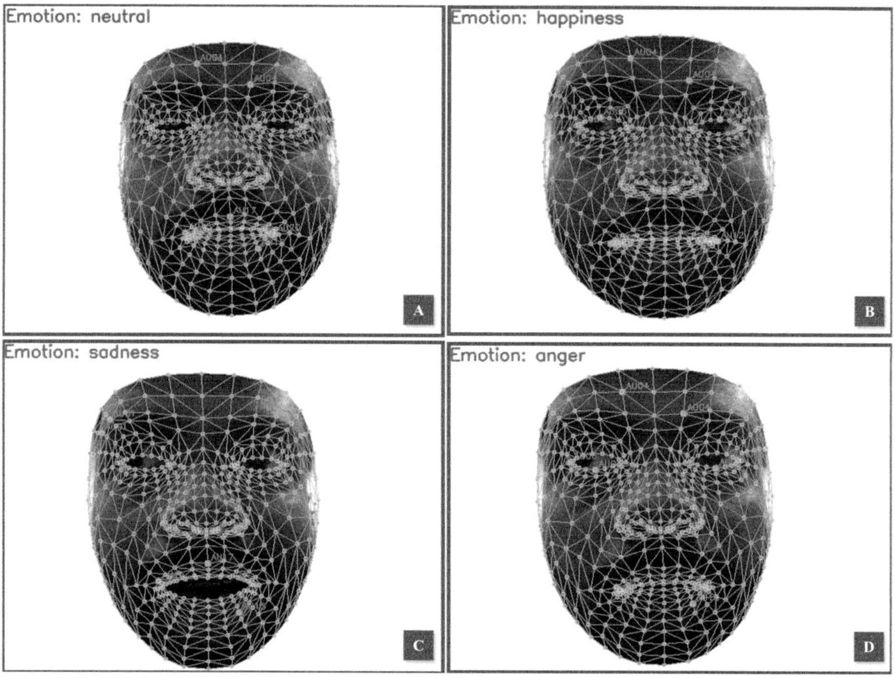

FIGURE 3.7 Emotional variation of the users during the learning period.

The image shows the Action Unit mesh of the facial landmarks.

landmark analysis, enabling tailored responses that enhance STEM learning experiences. In a neutral state (A), the model encourages exploration by offering optional resources while safeguarding emotional well-being. When detecting happiness (B), it acknowledges positive affect, reinforcing self-confidence and suggesting strategies that foster emotional and behavioral engagement. For sadness (C), the model identifies emotional distress and recommends supportive approaches to build resilience and address behavioral needs. In cases of anger (D), it recognizes challenges in emotional regulation and adapts responses to help students develop coping strategies. This emotionally aware adaptation highlights the model's potential to create a supportive, personalized, and responsive learning environment.

Table 3.5 illustrates how a GenAI model adapts responses based on students' emotional states during STEM learning. When students express happiness, the model acknowledges their emotional well-being and suggests strategies that promote emotional and behavioral engagement. In a neutral state, the model offers general encouragement and optional resources, while emphasizing the importance of maintaining personal well-being. When students express anger or sadness, the model identifies emotional distress and, particularly for sadness, recommends strategies to support emotional resilience and behavioral needs. These tailored responses demonstrate the model's potential to offer emotionally responsive support that aligns with students' affective states, ultimately enhancing the learning experience.

TABLE 3.5
GenAI Model Responses According to the Students' Emotions During STEM Learning

Emotion	Model Response
Neutral (see Figure 3.3(a))	• If you want to learn more about this topic, please visit the links below. • The student will not compromise the student's personal and emotional health.
Happiness (see Figure 3.3(b))	• The student is experiencing a sense of self, independence, and self-confidence. • The student is experiencing happiness. Provide a learning strategy that supports both emotional and behavioral needs.
Sadness (see Figure 3.3(c))	• The student is in distress. • The student is experiencing sadness. Provide a learning strategy that supports both emotional and behavioral needs.
Anger (see Figure 3.3(d))	• The student is experiencing difficulties learning to handle.

3.8 CHALLENGES AND ETHICAL CONCERNS

GenAI holds transformative potential for identifying and addressing emotional and behavioral barriers in STEM education. By monitoring student engagement, detecting affective states, and personalizing learning experiences, these advanced systems can provide support that extends far beyond the capabilities of traditional methods. However, alongside this promise comes significant complexity. As GenAI becomes more deeply integrated into educational settings, it introduces various technical, ethical, and social challenges that must be carefully navigated. Data privacy, algorithmic bias, transparency, and fairness are particularly critical when working with sensitive emotional and behavioral data. Without responsible design and implementation, the use of AI in emotionally charged learning environments risks causing unintended harm or reinforcing existing inequalities. Table 3.6 provides an overview of the key challenges and ethical concerns related to GenAI in STEM education, highlighting each issue and its potential risks or consequences [64–66].

Table 3.6 highlights that while GenAI offers innovative tools for improving student outcomes, its deployment in STEM education is not without critical risks. The most immediate concerns relate to privacy and data security, mainly when AI systems rely on real-time, sensitive inputs such as facial expressions or emotional tone. Without strong data governance, such practices could undermine trust and student autonomy. Equally concerning is the issue of bias and fairness; AI tools trained on limited or non-inclusive datasets may inaccurately assess students from diverse cultural or neurodiverse backgrounds, perpetuating inequities rather than resolving them. Additionally, the lack of transparency and explainability in AI decision-making can make it difficult for educators and students to understand or challenge outcomes. Overreliance on AI systems may further erode the critical role of human judgment in teaching, reducing nuanced engagement with learners. Ultimately, ethical concerns regarding manipulation, labeling, and equity of access

TABLE 3.6
Key Challenges and Ethical Concerns in Using GenAI for Emotional and Behavioral Analysis in STEM Education

Challenge/Ethical Concern	Description	Risks/Potential Impacts
Privacy and data security	Collection of sensitive data (e.g., facial expressions, biometrics, language use).	Data breaches, loss of student trust, perceived surveillance, and legal noncompliance.
Bias and fairness	AI models may reflect biases from nondiverse or unbalanced training data.	Misinterpretation of emotions or behaviors, especially across cultures or neurotypes.
Informed consent and autonomy	Students must understand and agree to how their data is used and analyzed.	Coerced participation, lack of transparency, and erosion of student agency.
Overreliance on automation	Teachers may depend too heavily on AI recommendations without critical evaluation.	Missed contextual cues, reduced educator discretion, and diminished teacher–student relationships.
Transparency and explainability	Many AI models lack human-readable reasoning for their outputs.	Difficulty in understanding or making challenging decisions, resulting in reduced trust in AI-generated feedback.
Emotional manipulation	AI may adjust content or tone based on detected emotional states.	Risk of nudging or manipulating behavior, potential emotional harm, or dependency.
Labeling and stigmatization	Categorizing students based on emotional or behavioral profiles.	Negative labeling, self-fulfilling prophecies, and biased treatment by educators or peers.
Equity in access and use	Not all schools or students have equal access to reliable AI tools or data safeguards.	Widening the digital divide leads to disproportionate harm for underserved or marginalized communities.

underscore the need for robust regulatory frameworks and inclusive design practices. As such, implementing GenAI in STEM education must be approached cautiously, ensuring it supports human-centered, ethical learning environments rather than supplanting them.

As GenAI continues to expand its role in STEM education, especially in emotional and behavioral analysis, ethical design and responsible implementation are paramount. These technologies should empower, not exploit; support, not surveil. Navigating these challenges requires collaboration among AI developers, educators, ethicists, and policymakers to ensure that the benefits of innovation do not come at the cost of students' dignity, equity, and autonomy.

3.9 CONCLUSION

As STEM education increasingly moves into digital and hybrid spaces, integrating GenAI for emotional and behavioral analysis represents a powerful evolution in learner-centered design. Instead of treating emotions and behaviors as secondary to academic outcomes, educators can now treat them as integral components of the learning process, measurable, interpretable, and improvable. By identifying when students are struggling emotionally, disengaging behaviorally, or doubting themselves, GenAI can help educators intervene earlier, with greater precision and compassion. This shift can improve academic outcomes and cultivate more confident, resilient, and emotionally intelligent learners.

In the long term, GenAI can help reframe STEM education, not as a cold, technical journey but as a profoundly human one, where emotional and behavioral well-being is essential to intellectual growth. When used thoughtfully, this technology can help unlock a more inclusive and adaptive future for STEM education, where every student has the opportunity to thrive.

NOTES

1 https://www.ibm.com/think/insights/how-ibm-is-shaping-ai-governance-in-education-with-smarter-balanced.
2 https://www.ibm.com/think/news/tech-companies-supercharge-ai-in-classroom.

REFERENCES

1. Johnson, S. L., Bishop, J. P., & Rogers, K. D. (2025). Shifting pedagogically: Incorporating the social, cultural, and emotional dimensions of student learning to develop STEM-identities in computer science. *Journal of Applied Developmental Psychology*, 97, 101757–101757. https://doi.org/10.1016/j.appdev.2025.101757
2. Pleasants, K. (2023). Integrative approaches in education: Bridging STEM and the arts. *Xpertno International Journal of Interdisciplinary Research (XIJIR)*, 1(1), 30–42. https://doi.org/10.5281/zenodo.10053569
3. Sokolova, E. V., Blaginin, V. A., & Shatrova, A. Y. (2025). Evolution and current trends in STEM education: A retrospective and bibliometric analysis. *Journal of Hypermedia & Technology-Enhanced Learning (J-HyTEL)*, 3(1), 90–107. https://doi.org/10.58536/j-hytel.169
4. Ayeni, O. O., Chisom, O. N., Al Hamad, N. M., Osawaru, B., & Adewusi, O. E. (2024). Enhancing STEM education through emotional intelligence and counseling techniques. *World Journal of Advanced Research and Reviews*, 21(2), 903–916.
5. Murphy, S., MacDonald, A., Wang, C. A., & Danaia, L. (2019). Towards an understanding of STEM engagement: A review of the literature on motivation and academic emotions. *Canadian Journal of Science Mathematics and Technology Education*, 19(3), 304–320. https://doi.org/10.1007/s42330-019-00054-w
6. Garner, P. W., Nuria G., Gupta, A., & Wood, T. (2017). Innovations in science education: Infusing social emotional principles into early STEM learning. *Cultural Studies of Science Education*, 13(4), 889–903. https://doi.org/10.1007/s11422-017-9826-0
7. Friedlaender, G. E., & Friedlaender, L. K. (2018). Edvard munch and the scream: A cry for help. *Clinical Orthopaedics & Related Research*, 476(2), 200–202. https://doi.org/10.1007/s11999.0000000000000046

8. Borah, A. R., Nischith, N. T., & Gupta, S. (2024). Improved learning based on GenAI. 1527–1532. https://doi.org/10.1109/idciot59759.2024.10467943
9. Hu, W., & Shao, Z. (2025). Design and evaluation of a GenAI-based personalized educational content system tailored to personality traits and emotional responses for adaptive learning. *Computers in Human Behavior Reports*, 100735–100735. https://doi.org/10.1016/j.chbr.2025.100735
10. Zhang, Y., Liu, H., Li, X., & Fan, Y. (2025). Learners' emotion and motivation while learning with GenAI. *Routledge EBooks*, 88–123. https://doi.org/10.4324/9781003632146-4
11. Divya, G. S. (2025). *Impact of GenAI on student outcomes*. Chapman and Hall/CRC EBooks, 139–175. https://doi.org/10.1201/9781003422433-7
12. L'Heureux, A., Katarina, G., Elyamany, H. F., & Miriam. (2017). Machine learning with big data: Challenges and approaches. *IEEE Access*, 5, 7776–7797. https://doi.org/10.1109/access.2017.2696365
13. Wilson, A., & Anwar, M. R. (2024). The future of adaptive machine learning algorithms in high-dimensional data processing. *International Transactions on Artificial Intelligence (ITALIC)*, 3(1), 97–107. https://doi.org/10.33050/italic.v3i1.656
14. Shethiya, A. S. (2024). Adaptive learning machines: A framework for dynamic and real-time ML applications. *Annals of Applied Sciences*, 5(1). https://annalsofappliedsciences.com/index.php/aas/article/view/23
15. Memon, T. D., & Kwan, P. (2025). A collaborative model for integrating teacher and GenAI into future education. *TechTrends*. https://doi.org/10.1007/s11528-025-01105-w
16. Vytautas, Š., Burbaitė, R., Mikas, B., & Giedrius, Z. (2025). Developing problem-solving skills to support sustainability in STEM education using generative AI tools. *Sustainability*, 17(15), 6935–6935. https://doi.org/10.3390/su17156935
17. Pabba, C., & Kumar, P. (2021). An intelligent system for monitoring students' engagement in large classroom teaching through facial expression recognition. *Expert Systems*. https://doi.org/10.1111/exsy.12839
18. Almasre, M., Alsaggaf, W., Al-Malki, N., & Brdesee, H. (2025). Emotional engagement prediction and LLM feedback in smart learning environments. *International Journal of Artificial Intelligence in Education*. https://doi.org/10.1007/s40593-025-00504-7
19. Zhang, Y., Liu, H., Xiao, Y., Amoon, M., Zhang, D., Wang, D., Yang, S., & Quek, C. (2024). LLM-enhanced multi-teacher knowledge distillation for modality-incomplete emotion recognition in daily healthcare. *IEEE Journal of Biomedical and Health Informatics*, 1–11. https://doi.org/10.1109/jbhi.2024.3470338
20. Mohan, M., Salah, B, Munkhjargal, G., & Alnajjar, F. (2025). Comparing emotion detection methods in online classrooms: YOLO models, multimodal LLM, and human baseline. *IEEE Global Engineering Education Conference (EDUCON)*, 2022, 1–7. https://doi.org/10.1109/educon62633.2025.11016401
21. Abdelrahman, L., Ashraf, A., Barakat, M., Saleh, K., Ahmed, E., Sherif, B., Badawy, A. N., & Ghada, K. (2024). A comparative analysis of large language models for automated course content generation from books. 437–442. https://doi.org/10.1109/niles63360.2024.10753166
22. Trust, P., & Minghim, R. (2024). A study on text classification in the age of large language models. *Machine Learning & Knowledge Extraction*, 6(4), 2688–2721. https://doi.org/10.3390/make6040129
23. Aist, G., Kort, B., Reilly, R., Mostow, J., & Picard, R. (2025). Experimentally augmenting an intelligent tutoring system with human-supplied capabilities: adding human-provided emotional scaffolding to an automated reading tutor that listens. *Proceedings. Fourth IEEE International Conference on Multimodal Interfaces*, 483–490. https://doi.org/10.1109/icmi.2002.1167044

24. Mostow, J., & Aist, G. (2001). Evaluating tutors who listen: An overview of project LISTEN. In K. D. Forbus & P. J. Feltovich (Eds.), *Smart machines in education: The coming revolution in educational technology* (pp. 169–234). The MIT Press.
25. Marquez-Carpintero, L., Viejo, D. Y., Cazorla, M. (2025). Enhancing engineering and STEM education with vision and multimodal large language models to predict student attention. *IEEE Access*, 13, 114681–114695. https://doi.org/10.1109/access.2025.3584025
26. Ortega-Ochoa, E., Sabaté, J.-M., Arguedas, M., Conesa, J., Daradoumis, T., & Caballé, S. (2024). Exploring the utilization and deficiencies of Generative Artificial Intelligence in students' cognitive and emotional needs: A systematic mini-review. *Frontiers in Artificial Intelligence*, 7. https://doi.org/10.3389/frai.2024.1493566
27. Ralston, K., Chen, Y., Haruna, I., & Farhana, Z. (2019). A Voice Interactive Multilingual Student Support System using IBM Watson. *2021 20th IEEE international conference on machine learning and applications (ICMLA)*. https://doi.org/10.1109/icmla.2019.00309
28. University of Illinois at Urbana-Champaign (UIUC). (n.d.). SALT Lab. Retrieved April 10, 2025, from https://salt.ischool.illinois.edu/research.html
29. Curry, A. C., & Curry, A. C. (2023). Computer says "No": The case against empathetic conversational AI. *Findings of the Association for computational linguistics: ACL 2022* (pp. 8123–8130). https://doi.org/10.18653/v1/2023.findings-acl.515
30. Conati, C., & Zhao, X. (2004, January). Building and evaluating an intelligent pedagogical agent to improve the effectiveness of an educational game. In *Proceedings of the 9th international conference on intelligent user interfaces* (pp. 6–13).
31. Baker, R. S. D., Corbett, A. T., Koedinger, K. R., Evenson, S., Roll, I., Wagner, A. Z., ... & Beck, J. E. (2006, June). Adapting to when students game an intelligent tutoring system. In *International conference on intelligent tutoring systems* (pp. 392–401). Berlin, Heidelberg: Springer Berlin Heidelberg.
32. Lee, H.-P. H., Sarkar, A., Lev Tankelevitch, Drosos, I., Rintel, S., Banks, R., & Wilson, N. (2025). *The impact of generative AI on critical thinking: Self-reported reductions in cognitive effort and confidence effects from a survey of knowledge workers* (pp. 1–22). https://doi.org/10.1145/3706598.3713778
33. Conati, C. (2002). Probabilistic assessment of user's emotions in educational games. *Applied Artificial Intelligence*, 16(7–8), 555–575. https://doi.org/10.1080/08839510290030390
34. Ahuja, K., Kim, D., Xhakaj, F., Varga, V., Xie, A., Zhang, S., Townsend, J. E., Harrison, C., Ogan, A., & Agarwal, Y. (2019). EduSense. *Proceedings of the ACM on Interactive, Mobile, Wearable and Ubiquitous Technologies*, 3(3), 1–26. https://doi.org/10.1145/3351229
35. Schubert, M., Durruty, D., & Joyner, D. A. (2018, June). Measuring learner tone and sentiment at scale via text analysis of forum posts. In *CEUR workshop proceedings* (Vol. 2141, pp. 30–34).
36. Fischer, I., Sweeney, S., Lucas, M., & Gupta, N. (2024). Making sense of generative AI for assessments: Contrasting student claims and assessor evaluations. *The International Journal of Management Education*, 22(3), 101081–101081. https://doi.org/10.1016/j.ijme.2024.101081
37. Bosch, N., D'Mello, S. K., Baker, R. S., Ocumpaugh, J., Shute, V., Ventura, M., Wang, L., & Zhao, W. (2016). Detecting student emotions in computer-enabled classrooms. *IJCAI international joint conference on artificial intelligence*, 2016-January, 4125–4129.
38. Bhatt, P., Sethi, A., Vaibhav, T., Shroff, J., Isha, P., Desai, A., Sinha, P., Deshpande, A., Joshi, G., Anil, R., Jain, P., Rahee, W., Kotecha, K., & Jain, N. K. (2023). Machine learning for cognitive behavioral analysis: datasets, methods, paradigms, and research directions. *Brain Informatics*, 10(1). https://doi.org/10.1186/s40708-023-00196-6

39. Wang, K. D., Wu, Z., Tufts, L., Wieman, C., Salehi, S., & Haber, N. (2025). Scaffold or crutch? Examining college students' use and views of generative AI tools for STEM education. *2022 IEEE global engineering education conference (EDUCON)* (pp. 1–10). https://doi.org/10.1109/educon62633.2025.11016406
40. Takara, M. Y., Fethiye, O., & Connell, A. E. (2025, June 22). Harnessing the power of GenAI: A new era for data science education for civil and environmental engineering. *Asee.org*. https://doi.org/10.18260/1-2--56684
41. Changkui, L. C.. (2025). Applications of Large Multimodal Models (LMMs) in STEM education: *From Visual Explanations to Virtual Experiments*, 1(2), 1–18. https://doi.org/10.6914/aiese.010201
42. Heilala, V., Araya, R., & Hämäläinen, R. (2025). Beyond Text-to-Text: An overview of multimodal and generative artificial intelligence for education using topic modeling. *Proceedings of the 40th ACM/SIGAPP Symposium on Applied Computing*, 54–63. https://doi.org/10.1145/3672608.3707764
43. Gao, Y., Zhai, X., Li, M., Lee, G., & Liu, X. (2025). A multimodal interactive framework for science assessment in the era of generative artificial intelligence. *Journal of Research in Science Teaching* https://doi.org/10.1002/tea.70009
44. Ching, K., Pun, J., Wangyin, K.-L., & Mai, J. (2024). Exploring students' multimodal representations of ideas about epistemic reading of scientific texts in generative AI tools. *Journal of Science Education and Technology*. https://doi.org/10.1007/s10956-024-10182-0
45. Chu, H.-C., Lu, Y.-C., & Tu, Y.-F. (2025). How GenAI-supported multi-modal presentations benefit students with different motivation levels: Evidence from digital storytelling performance, critical thinking awareness, and learning attitude. *Educational Technology & Society*, 28(1), 250–269. https://www.jstor.org/stable/48810718
46. Lee, U., Jeong, Y., Kim, S., Son, Y., Byun, G., Kim, H., & Lim, C. (2025). How can video generative AI transform K-12 education? examining teachers' perspectives through TPACK and TAM. ArXiv.org. https://arxiv.org/abs/2503.08003
47. Rajesh, S. G., Smriti, V. M., Gauri, S. P., & Rolla, S. (2025). Enhancement of virtual assistants through MultiModal AI for emotion recognition. *IEEE Access*, 102159–102179. https://doi.org/10.1109/access.2025.3577664
48. Spanio, M. (2024). Towards emotionally aware AI: Challenges and opportunities in the evolution of multimodal generative models. *Proceedings of the AIxIA doctoral consortium, 2024.*
49. Choudhury, A. (2025). Data collection and preprocessing for generative AI. *Advances in Business Strategy and Competitive Advantage Book Series*, 1–32. https://doi.org/10.4018/979-8-3693-7026-1.ch001
50. Culjak, I., Abram, D., Pribanic, T., Dzapo, H., & Cifrek, M. (2012, May). A brief introduction to OpenCV. In *2012, proceedings of the 35th International Convention MIPRO* (pp. 1725–1730). IEEE.
51. Lugaresi, C., Tang, J., Nash, H., McClanahan, C., Uboweja, E., Hays, M., Zhang, F., Chang, C.-L., Yong, M. G., Lee, J., Chang, W.-T., Hua, W., Georg, M., & Grundmann, M. (2019). MediaPipe: A framework for building perception pipelines. ArXiv.org. https://arxiv.org/abs/1906.08172
52. Pawar, V., Abhijit, V., Chavan, P., Siddhi, G., & Nair, S. (2024). The Future of Emotional Engineering: Integrating Generative AI and Emotional Intelligence. *2022 6th international conference on computing, communication, control and automation (ICCUBEA)*, 1–6. https://doi.org/10.1109/iccubea61740.2024.10775105
53. Li, X., & Bryan-Kinns, N. (2025). Generative AI for affective vibration: Human-centered evaluation of LLM and VAE models. *Proceedings of the 2025 conference on creativity and cognition*, 377–383. https://doi.org/10.1145/3698061.3734410

54. Zohar, E., Elad, R., Kfir, A., Lvovsky, M., Yoav, S., & Dorit, H.-S. (2023). Capacity of generative AI to interpret human emotions from visual and textual data: Pilot evaluation study. *JMIR Mental Health*, 11, e54369. https://doi.org/10.2196/54369
55. Markowitz, D. M. (2024). Can generative AI infer thinking style from language? Evaluating the utility of AI as a psychological text analysis tool. *Behavior Research Methods*, 56(4), 3548–3559. https://doi.org/10.3758/s13428-024-02344-0
56. Mikeska, J. N., Klebanov, B. B., Bhatia, A., Halder, S., & Suhan, M. (2025). Evaluating the use of generative artificial intelligence to support learning opportunities for teachers to practice engaging in key instructional skills. *Lecture Notes in Computer Science*, 378–391. https://doi.org/10.1007/978-3-031-98417-4_27
57. Pathak, A., Hardik, M., Bhavnish, S., Sahil, B., & Venkatesan, M. (2024). Emotion-aware text to speech: Bridging sentiment analysis and voice synthesis. 1–7. https://doi.org/10.1109/inocon60754.2024.10512224
58. Guo, Y., Li, G., Xie, C., & Sun, Q. (2025). Evolution and perspectives of speech synthesis technology: From parametric synthesis to the era of large language models. 350–353. https://doi.org/10.1109/icaid65275.2025.11034615
59. Melton, M., & Dorodchi, M. M. (2025, June). The Role of Predictive and Generative AI in Shaping Modern Education: Current Applications and Opportunities. Paper presented at *2025 ASEE annual conference & exposition*, Montreal, Quebec, Canada.
60. Bond-Taylor, S., Leach, A., Long, Y., & Willcocks, C. G. (2021). Deep generative modelling: A comparative review of VAEs, GANs, normalizing flows, energy-based and autoregressive models. *IEEE Transactions on Pattern Analysis and Machine Intelligence*, 44(11), 7327–7347. https://doi.org/10.1109/tpami.2021.3116668
61. Akbari, F., Sartipi, K., & Archer, N. (2022). Synthetic behavior sequence generation using generative adversarial networks. *ACM Transactions on Computing for Healthcare*. https://doi.org/10.1145/3563950
62. Alessandro, S., Wang, Y., Wichern, G., Toshiaki, K.-A., Ohta, Y., Kaneko, Y., Laughman, C., & Chakrabarty, A. (2023). Synthesizing building operation data with generative models: VAEs, GANs, or something in between? 125–133. https://doi.org/10.1145/3599733.3600260
63. Choi, J.-G., Nah, Y., Ko, I., & Han, S. (2021). Deep learning approach to generate a synthetic cognitive psychology behavioral dataset. *IEEE Access*, 9, 142489–142505. https://doi.org/10.1109/access.2021.3120083
64. Olohunfunmi, I. A., & Khairuddin, A. Z. (2024). Exploring ethical dilemmas of AI generative tools among higher education students: A systematic review. *Advances in Computer Science Research*, 255–275. https://doi.org/10.2991/978-94-6463-589-8_24
65. Farangi, M. R., Nejadghanbar, H., & Hu, G. (2024). The use of generative AI in research: Ethical considerations and emotional experiences. *Ethics & Behavior*, 1–17. https://doi.org/10.1080/10508422.2024.2420133
66. Henriksen, D., Creely, E., Gruber, N., & Leahy, S. (2025). Social-emotional learning and generative AI: A critical literature review and framework for teacher education. *Journal of Teacher Education*. https://doi.org/10.1177/00224871251325058

4 Generative AI for STEM Learning Among Visually, Hearing, and Speech-Impaired Students

4.1 INTRODUCTION

STEM education, comprising science, technology, engineering, and mathematics, remains a cornerstone of global innovation. Yet this domain too often proves exclusionary for students with visual, hearing, or speech impairments [1, 2]. The traditional reliance on visual diagrams, auditory lectures, and sensory-rich experiments erects significant barriers to participation. Physics is taught through force diagrams and sound waves; chemistry is taught through molecular models and vibrant reactions; mathematics is taught through equations and graphs; engineering is taught through intricate schematics [3, 4]. While these tools are commonplace for sighted and hearing learners, they present daunting obstacles for those with sensory or communicative disabilities. Although accommodations such as braille textbooks, tactile graphics, captioning, and interpreters offer partial relief, they are often resource-intensive, static, and provided reactively, long after the lesson has progressed.

Recent scholarship underscores these limitations. A systematic review by Voultsiou [5] of AI, VR, and LLMs in special education highlighted how personalization and adaptability are essential in meeting learners' unique needs, yet conventional tools remain insufficiently inclusive. Buzzi et al. [6] discussed AI-supported STEM tools for students with disabilities, noting persistent accessibility gaps and reinforcing the need for more adaptive and inclusive interventions.

Here, GenAI offers not just incremental improvement but truly transformative potential. Unlike earlier assistive technologies, GenAI is dynamic, flexible, multimodal, and capable of creating customized content on demand. It adapts across sensory modalities and responds interactively and immediately to learners' needs. For instance:

- It can generate tactile, 3D-printable models of molecules or graphs for visually impaired students.
- It can convert data into auditory sonifications, enabling learners to "hear" abstract patterns, techniques rooted in sensory substitution research and sonification methods [5–8].

DOI: 10.1201/9781003641490-4

- It can produce narrative descriptions that make complex concepts tangible.
- For deaf students, GenAI can offer real-time captioning enriched with STEM vocabulary, animated sign-language avatars, and translate sound-based demonstrations into real-time visual animations.

These capabilities are supported by emerging assistive devices, such as Audo-Sight, which integrates multimodal LLMs to deliver context-aware interaction for visually impaired users in real time [9], and Audemy. This AI-powered audio-based learning platform personalizes content for visually impaired students based on engagement and pacing [8, 10]. In contrast to traditional tools, braille arrives late, tactile visuals can't capture dynamic discourse, captions often miss technical precision, and interpreters may be unavailable. GenAI closes this "access gap" by delivering simultaneous and modality-rich content, descriptions, sounds, and tactile models, allowing students to access complex STEM content alongside their peers, not retrospectively.

This immediacy has profound implications for classroom participation and the development of learner identity. Research on inclusive education indicates that delayed access can diminish comprehension, undermine participation, and erode confidence. By enabling real-time engagement, GenAI helps learners ask questions, contribute meaningfully, and nurture a sense of belonging in STEM contexts. It transforms learners' perceptions, helping them see themselves not as outsiders, but as scientists, mathematicians, and engineers. From a pedagogical perspective, GenAI also eases the burden on educators and institutions. Accessibility planning often demands specialized training and extensive prep time. AI's real-time content adaptation allows teachers to concentrate on pedagogy rather than formatting. Institutions benefit from scalable, cost-effective tools that supersede bespoke, labor-intensive accommodations, making inclusive STEM learning feasible even in underserved or rural settings.

Yet, meaningful integration of GenAI requires vigilance. Tools must be accurate, ethically designed, compatible with accessibility standards, and transparent in their operation. Research emphasizes the importance of incorporating accessibility principles from the outset, not as an afterthought. For example, studies applying Web Content Accessibility Guidelines (WCAGs) 2.2 to GenAI tools found systemic accessibility barriers and emphasized the need for proactive, inclusive design aligned with regulatory and ethical imperatives [11]. Moreover, frameworks that combine AI and universal design advocate for adaptable, configurable systems that support diverse user needs while addressing privacy, bias, and ethics [12].

As this chapter unfolds, we will explore challenges, solutions, case studies, and future directions, ranging from real-time captioning and sign-language avatars to tactile models and sonified graphs. The innovations affirm a powerful truth: accessibility in STEM isn't a separate pathway but a catalyst for richer, more creative education for all. The journey is just beginning, but the vision is clear: a world where no learner, no matter their sensory or communicative ability, is left outside the lab, the lecture hall, or the equation.

4.2 CHALLENGES IN STEM FOR VISUALLY, HEARING, AND SPEECH-IMPAIRED LEARNERS

STEM subjects present some of the most rewarding yet complex areas of study. They are inherently multisensory, often requiring students to visualize, listen, manipulate, and analyze simultaneously. While this dynamic approach stimulates curiosity for many learners, it can also be a source of exclusion for students with sensory impairments. For visually and hearing-impaired learners, the barriers are not simply about "missing out" on one sensory input; they compound into structural disadvantages that affect confidence, participation, and long-term achievement in science and mathematics [13, 14].

Below, the authors explore the specific challenges faced by visually impaired students, as well as those faced by D/HH students, and the overlapping systemic obstacles that affect both groups.

4.2.1 Barriers for Visually Impaired Students

STEM subjects present some of the most rewarding yet complex areas of study. They are inherently multisensory, often requiring students to visualize, listen, manipulate, and analyze simultaneously. While this dynamic approach stimulates curiosity for many learners, it can also be a source of exclusion for students with sensory impairments. For visually and hearing-impaired learners, the barriers are not simply about "missing out" on one sensory input; they compound into structural disadvantages that affect confidence, participation, and long-term achievement in science and mathematics [15–17].

Below, we explore the challenges faced by visually impaired and deaf students, as well as the overlapping systemic obstacles that affect both groups.

- **Diagram-Heavy Content**: One of the most striking challenges is the reliance on visual representations in STEM. Physics concepts such as force vectors are almost always taught using arrows and diagrams. Chemistry lessons rely on visualizations of molecules, bonding structures, and orbital configurations. Biology lessons include detailed illustrations of cells, organs, or ecosystems. These diagrams provide sighted students with a quick, "big picture" view of abstract ideas. However, these images may be inaccessible for visually impaired students or reduced to simplified descriptions that strip away nuance. Imagine repeatedly hearing the words "as shown in the diagram" in class, with no tactile or auditory equivalent. Without alternatives, students are left building incomplete mental models of complex concepts [18, 19]. As shown in Table 4.1, these challenges span multiple STEM disciplines, where reliance on visual symbols or illustrations creates consistent obstacles to comprehension.
- **Laboratory Work**: Laboratory activities, often considered the heart of STEM learning, pose another set of challenges. Experiments usually rely on visual cues, such as a color change in a chemical reaction, the movement of liquid in a burette, or the appearance of a flame. Equipment like

TABLE 4.1
Examples of Diagram-Heavy Content in STEM and Their Impact on Visually Impaired Learners

Example of Barrier	Impact
Vector diagrams in physics	Concepts remain abstract without tactile or auditory substitutes.
Molecular models in chemistry	Oversimplification through verbal descriptions.
Biological illustrations	Nuanced understanding of structures lost.

oscilloscopes, thermometers, or pressure gauges often rely on analog dials or digital displays but lack auditory alternatives. This can lead to partial participation or exclusion for a visually impaired learner. Teachers may hesitate to allow independent work due to safety concerns, but this effectively denies students the hands-on experiences that make STEM engaging.

- **Graph and Data Interpretation**: Graphs, charts, and data tables are essential in STEM because they summarize results and highlight patterns. Yet, interpreting a graph is primarily a visual process: students must see slopes, clusters, or intersections to grasp its meaning. Visually impaired students often rely on screen readers, which can only relay text labels sequentially, not the shape of the data. This creates a barrier to higher-order analysis, where students must interpret trends rather than isolated points.

4.2.2 Barriers for Hearing-Impaired Students

STEM education presents unique challenges for deaf students, not because of a lack of ability, but due to the barriers inherent in traditional teaching methods. Lecture-heavy instruction, group-based learning, and sound-dependent experiments are standard in science and engineering classrooms, yet each of these formats assumes full auditory access. When accurate captions, interpreters, or adaptive tools are missing, or when the classroom environment itself hinders inclusion, D/HH learners face disproportionate obstacles in keeping pace with their peers [20–23].

- **Lecture-Based Delivery**: The lecture format remains a double-edged sword for deaf students. While efficient for teachers, lectures depend on spoken delivery. Without accurate real-time captions or interpreters, students quickly fall behind in their learning. Even with captions, misinterpreting technical vocabulary is common; confusing "ion" with "iron" can derail entire explanations in chemistry.
- **Group Work**: STEM classrooms often encourage collaborative problem-solving. Yet, group discussions can be chaotic environments for D/HH learners. Multiple voices overlap, some students speak without facing them, and side conversations are easily missed. Even strong lip-readers struggle to keep pace with several speakers at once.

TABLE 4.2
Examples of Sound-Based STEM Tasks and Barriers for Deaf and Hard-of-Hearing Learners

Sound-Based STEM Task	Barrier for Hearing-Impaired Learners
Physics of resonance	Cannot perceive tones or beats.
Electronics circuits	Misses audible alerts or signals.
Acoustic wave labs	Disconnected from experimental results.

- **Auditory Experiments**: Certain branches of STEM rely directly on sound. Physics lessons on resonance, acoustics, or interference depend on the ability to hear tones or echoes. Electronics labs may involve recognizing beeps or hums as feedback.

Without visual or haptic substitutes, D/HH students are cut off from key experiences. Too often, these accommodations are overlooked, reinforcing feelings of exclusion. As summarized in Table 4.2, many auditory-based STEM tasks present barriers that require thoughtful redesign to ensure inclusion.

4.2.3 Barriers for Speech-Impaired Students

Speech-impaired students encounter distinct barriers in STEM classrooms, where speech-centered practices still predominate. Expectations surrounding oral presentations, viva voce assessments, and rapid-fire questioning can mask genuine understanding when learners are unable to demonstrate their knowledge verbally or are not offered flexible assessment options (e.g., written, digital, or AAC-supported responses[1]). Similarly, collaborative tasks often prioritize quick turn-taking, leaving students who communicate via speech-generating devices vulnerable to misinterpreting processing time as a sign of disengagement. In day-to-day participation, active-learning routines that reward immediacy over accessibility can compound frustration and exclusion. Recognizing these dynamics and redesigning assessment, collaboration norms, and participation structures accordingly is essential to ensure that communication differences do not become de facto barriers to success [24–27].

- **Oral Presentations and Explanations**: STEM education often evaluates students' understanding through oral presentations, lab viva-voce, or spontaneous classroom questioning. Speech-impaired learners may understand the concepts deeply but face difficulty demonstrating knowledge in these formats. Without flexible assessment methods (e.g., written, digital, or AAC devices), their competence risks being underestimated.
- **Collaborative Problem-Solving**: Group projects frequently rely on rapid verbal exchanges. For students using speech-generating devices or alternative communication methods, delays in participation can be misinterpreted as disengagement or a lack of ability, thereby undermining their inclusion in teamwork.

TABLE 4.3
Barriers for Speech-Impaired Learners in STEM

STEM Activity	Typical Expectation	Barrier for Speech-Impaired Learners	Potential Alternative
Lab viva-voce	Oral defense of results.	The student cannot demonstrate knowledge orally.	Written defense, AAC responses.
Oral presentations	Verbal delivery of project work.	Exclusion from the assessment criteria.	Multimedia/video with captions.
Brainstorming sessions	Rapid verbal idea exchange.	A delay in AAC entry disrupts the group flow.	Digital collaboration boards.
Classroom questioning	Quick spoken answers.	Responses delayed or absent.	Pre-submitted or text-based responses.
Group coding/ debugging	Real-time spoken troubleshooting.	Student excluded from active debugging.	Shared coding platforms with chat.

- **Classroom Participation**: Active learning strategies, such as Socratic questioning or oral brainstorming, privilege quick verbal responses. Speech-impaired students may experience frustration or exclusion when peers and teachers do not allow adequate time for their contributions.

Table 4.3 shows the barriers experienced by speech-impaired learners in STEM activities, highlighting the gap between traditional expectations and students' opportunities for participation, and suggesting alternative strategies for equitable engagement.

4.3 GenAI SOLUTIONS FOR VISUAL IMPAIRMENT IN STEM

STEM fields are highly visual, often relying on diagrams, graphs, formulas, and spatial representations to convey complex concepts. For visually impaired students, this creates significant barriers to participation and understanding. Traditional accessibility tools, such as Braille translations, tactile graphics, and screen readers, provide partial support but often fail to convey the complexity and dynamism of STEM content [28, 29].

GenAI provides transformative solutions, enabling adaptive, personalized, and multimodal learning experiences tailored to individual needs. Unlike conventional assistive technologies, GenAI can create new content, such as descriptions, sonified data, tactile-ready diagrams, and interactive simulations, tailored to the learner's needs [30, 31]. This section explores how GenAI solutions advance accessibility for visually impaired learners in STEM education and practice.

GenAI leverages LLMs, TTS systems, image-to-text models, and multimodal AI systems to create accessible representations dynamically.

4.3.1 Generative AI as a Transformative Accessibility Tool

GenAI represents a significant breakthrough in accessibility for visually impaired learners, particularly in STEM disciplines where abstract reasoning and visual information are central. Unlike traditional assistive technologies that merely adapt existing content into limited formats, GenAI actively creates new representations tailored to individual learners' needs. By leveraging LLMs, advanced TTS systems, image-to-text algorithms, and multimodal frameworks, GenAI can dynamically transform inaccessible material into multimodal experiences. This adaptability enables not only bridging accessibility gaps but also enriching learning with innovative, interactive modalities [32–34].

Table 4.4 highlights the core capabilities of GenAI in enhancing accessibility for visually impaired learners in STEM. Each capability demonstrates how GenAI moves beyond traditional assistive tools by adapting content and actively generating new, multimodal representations. Text-to-audio conversion provides enriched narration of complex mathematical expressions, while visual-to-description transformation ensures that diagrams and graphs become meaningfully interpretable. Similarly, text-to-tactile

TABLE 4.4
Core Capabilities of GenAI for Accessibility in STEM

Capability	Description	Transformative Impact for Visually Impaired Learners
Text-to-audio conversion with contextual enrichment	AI-generated speech incorporates intonation, pauses, and contextual cues when reading equations or complex STEM text.	Makes mathematical expressions and technical explanations clearer, more engaging, and easier to follow than monotonous screen reader outputs.
Visual-to-description transformation	Vision-language models (e.g., CLIP, BLIP, GPT-Vision) translate images, graphs, and diagrams into detailed, natural-language narratives.	Enables learners to understand the meaning behind graphs, charts, and visual data, capturing relationships and trends rather than only static labels.
Text-to-tactile generation	AI converts inaccessible diagrams or images into tactile-ready outputs for embossing printers or 3D printing.	Allows learners to physically explore diagrams, molecules, and geometric shapes, thereby enhancing their comprehension of spatial and structural concepts.
Data sonification	Converts numerical data or patterns into auditory forms such as pitch, rhythm, and tempo.	Empowers students to "hear" trends in datasets, recognize fluctuations, and grasp abstract mathematical patterns without visual input.
Conversational tutoring	AI-powered tutors provide interactive, real-time explanations, generate practice problems, and adapt responses to learner queries.	Creates a personalized, dynamic learning experience comparable to human tutoring, bridging gaps in accessibility and engagement.

generation and data sonification extend accessibility into the physical and auditory domains, offering learners alternative pathways to engage with abstract concepts. Ultimately, conversational tutoring highlights the adaptive and interactive nature of GenAI, positioning it as a transformative force in accessible STEM education.

4.3.2 Possible Approaches of GenAI in Visual Impairment in STEM

4.3.2.1 Tactile Diagram Generation

GenAI models trained on image-to-3D translation can interpret complex STEM visuals and generate tactile-friendly representations [35]. Diagrams such as molecular structures, geometric figures, or physics illustrations are converted into 3D-printable or braille-embossable files. For example, a force arrow in a free-body diagram might be rendered as a raised, textured line. The line's width and texture can represent the magnitude and direction of force, enabling a physical interpretation of abstract concepts. Figure 4.1 illustrates the concept of the development approach for a visual diagram of a 3D braille embosser, which can be utilized in STEM teaching and learning.

Tactile interaction allows visually impaired learners to build mental models of complex systems [36]. This method supports the development of spatial reasoning skills, which are critical in physics, engineering, and biology.

4.3.2.1.1 Proposed Example

The methodology begins with a preprocessing stage, where complex equations and scientific symbols are converted into descriptive language that is both unambiguous and easy to interpret non-verbally. For example, "→" becomes "yields," "×" becomes "times," and exponents are verbalized as "to the power of." This ensures that learners relying on screen readers or Braille can follow the meaning of equations without requiring prior visual reference. Braille conversion is then applied. Where available, Liblouis tables enable Nemeth or Unified English Braille for complete technical accuracy, while a Unicode Braille fallback ensures baseline accessibility in any environment.

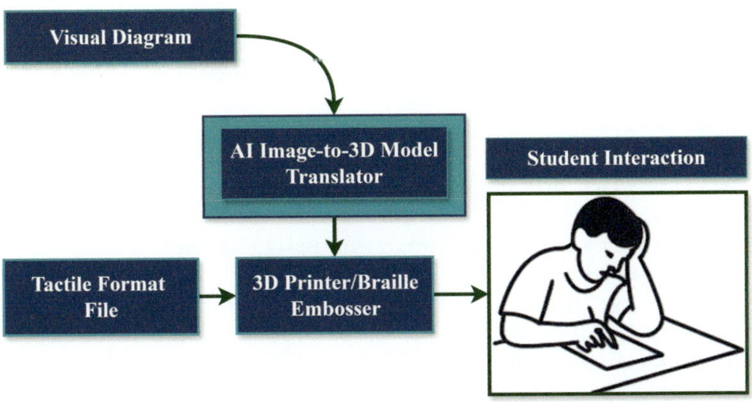

FIGURE 4.1 Workflow for tactile diagram generation.

The second stage involves GenAI descriptions, providing plain, tactile-friendly explanations that supplement raw text and diagrams. AI-generated chemistry explanations describe molecules in terms of bonds, shape, and electron pairs, avoiding reliance on symbols. For instance, water (H_2O) is explained as having two hydrogen atoms bonded to an oxygen atom with two lone electron pairs, which create a bent molecular shape. In physics, AI explains free-body diagrams by verbalizing the functions and directions of forces: "friction acts to the left, normal force acts upward, applied force acts to the right, and weight acts downward." These explanations are concise, typically two to three sentences, and can be embedded directly into diagram metadata for screen readers, or optionally displayed on canvas as Braille summaries for tactile exploration.

Finally, tactile-friendly Scalable Vector Graphics (SVG)[2] rendering ensures that diagrams are usable by touch. Labels are converted into Braille and placed on white background plates to avoid overlaps with arrows or bonds, thereby preventing tactile confusion. Chemistry diagrams display structural features, such as lone pairs, using distinct dots. In contrast, physics diagrams emphasize bold arrows with separated Braille labels. This end-to-end system, text preprocessing, AI-generated descriptions, Braille translation, and tactile rendering, creates multimodal access to STEM content. From an educational perspective, this methodology embodies universal design, as learners access information through multiple pathways, thereby enhancing comprehension and equity. By combining GenAI with tactile graphics and Braille translation, educators can deliver chemistry and physics lessons that are inclusive, scalable, and adaptable to diverse classroom needs, ensuring students with visual impairments fully participate in STEM learning.

The proposed system's methodology is described in Algorithm 4.1.

ALGORITHM 4.1 GENAI PIPELINE FOR BRAILLE-FRIENDLY STEM DIAGRAMS

```
 1. Inputs: chemExpr, physExpr, opts
 2. Outputs: molecule water.svg, physics free body.svg
 3. Preprocess: normalize symbols, compress whitespace
 4. Prompt Construction: build plain-language prompts
    (sentences, tactile cues)
 5. LLM Inference: generate or fallback to deterministic
    output
 6. Guardrails: enforce length, no symbols, filter
    profanity
 7. Braille Translation: Unicode Braille map
 8. SVG Rendering:
 9. Chemistry: draw atoms/bonds; Braille labels; save
10. Physics (FBD): draw block/forces; Braille labels; save
    physics free body.svg
```

As shown in Figure 4.2, the authors present tactile, high-contrast diagrams with integrated Braille labels for STEM learning. Figure 4.2(A) illustrates a free-body diagram of a block on a horizontal surface: the normal force acts upward, the weight acts downward, the applied force points to the right, and the friction opposes motion to the left. Figure 4.2(B) depicts a H_2O molecule with a central oxygen atom bonded to two hydrogens; the two lone-pair electrons on oxygen are rendered as raised dots above the atom. In both panels, labels are provided in Braille. They are automatically

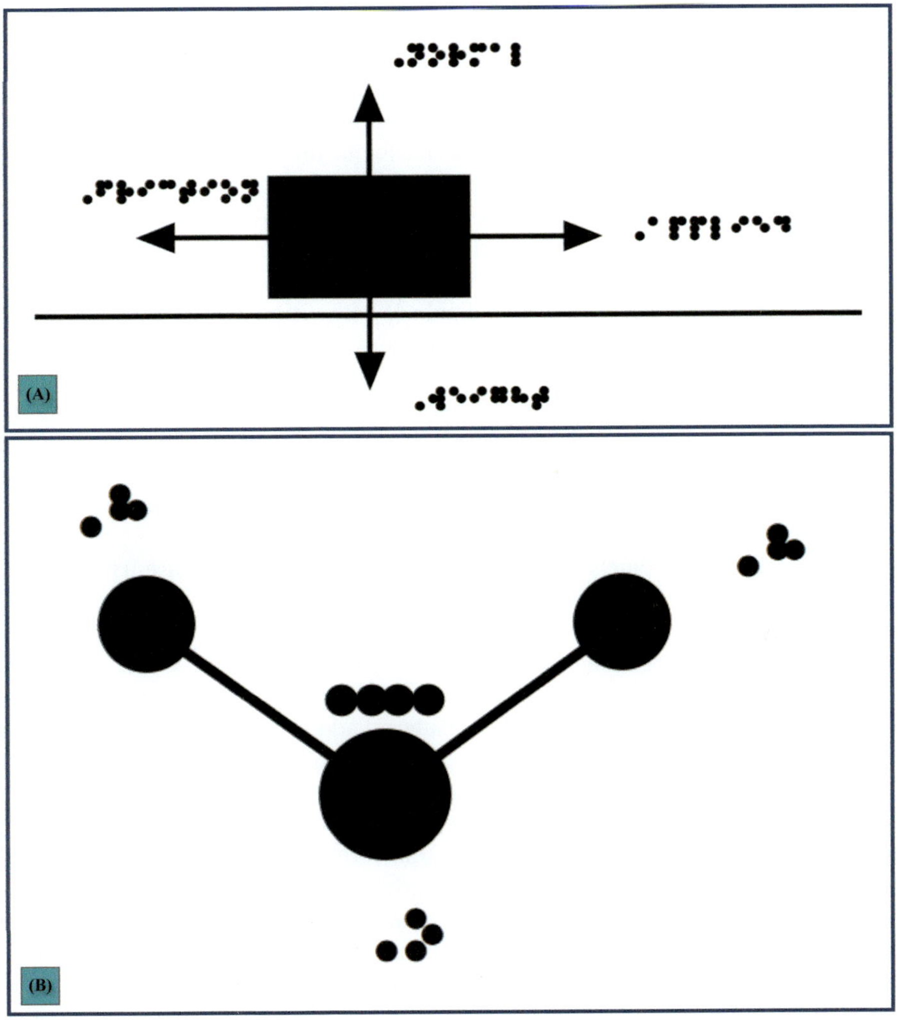

FIGURE 4.2 Braille text–integrated tactile diagrams for STEM learning. (a) Free-body force diagram of a block on a horizontal surface with four labeled forces: normal (up), weight (down), applied (right), and friction (left). (b) Stylized water molecule showing a bent H_2O structure with two O–H bonds and oxygen's lone-pair electrons; atom labels are presented in Braille.

positioned on back-plated text blocks so arrows and bonds never cross the text, enabling clear tactile tracing and easy association between labels and features.

4.3.2.2 Data Sonification

Sonification using GenAI, particularly with models like BERT, represents an innovative fusion of data science, audio processing, and AI [37, 38]. This technique involves transforming structured numerical data into sound by leveraging semantic embeddings produced by AI models [39]. One of the most impactful applications of this technology lies in education. Educators can provide students with a multi-sensory learning experience by converting data into audio. This approach supports auditory learners and reinforces complex concepts in data analysis, making abstract patterns more intuitive and accessible. In STEM education, for example, hearing changes in temperature or humidity values over time helps students understand fluctuations more naturally than through charts alone. Furthermore, this technique promotes AI literacy by exposing students to practical and creative applications of language models, thereby bridging the gap between theoretical AI knowledge and real-world implementation [40].

Another robust use case of AI-based sonification is accessibility, particularly for individuals who are visually impaired. Traditional data visualization tools, such as graphs and tables, are inaccessible to individuals with vision loss. Sonification offers an inclusive alternative by turning numerical values into audible frequencies or tones. This enables blind users to "listen" to trends or anomalies in datasets, allowing for independent exploration of scientific or statistical information. With tactile graphics or Braille materials, sonification adds another sensory dimension, fostering a richer and more accessible data interaction environment. Moreover, real-time sonification can deliver alerts and updates in live applications such as environmental monitoring or IoT systems without relying on visual cues.

In the realm of data analysis, sonification also holds great promise. Humans are adept at recognizing patterns in sound, often more quickly than they can visually perceive them [41]. This can identify anomalies, shifts, or trends in time-series data such as temperature logs, heart rate signals, or financial metrics. When embedded with AI representations (such as BERT embeddings), the resulting sounds reflect numerical changes and deeper contextual patterns, adding a layer of semantic understanding. Analysts could use sound to complement traditional dashboards, offering a novel way to "hear" what the data is doing.

From an artistic perspective, AI-generated sonification opens new possibilities in generative art and music. Datasets can be transformed into musical compositions, where each data point corresponds to a note, rhythm, or harmonic structure. Artists can use real-world information, such as climate change statistics or population trends, to create immersive, data-driven soundscapes. This creative expression is both engaging and powerful, making data emotionally resonant and relatable for storytelling and public engagement.

4.3.2.2.1 Proposed System

The data sonification system described in this section integrates structured numerical processing with GenAI to convert temperature data into an audio signal. The pipeline begins by creating a synthetic dataset comprising 15 temperature measurements ranging from 15°C to 35°C. Each row of this dataset is converted into a natural language text string, such as "temperature: 28.65," to enable processing by a language model. These text-based descriptions are passed through a pre-trained GenAI model, specifically BERT, which generates dimensional embeddings that capture the semantic structure and contextual relationships of the input data.

Instead of using raw temperature values for sonification, the system leverages the semantic embeddings produced by BERT. These embeddings represent a high-level, learned abstraction of the data that goes beyond simple numerical value encoding. The L2 norm (magnitude) of each embedding vector is calculated to reduce the dimensionality to a single scalar feature. This magnitude is then normalized to a [0, 1] range and mapped to an audible frequency range of 220 Hz to 1100 Hz, corresponding to musical pitches from low A to high C#.

Each frequency is synthesized as a sine wave tone lasting 300 milliseconds, and these tones are concatenated in temporal sequence, preserving the original dataset's order. The final output is an audio waveform that audibly reflects the variation in temperature as perceived through the lens of BERT's generative understanding of the input. A spectrogram is computed from this audio signal using the Short-Time Fourier Transform (STFT), offering a visual representation of the sonified data [42]. The result is a multi-layered representation that combines numerical data, natural language interpretation, semantic embedding, and acoustic mapping, enabling users to explore complex data trends through hearing and visualization.

The proposed methodology is described in Algorithm 4.2.

ALGORITHM 4.2 TEMPERATURE DATA SONIFICATION USING BERT

```
Input: scalar temperature series Output: WAV audio
Load BERT tokenizer & encoder
for each temperature t do
    x ← temperature
    h ← BERT(x); z ← h[CLS]
    a ← ||z||₂; ã ← min_max_normalize(a)
    f ← linear map(ã, [220, 1100] Hz)
    y ← sine_osc(f, 0.3 s); append y to stream
Write stream to.wav (mono)
```

Figure 4.3 illustrates the transformation of numerical temperature data into an audio signal through the sonification pipeline. Figure 4.3(A) shows the original temperature values for 15 synthetic samples ranging from approximately 15°C to 35°C. These values are normalized and mapped to audio frequencies between 220 and 1100 Hz. Figure 4.3(B) presents the spectrogram of the resulting sound file, where each horizontal band represents a single tone corresponding to a temperature value. The x-axis indicates the time sequence of tones, the y-axis shows the frequency content, and the color intensity reflects the sound power at each frequency. This visual directly

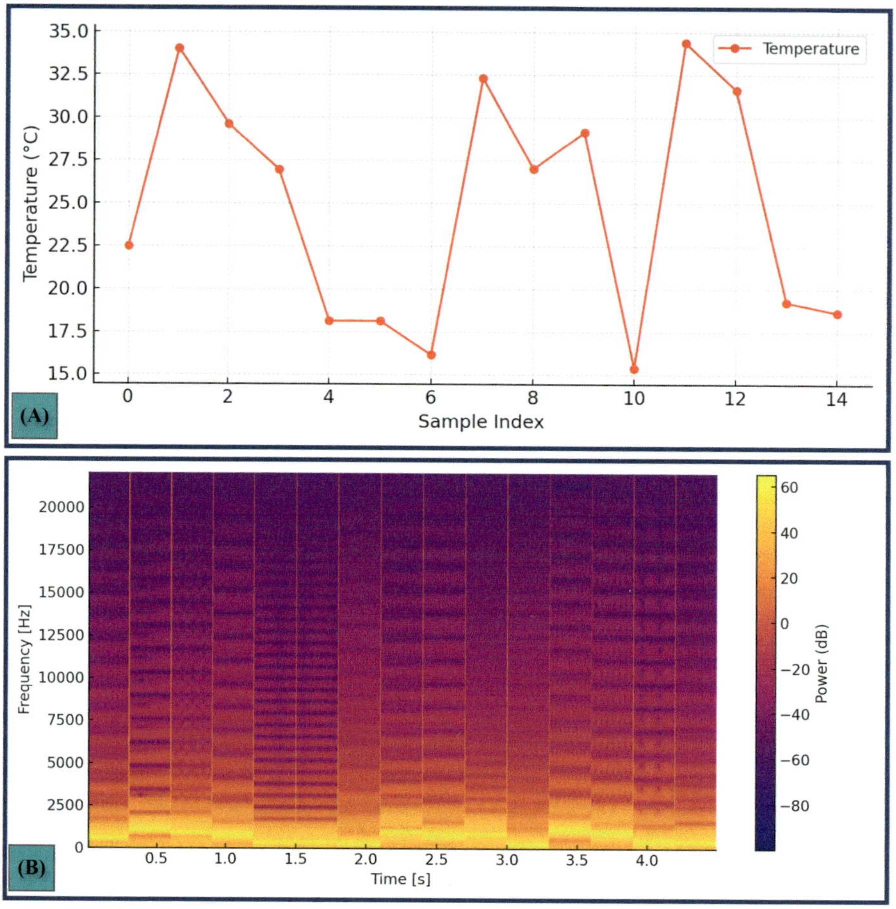

FIGURE 4.3 (a) Plot of temperature values across 15 samples, representing a synthetic dataset. Each point corresponds to a distinct time-stamped observation. (b) A spectrogram of the audio is generated by mapping each temperature value to a unique tone frequency (220–1100 Hz). The horizontal bands represent the pitch of each tone over time, while the color intensity indicates the amplitude in decibels.

represents how raw numerical data can be perceived and analyzed through sound, demonstrating a core principle of AI-assisted data sonification.

4.3.2.3 Context-Aware Audio Descriptions for STEM Accessibility

GenAI is opening up powerful new ways to support people with visual impairments in STEM. Instead of only reading text or describing an image in basic terms, AI can now give context-aware audio descriptions, meaning the narration adapts to the situation, explains what is important, and even offers guidance for next steps. For example, imagine a chemistry student in a lab. Traditional tools might say, *"There is a flask and a burette."* But with context, AI could describe: *"This is an acid–base titration setup. The pH reading is 7.2, and you are close to the endpoint. Add just a few more drops to complete the process."* This type of narration is far more helpful because it connects what the student sees with what they need to do. In mathematics, when a student writes an integral on paper, the system doesn't just say, "*an equation is visible.*" Instead, it might say: "*This is the integral of sine from zero to pi. The answer is two, because the curve's positive and negative areas cancel except for two units above zero.*" In biology, when looking at a slide under the microscope, instead of "*cells are present,*" the narration could be: "*About thirty onion skin cells are visible. Most have nuclei. One cell is in the middle of dividing.*" Physics experiments could turn measurements into insight: "*The cart on the inclined plane is accelerating more slowly than predicted, which suggests friction is affecting the result.*" The system can even point out the real story for data graphs: "*The red line rises quickly, levels of around 35 minutes, then drops slightly. The blue line stays nearly flat. The biggest gap is at 30 minutes.*"

Here, we translate that idea from concept to implementation in a concrete STEM use case. Building on the examples above, where narration adapts to the task and offers next steps, we focus on chemistry notation. In this domain, small visual cues (such as subscripts, charge, and layout) carry significant meaning. Our goal is to transform a fuzzy, hard-to-read snapshot into two things a learner can immediately act on: a clear, accessible representation of the equation and a plain-language explanation that situates it within the current task. This moves beyond "what's on the page" to "what it means and what to do next," preserving the spirit of context-aware guidance while addressing the practical barriers of low-quality images and handwriting. The workflow below operationalizes this: it detects and interprets the equation, normalizes it for accessibility, and delivers guidance in formats that are usable with screen readers and print. With this bridge from principle to practice in place, Figure 4.4 outlines the end-to-end pipeline that enables these capabilities.

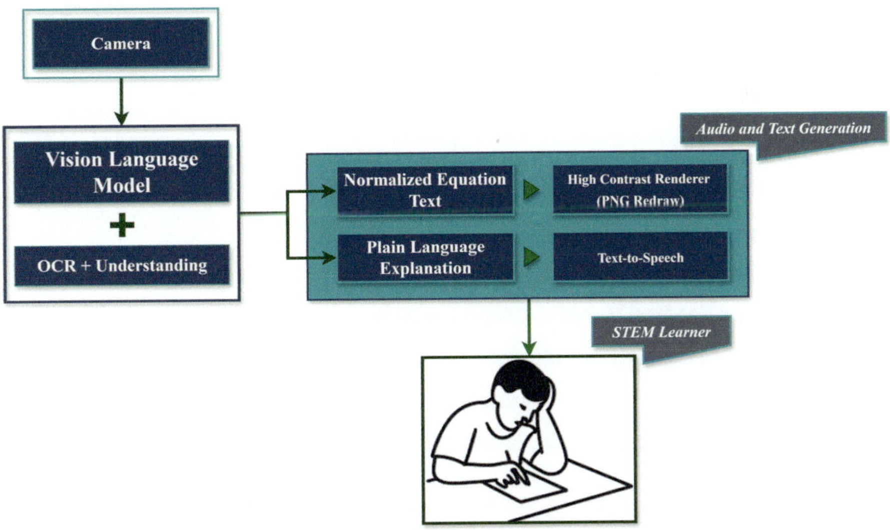

FIGURE 4.4 Overall pipeline for accessible chemistry equation support: a camera captures an image, which is fed to a vision–language model (OCR + understanding), producing normalized equation text and a plain-language explanation.

An image captured by a camera is analyzed by a vision–language model that combines OCR with contextual reasoning. The model emits two products: a normalized, machine-readable equation string and a concise explanation in everyday language. The equation is redrawn as a high-contrast Portable Network Graphics (PNG) for screen viewing or print, while the explanation is converted to audio via TTS. Together, the text and audio provide actionable guidance and an apparent visual reference, enabling learners to understand what the equation means without relying on low-quality photos or small handwriting. The modular design also allows extensions such as automatic balancing, MathML/Braille export, or safety prompts for laboratory settings.

A photograph of a chemistry equation, for example, the whiteboard showing benzene laboratory preparation by reducing phenol with zinc ($C_6H_5OH + Zn \rightarrow C_6H_6 + ZnO$), is captured via webcam or uploaded. A vision–language model (Qwen2-VL-2B-Instruct) performs OCR and context understanding to output both a normalized equation string and a concise, plain-language explanation for blind or low-vision learners. The equation is redrawn as a high-contrast PNG using PIL, and the explanation is synthesized into speech with Google Text-to-Speech (gTTS)[3] to produce an MP3 (see Figure 4.5).

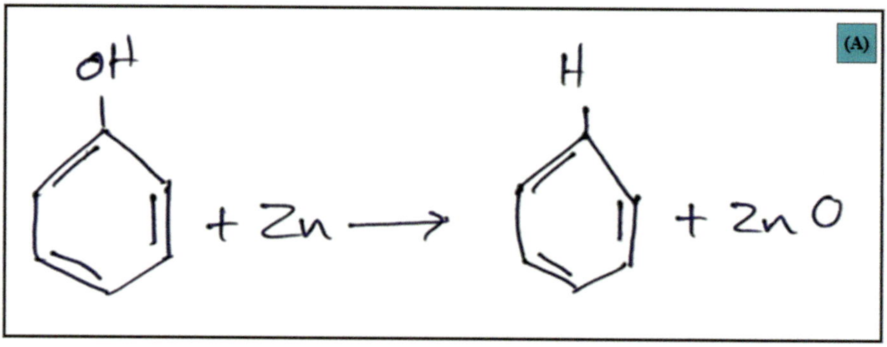

(B)

Preparation of Benzene from Phenol

Equation: C6H5OH + Zn -> C6H6 + ZnO (balanced)

Plain-language explanation:

- Start with phenol (a benzene ring with an –OH group). Zinc acts as a reducing agent.
- Zinc removes oxygen from phenol's –OH group and becomes zinc oxide (ZnO).
- The ring stays intact and becomes benzene (C6H6). The equation is already balanced 1:1:1:1.
- This is called a reduction because oxygen is taken away from the organic molecule.

Notes: Benzene is flammable and toxic; handle in a fume hood. Dispose of ZnO according to lab rules.

FIGURE 4.5 (a) Preprocessed input image from the camera. (b) GenAI generated an explanation for visually impaired students (the exact text will be used with TTS so students can hear what is shown in the equation).

The result is not just accessibility, but actual participation and independence. Learners with visual impairments can participate in experiments, solve problems, and interpret data alongside their peers. Teachers and institutions can feel confident that students receive accurate, safe, and fair support. When applied thoughtfully, GenAI can transform STEM learning and work environments into spaces where everyone has the tools to succeed.

4.3.2.4 Multimodal AI: Combining Touch and Sound

One of the most promising frontiers in inclusive STEM education is the use of multimodal AI systems [43, 44]. These platforms combine multiple sensory channels, such as touch and sound, to create a richer and more accessible learning experience. For visually impaired learners, neither sound nor tactile diagrams alone provides the whole picture [45]. Sound can convey trends, relationships, or sequences, while tactile interaction allows for spatial and structural understanding. Combined, the two create an immersive learning environment that closely mirrors the multi-sensory input experienced by sighted students.

This integration is compelling in STEM domains where concepts are inherently spatial and dynamic. In mathematics, tactile graphs enhanced with sonification help students perceive functions, slopes, and intersections in ways that transcend the limitations of either medium alone. In chemistry, 3D molecular models paired with audio explanations provide both structural detail and conceptual clarity. In physics, tactile models of waveforms, coupled with sound-based sonification, replicate phenomena of motion and frequency, allowing learners to both feel and hear oscillations [46–49]. Consider the sine wave: a tactile diagram can show its shape, but it is static. Sonification can provide the rhythm of rising and falling pitch, but lacks a sense of periodicity in space. However, when these channels are combined, students can feel the curve with their fingers while simultaneously hearing the oscillation, reinforcing comprehension through parallel sensory pathways.

Table 4.5 shows multimodal accessible tools for STEM learning in mathematics, chemistry, and physics, demonstrating the breadth of potential applications.

The authors propose a concept for a multimodal STEM system that combines tactile and audio elements for teaching mathematics, chemistry, and physics. The development of the multimodal STEM learning system, featuring tactile graphics, Braille outputs, voice descriptions, and interactive diagrams, was grounded in an

TABLE 4.5
Multimodal Accessibility Tools for STEM Learning

Domain	Uses
Mathematics	Tactile graphs combined with sonification help learners grasp functions, slopes, and intersections.
Chemistry	Three-dimensional models of molecules, paired with audio explanations, provide both structural and conceptual clarity.
Physics	Tactile models of waveforms, coupled with sound-based sonification, replicate the phenomena of motion and frequency in an experientially meaningful way.

inclusive-by-design methodology augmented by the power of GenAI. The central goal was to create an educational interface that allows visually impaired students to explore mathematics, physics, and chemistry concepts in an interactive, intuitive, and independent way. The development followed a multi-stage cycle involving need assessment, AI model integration, user feedback, accessibility validation, and the synthesis of multimodal output.

At the system's core is a GenAI layer responsible for automatically producing semantic descriptions of STEM diagrams (e.g., function plots, atomic bonds, waveforms). When a teacher or learner inputs a graph or equation, the GenAI model interprets the content and generates clear, instructional text such as: *"This is a sine curve. The function reaches a maximum value of 1 at x equals 1.57."* This output is available in three parallel formats: TTS, Braille translation, and captioning, providing universal access. The Braille content is verified via Liblouis round-trip translation, ensuring that what is printed tactilely matches the original input's meaning.

For teachers, this automation drastically reduces preparation time. Traditionally, producing accessible STEM materials required manual Braille transcription, verbalization of diagrams, and coordination with special education teams. With GenAI embedded, a teacher inputs the lesson content, such as a function like $y = \sin(x)$ or a chemical bond type, and receives prestructured output ready for audio playback, Braille embossing, or visual display with tactile export (SVG for swell paper or embossers). Additionally, the GenAI system features context-aware snapping for touch-beam interactivity, enabling learners to precisely land on features such as graph zeros, extrema, or molecular bond centers, where detailed verbal or Braille descriptions are provided. Algorithm 4.3 outlines the proposed methodology and approach for developing the multimodal system.

ALGORITHM 4.3 MULTIMODAL STEM ACCESSIBILITY PIPELINE WITH GENAI

1. **Input:** STEM content *C* (e.g., function, diagram, equation)
2. **Output:** Tactile diagram *D*, Audio narration *A*, Braille description *B*
3. **Step 1: Preprocessing**
4. Parse *C* to identify domain-specific structure (e.g., graph type, math formula, molecule)
5. **Step 2: Generative AI Description Synthesis**
6. *T* ← GenAI(*C*) ▷ Use LLM to generate instructional-level textual explanation
7. *T* ← PostProcess(*T*) ▷ Simplify, format, and align with accessibility rules
8. **Step 3: Modality Conversion**
9. *D* ← GenerateTactileDiagram(*C*) ▷ Plot and export SVG with haptic grid alignment
10. *A* ← TextToSpeech(*T*) ▷ Convert description to speech via TTS engine

```
11. B ← BrailleTranslate(T, Table) ▷ Translate to Braille
    using Liblouis
12. Assert: BackTranslate(B) ≈ T
13. Step 4: Export
14. Save (D, A, B) as SVG, WAV, BRF respectively return
    (D, A, B)
```

The result is a self-contained, AI-powered toolkit that transforms standard STEM material into multimodal learning experiences. Learners can explore diagrams tactually, hear precise explanations at each feature, and read Braille output aligned with their cognitive map of the content. For example, when examining a titration curve, the GenAI system not only plots the curve but also describes buffer zones and equivalence points both in voice and Braille, with beam snapping to chemically significant regions (see Figure 4.6).

4.4 GenAI Solutions for Hearing Impairment in STEM

STEM education has always posed unique challenges for students who are D/HH. Mathematics, chemistry, physics, or engineering classes often rely on rapid spoken explanations, complex diagrams narrated aloud, and fast-moving group discussions. Laboratory sessions and fieldwork further complicate matters by embedding critical information in auditory alerts, spontaneous instructor guidance, and safety warnings. For special needs students, missing even a few seconds of explanation can mean losing the thread of an entire derivation or misunderstanding a lab protocol. Traditional accommodations, such as human interpreters, captioning services, and note-takers, have been invaluable; however, they remain limited by cost, availability, accuracy, and their inability to adapt to the specialized vocabulary of STEM fields [50–53].

GenAI, particularly LLMs and multimodal systems, has opened a new frontier in accessibility. Instead of static captions or generic transcripts, students can now access dynamically generated content that cleans technical speech, formats mathematical equations, integrates visual aids, and converts written or spoken language into sign language avatars. These technologies promise to make learning not only accessible but also inclusive, enabling students who are D/HH to participate fully in STEM classrooms, labs, and online environments. The following sections examine how GenAI can be applied, with concrete examples, case studies, and Python code snippets using Hugging Face models to illustrate practical workflows.

4.4.1 Speech-to-Text with STEM Uses for Mathematics

A significant challenge for individuals with hearing impairments in STEM fields is accurately transcribing complex lectures, seminars, and technical meetings. Standard STT systems often mistranscribe mathematical symbols, chemical formulas, or specialized jargon. GenAI can enhance transcription by contextualizing speech within the STEM domain [54–57]. For example, when a professor says "*integral from*

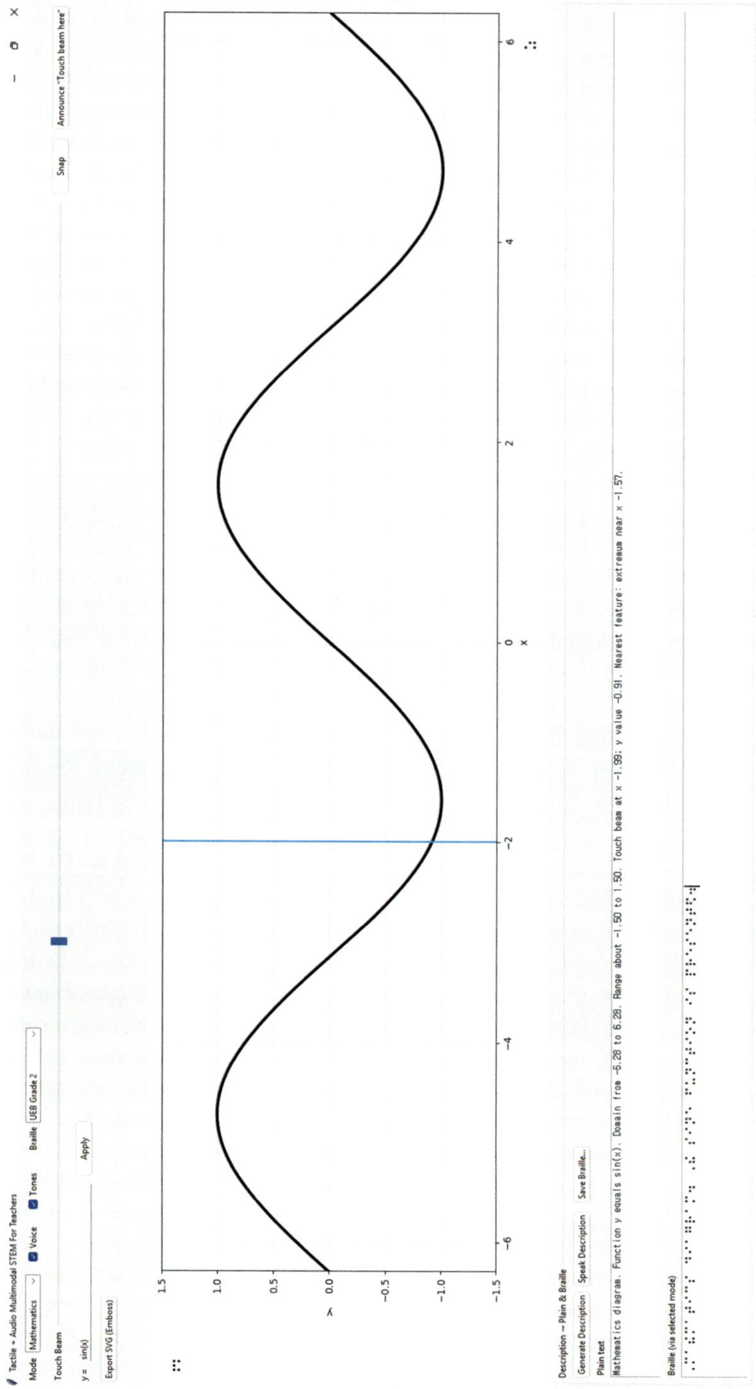

FIGURE 4.6 Tactile + audio multimodal STEM system for teachers.

zero to infinity of e to the negative x squared dx," a naive transcription may render gibberish. A fine-tuned GenAI model, however, can convert this directly into the mathematical expressions shown in Eqs. (4.1) and (4.2):

$$\int_0^\infty e^{-x^2}\,dx \tag{4.1}$$

$$y'' - 3y' + 2y = 0 \tag{4.2}$$

Figure 4.7 shows a complete workflow for extracting mathematical equations from a transcript using LLMs, with multiple fallback strategies to ensure reliability. It starts by setting up imports, handling user input, and modeling candidates. The script attempts to load a text-generation model in three tiers: first, it tries a GPU-optimized 4-bit quantized model via bitsandbytes, then falls back to standard transformer models (CPU/GPU), and finally to llama.cpp GPT-Generated Unified Format (GGUF) models if needed. Once a model is loaded, it generates a structured prompt that asks the LLM to extract and format equations in LaTeX with short captions, returning results strictly in JSON. If the model fails or produces unusable output, a heuristic fallback scans the transcript for text that resembles equations. Extracted equations

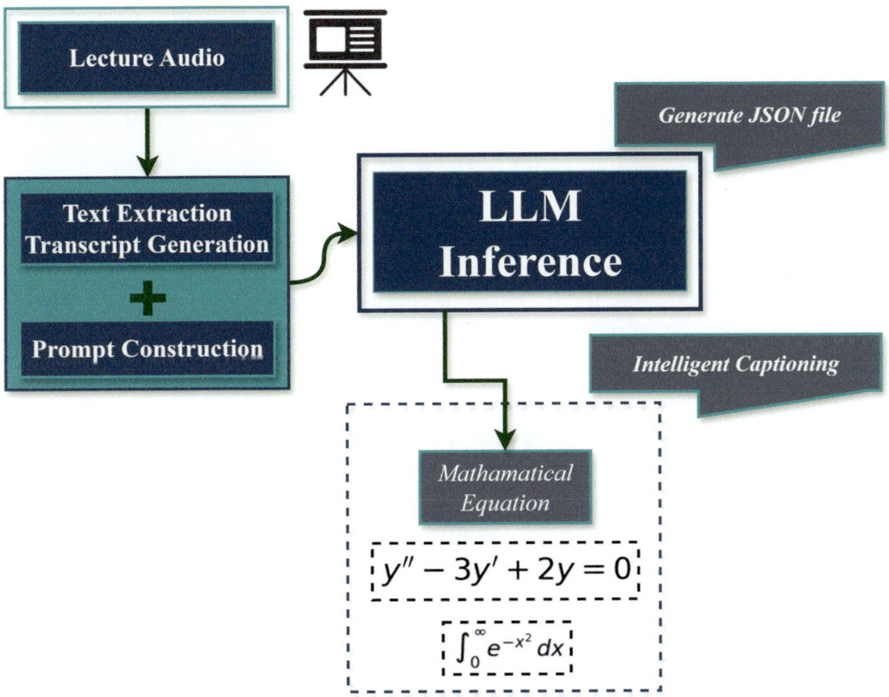

FIGURE 4.7 Methodology for transcript-to-equation extraction and rendering.

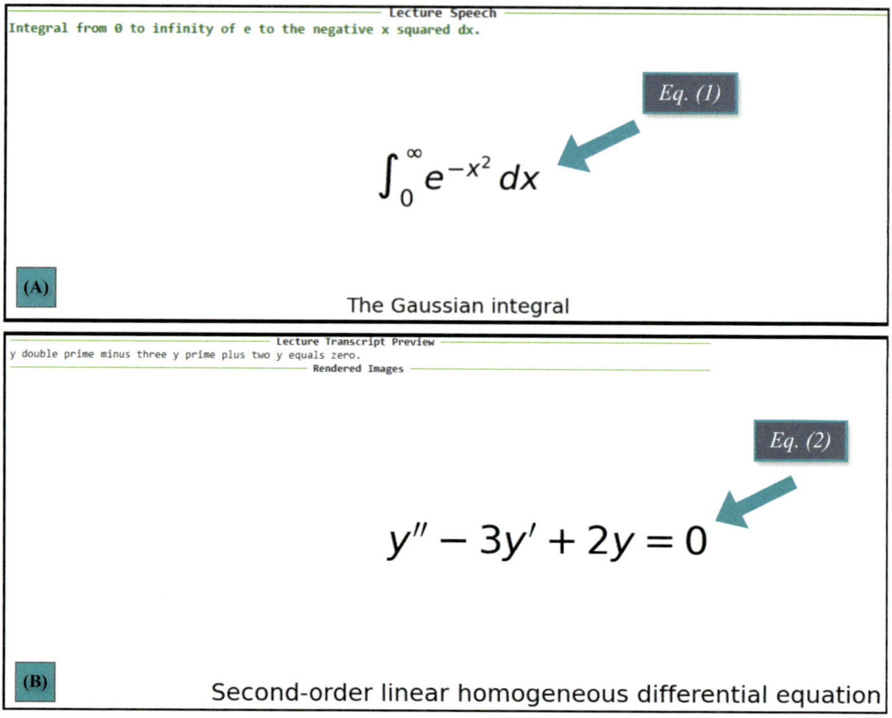

FIGURE 4.8 Enhanced auto-captioning for deaf STEM learners. The output results for (a) the Gaussian integral, (b) the second-order linear homogeneous equation.

are saved to equations.json and rendered as PNG images with captions for visualization. The process concludes by displaying a preview of the transcript, the detected equations, and the rendered equation images, ensuring that users consistently receive usable results from the LLM or heuristics.

As shown in Figure 4.8, the output auto-captioning of the lecture is more visualized by generating equations, allowing STEM learners who can't attend to interact with the lecture more efficiently.

4.5 GENERATIVE AI SOLUTIONS FOR SPEECH IMPAIRMENT IN STEM

GenAI can dramatically lower the communication barriers faced by learners and professionals with speech impairments across STEM. STEM is naturally collaborative, including lab meetings, code reviews, oral defenses, research seminars, and design critiques. Much of that collaboration relies on precise, rapid, and often technical spoken exchanges. When speech is dysarthric, apraxic, stuttered, or otherwise atypical, participation can be constrained not by knowledge or skill but by communication friction. Modern AI gives us a toolkit to reduce that friction: accurate STT or Automatic Speech Recognition (ASR) systems tuned for atypical speech, TTS, and voice banking to provide a consistent professional voice, multimodal interfaces that blend typing, captioning, and synthesized audio, and adaptive tutoring systems that explain complex ideas in multiple modalities. Importantly, these systems must be designed for accessibility, privacy, robustness, and domain specificity, because STEM communication is loaded with jargon (e.g., "Fourier transform," "electrophoresis," "nanofabrication") that general-purpose models often mishandle. Recent projects and datasets focused on atypical speech (e.g., Google's Project Euphonia and widely used corpora like UA-Speech and TORGO) have accelerated progress by enabling the personalization of recognition and benchmarking models in realistic conditions [57–62].

As shown in Table 4.6, GenAI has begun transforming speech technology by enabling the recognition and enhancement of atypical speech, creating high-quality synthetic voices, and developing multimodal conversational agents. As shown in

TABLE 4.6
Capabilities Enabled by GenAI for Speech Technologies

Area	Description	Examples/Tools	Applications
Recognition and enhancement	Self-supervised speech models learn from unlabeled audio, then fine-tune on small-labeled sets (including atypical speech). They outperform older pipelines in accuracy and latency.	**wav2vec 2.0** and similar models.	High-accuracy, low-latency captioning is available in classrooms or on Zoom, even for individuals with disordered speech, once the system has been properly adapted.
Synthetic speech and voice banking	TTS systems can generate clear, natural, or personalized speech. Combined ASR → LLM → TTS pipelines enable flexible input while maintaining a consistent professional voice output.	Tacotron-like models, VITS, and multi-speaker TTS.	Assistive communication, professional-sounding speech in meetings.
Multimodal conversational tools	Conversational agents integrate ASR, LLMs, and TTS to create interactive copilots that answer questions and explain concepts aloud.	ASR + LLM + TTS stacks.	Useful in labs or hands-busy environments where typing isn't practical.
Personalized domain language	Domain-specific customization enhances recognition of rare or technical terms (e.g., STEM, medicine, genetics).	Lexicon boosting, domain-specific LMs, post-hoc reranking.	Accurate handling of rare symbols, jargon, and gene names.
Evidence base	Large, consented datasets of atypical speech support reproducible research and benchmarking.	UA-Speech, TORGO, and Project Euphonia.	Training, evaluation, and advancement of speech technology for atypical speech.

The Table Summarizes How Self-Supervised, TTS, and Multimodal AI Systems Expand Accessibility, Personalization, and Reproducibility in Speech Applications.

Table 4.1, these advances are powered by self-supervised models (e.g., wav2vec 2.0), cutting-edge TTS pipelines (such as Tacotron-like models and VITS), and domain-adapted language models. Importantly, evidence-based approaches such as UA-Speech,[4] TORGO,[5] and Project Euphonia[6] provide the datasets necessary for reproducible evaluation, ensuring that progress extends to diverse and disordered speech contexts [62, 63].

4.5.1 Generative AI-Enabled Sign Language Translation for STEM Presentation Support

The demand for inclusive learning environments in STEM disciplines has prompted researchers to explore advanced ATs. Among these, GenAI-powered sign language presentation systems are emerging as transformative tools that allow speech-impaired students to deliver technical content autonomously [64, 65]. This section presents a novel multimodal communication framework that leverages deep learning, natural language generation, TTS synthesis, and realistic 3D avatar animation for real-time sign language interpretation in STEM classrooms.

At the heart of the system lies a modular architecture (see Figure 4.9) composed of four integrated components: (1) hand gesture recognition, (2) generative language modeling, (3) voice synthesis, and (4) 3D avatar lip-sync rendering. The objective is

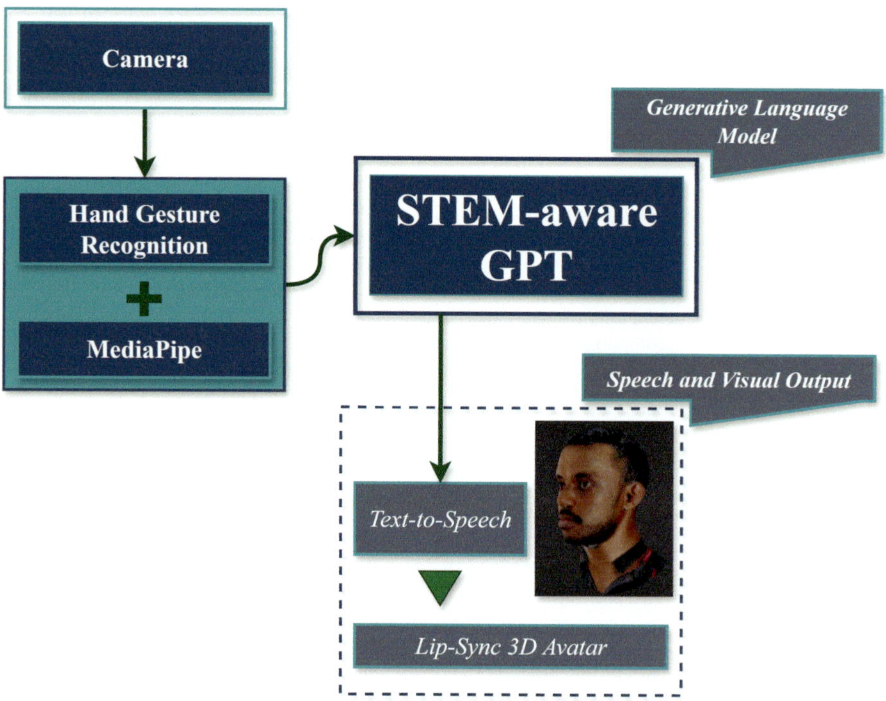

FIGURE 4.9 System architecture for GenAI-enabled sign language presentation.

to capture sign language input in real time, translate it into coherent spoken STEM content, and express it visually and audibly through an animated virtual presenter.

The end-to-end system is designed to be lightweight, portable, and real-time, enabling fluid communication without perceptible delay.

4.5.1.1 Gesture Recognition Module

The system begins with gesture acquisition using a webcam. Real-time video frames are processed through the MediaPipe framework to extract 21 2D landmarks per hand, representing joints, knuckles, and fingertips [66]. These coordinates form the feature set input to a Random Forest classifier, trained to recognize all 26 American Sign Language (ASL) alphabet signs and a "space" gesture. The classifier achieved an overall accuracy of 96.3%, with specific letters, such as C, O, W, and H, achieving 100% accuracy. Lower accuracy was observed for visually similar gestures, such as M and N (≈approximately 60%). A temporal smoothing strategy is applied to improve prediction reliability during live use: a letter is only confirmed after five consistent predictions across sequential frames. This filtering prevents jittery outputs and enhances user experience.

4.5.1.2 Contextual Sentence Generation Using Generative AI

Unlike static gesture recognition systems that output raw letters or words, this model integrates a GenAI language component fine-tuned on STEM vocabulary. It takes gesture-recognized words and transforms them into grammatically and contextually accurate sentences. For example, if a student spells "DNA," the AI model might generate the sentence:

> DNA stands for Deoxyribonucleic Acid, which contains the genetic instructions essential for life.

This semantic enrichment ensures that STEM presentations are correct, explanatory, and audience-friendly, eliminating the need for manual transcription or human interpreters.

4.5.1.3 TTS Synthesis and Auditory Delivery

The sentence generated is passed into a TTS engine, implemented using Pyttsx3, a lightweight Python library capable of offline, real-time synthesis. The engine supports multiple voice profiles, allowing speech-impaired students to customize voice pitch, speed, and tone, thereby personalizing their presentation style. Average Clarity Rating: 4.6/5 (based on user evaluation with interpreters and non-signers).

Realistic 3D Avatar for Visual Expression and Lip-Sync: Simultaneously, the system drives a 3D animated avatar developed using Blender and FaceBuilder, designed to visually "speak" the generated content. This avatar is rigged with 11 shape keys (blend shapes) that control mouth movements like jaw open, smile, lip roll, and pucker. Each ASL-recognized letter is mapped to an approximate phoneme, and corresponding shape keys are activated. The avatar achieved a 92% lip-sync alignment accuracy, validating the realism of its phoneme-to-mouth shape mapping. The synchronization ensures that spoken audio and lip movements are tightly aligned,

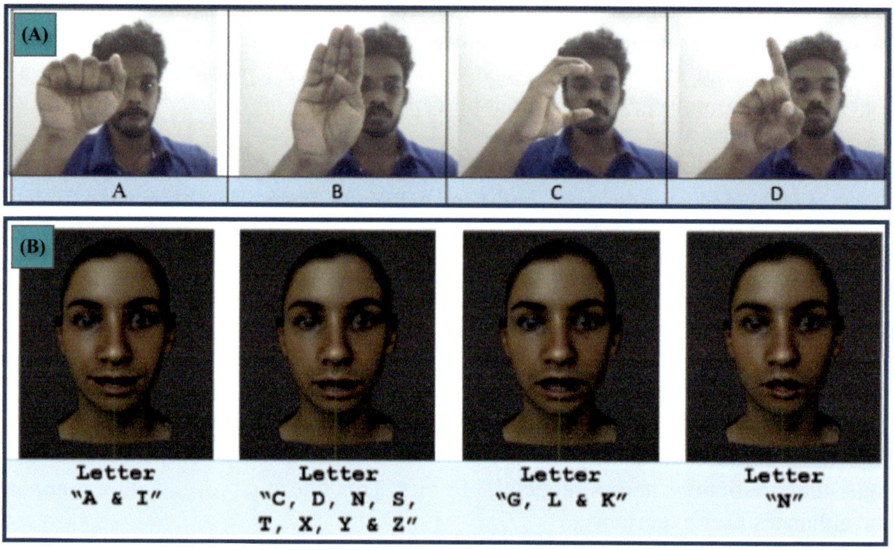

FIGURE 4.10 (a) Demonstration of manual sign gestures for letters A, B, C, and D in Sign Language. (b) The virtual avatar shows corresponding mouth patterns and letter facial expressions, with grouped representations.

enhancing accessibility for individuals with partial hearing loss and making the output more expressive.

The proposed system integrates gesture recognition and avatar-based visualization to facilitate communication in ASL. As shown in Figure 4.10(A), it illustrates the manual signing of selected alphabets (A, B, C, and D) captured from a signer using Sign Language. These gestures serve as the input for the recognition model. Figure 4.10(B) demonstrates the corresponding virtual avatar outputs, where mouth patterns and facial expressions are synchronized with the recognized gestures. For instance, the avatar maps single or grouped letters such as “A and I,” “C, D, N, S, T, X, Y, and Z,” “G, L, and K,” and “N,” thereby enabling more naturalistic and intelligible communication for hearing individuals. This dual representation underscores the system’s ability to bridge the gap between signers and non-signers through multimodal feedback.

4.6 GENERATIVE AI MODELS FOR CHEMISTRY INSTRUCTION TARGETING ELEMENTS AND BONDS IN SPECIAL EDUCATION CONTEXTS

This section outlines a generative, real-time chemistry learning model that integrates computer vision, symbolic chemistry rules, and an LLM to enable students to discover how elements form bonds and how molecular properties arise from their structure. At its core, the system turns inexpensive printed ArUco markers into "smart" atomic tiles: learners arrange markers on a table, and the model detects elements, proposes bonds, validates the resulting molecule, renders animated electron shells, and narrates the compound's name, properties, applications, and safety via structured LLM output.

The experience is deliberately tactile: students manipulate physical pieces while the software translates their layout into a chemical structure. As markers are added, removed, or moved, the system recomputes valence counts and bond possibilities, updates the Hill-notation formula, and provides live visual feedback, so misconceptions surface quickly and can be corrected through exploration.

4.6.1 Proposed Methodology

This section outlines the methodology of the proposed GenAI-enabled chemistry learning model for students with special needs in STEM. Algorithm 4.4 describes the model architecture, and the following sections point out the step-by-step development methodology.

ALGORITHM 4.4 GENERATIVE AI-ENABLED CHEMISTRY MODEL

```
procedure INIT
    Load AtomicDB (H.Ca); open camera
    Initialize UI (PyQt6); start LLM worker
        (rate-limited)
procedure MAINLOOP
    while camera open do
        frame ← ReadCamera()
        atoms ← DetectArucoAndMap(frame) ▷ threshold →
            contours → corners → pose
        bonds ← ProposeByGeometry(atoms)
        bonds ← ValidateByChemistry(bonds) ▷ valence +
            VSEPR + saturation
        formula ← HillNotation(atoms)
        if StructureStable() and not InCache() then
            EnqueueLLM({formula, atoms, bonds})
        RenderUI(frame, atoms, bonds, formula)
procedure LLMWORKER
    while running do
        req ← Dequeue()
        if req then
            resp ← CallLLM(req, temperature=0.2, timeout)
            CacheOrFallback(req.hash, resp);
                PostToUI(req.hash)
```

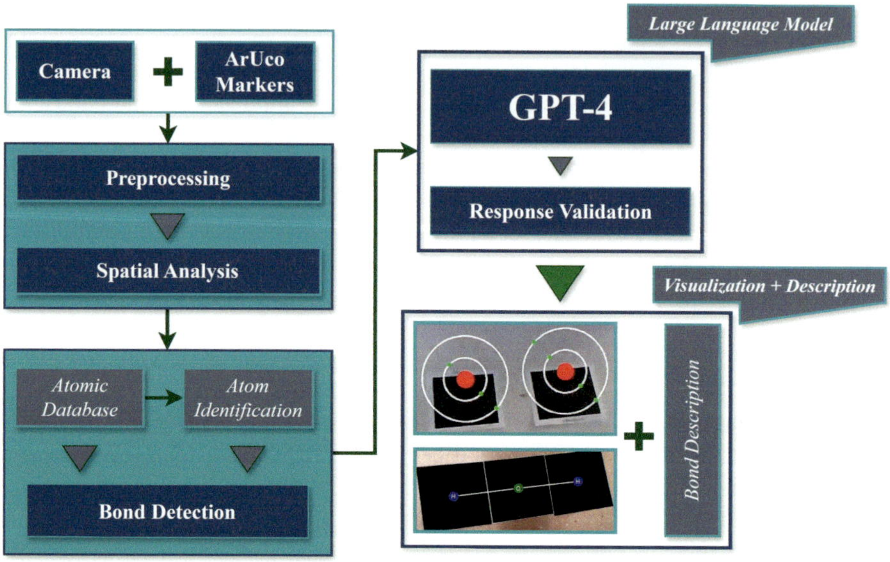

FIGURE 4.11 Architecture of the ArUco marker+GPT-4 enabled chemistry learning system.

4.6.1.1 Computer Vision Pipeline

The vision module uses the *DICT_4X4_50* ArUco dictionary (see Figure 4.11). Frames undergo adaptive thresholding and contour analysis, followed by corner refinement to ~0.1-pixel precision and pose estimation for robust identification under partial occlusion and variable classroom lighting. Each recognized ID maps to an atomic database that stores name, symbol, electron shell structure, RGB color, atomic mass, and valence. With atom identities established, centroids and pairwise distances are computed, and candidate bonds are hypothesized using Axis-Aligned Bounding-Box (AABB) overlap tests.

4.6.1.2 Chemical Analysis and Bond Validation

A rule-based engine filters and validates bonds using valence counts, noble-gas exclusion, and valence shell electron pair repulsion (VSEPR)-informed geometry checks (bond counts, angles, and saturation). A Hill-notation generator orders elements (C, then H, then alphabetical) and applies subscripts for multiplicities, so the displayed formula is always consistent with the current arrangement of markers. As the learner adds a hydrogen to carbon, for example, the system immediately updates the valence ledger, enforces saturation, and regenerates CH_4 with the expected tetrahedral geometry.

- **LLM-Backed Explanations**: When atoms and bonds stabilize into a plausible structure, the system packages a compact JSON prompt and calls the LLM at low temperature (~0.2) for factual stability. The response is validated for required fields. If parsing fails or connectivity drops, the app returns to the local database and performs partial analyses. Explanations are age-appropriate, featuring concise definitions and safety guidance that connect the visuals to real-world contexts.

- **Real-Time Visualization and UI**: A custom OpenGL-backed widget renders nuclei and animated electron shells; shells expand radially with stable spacing while geometric masking conceals raw markers to preserve immersion. The PyQt6 MVC design separates the ChemicalDataModel, the MolecularVisualizationView, and controllers for state/event management. Information panels track atom counts, current International Union of Pure and Applied Chemistry (IUPAC) name, and formula, while throttled refresh and double buffering maintain a steady 30 FPS.
- **Concurrency, Reliability, and Testing**: The camera/UI loop runs on the main thread; an LLMWorker on a QThread handles requests, guarded by mutexes and a FIFO queue with a cool-down to respect API limits. Hierarchical exception handling, exponential backoff, and graceful degradation keep the classroom experience resilient. Unit tests cover bond detection and formula generation; integration tests span camera and network behavior; and acceptance testing examines educational effectiveness, usability, and accessibility.

4.6.1.3 Results and Performance

Across multiple evaluation passes, the system consistently demonstrated real-time responsiveness, high accuracy, and stability, validating its suitability for interactive, classroom-grade deployment. The end-to-end throughput achieved the targeted 30 frames per second ($\approx$33.3 ms per frame), ensuring smooth operation with marker detection times typically under 10 ms and overall pipeline latency under 100 ms. This performance preserved the "live" feel required for hands-on learning environments where responsiveness is critical. Importantly, resource consumption remained modest: CPU utilization averaged 15–25% of a single core, while peak memory use remained around 50 MB during extended sessions. These metrics aligned well with the project's design goal of maintaining fluid performance even on modest, integrated-graphics laptops commonly found in classrooms. Complementary to these runtime outcomes, the technical specification summary confirmed 30 FPS rendering, over 95% marker recognition accuracy, a total latency of less than 100 ms, a memory footprint under 100 MB, and average LLM response times between 2 and 5 seconds, figures that matched the observed empirical behavior during evaluations. Figure 4.12 shows the ArUco marker for H and O, and its respective visualization using computer vision.

Detection accuracy and robustness were maintained by the ArUco pipeline, which integrated adaptive thresholding, contour analysis, subpixel corner refinement (with a precision of 0.1 pixels), and pose estimation. This pipeline proved resilient under realistic conditions such as partial occlusions and varied lighting, both of which are

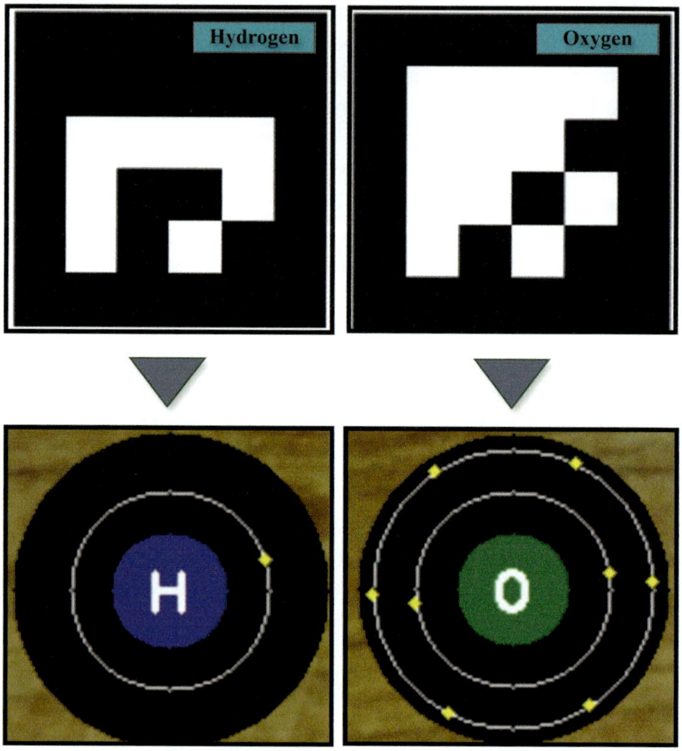

FIGURE 4.12 ArUco marker for H and O, and its respective visualization using computer vision.

frequent in classroom settings. The outcome was a consistently high marker recognition rate exceeding 95%, even when students dynamically overlapped or manipulated tiles. Furthermore, the spatial analysis stage, which computed centroids, Euclidean distances, and AABB overlaps, enabled stable bond proposals despite visual jitter. These geometric hypotheses were subjected to chemical validation rules based on valence and geometric constraints, ensuring the production of scientifically plausible results. This two-stage design significantly reduced false positives while retaining the responsiveness for live interaction.

On the visualization side, double-buffered rendering, alpha-blended overlays, and geometric masking sustained smooth and immersive graphics while hiding fiducials once atoms were identified. This provided a polished user experience, where students reported no perceptible frame drops during common manipulations, such as adding or removing tiles and testing bond arrangements. Frame buffer management, overlay compositing, and lightweight orbital animations supported the illusion of seamless interactivity, enhancing the overall experience. Update throttling and lazy loading further prevented unnecessary repaints, sustaining 30 FPS as chemical names, formulas, and labels were updated in real-time with the vision loop.

LLM interactions introduced modest delays of 2–5 seconds. However, the design preserved real-time interactivity by validating JSON outputs, applying schema checks, and falling back to local chemical data when parsing or connectivity issues arose. This prevented blocking failures, reducing disruptions to minor narrative delays. A robust exception hierarchy, network backoff mechanisms, state restoration, and user-facing notifications ensured resilience against network or camera issues. Unit and integration testing validated domain correctness and system performance: bond logic and formula generation were checked against references, while stress tests on camera capture, GUI rendering, and AI queuing demonstrated graceful degradation under load. Chemical accuracy was further cross-verified against NIST datasets, expert reviews, and literature spot checks, reinforcing its trustworthiness. Finally, user acceptance testing emphasized educational outcomes, usability, and accessibility, measuring whether learners could connect electron counts to bond formation, recognize valence limits, and interpret geometry shifts. WCAG-aligned reviews confirmed readability under diverse classroom display conditions. Collectively, these evaluations underscore not only the technical soundness but also the pedagogical readiness of the system for authentic classroom adoption.

Figure 4.13 illustrates the molecular composition of water, with hydrogen (H) and oxygen (O) atoms depicted in a structural bonding model. Water is a vital compound widely used in industrial, commercial, and laboratory applications, including cooling in power plants, chemical synthesis, and food production. Beyond its practical uses, the model also emphasizes safety considerations; though generally safe, water can cause damage when present in excess or in contact with reactive substances (e.g., metals susceptible to rusting). This visualization serves as both an educational aid and a reference for understanding the chemical and practical significance of water in diverse fields.

Figure 4.14 illustrates Lithium Hydride (LiH), an inorganic compound consisting of lithium and hydrogen atoms in a simple binary structure. Lithium hydride is a colorless solid (though commercial samples may appear gray) and represents the lightest ionic compound. It exhibits a small lattice constant and shares structural similarities with sodium chloride (NaCl). Due to its high hydrogen source density, LiH finds applications in aerospace, particularly space programs, and serves as a potent reducing agent in chemical synthesis. Its single covalent bond between lithium and hydrogen, as depicted, underlies its stability and utility in specialized chemical processes.

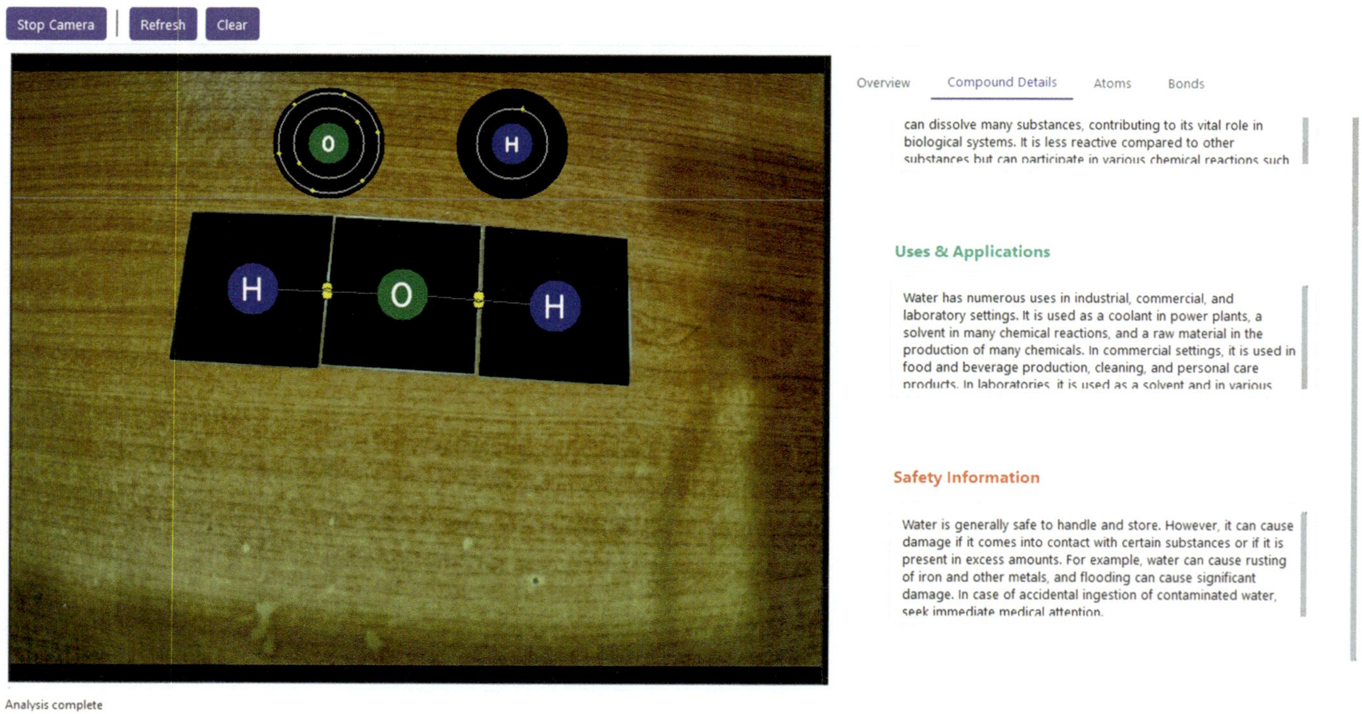

FIGURE 4.13 A GenAI-enabled digital simulation and model of the water molecule (H_2O), showing its atomic structure with two hydrogen atoms covalently bonded to one oxygen atom.

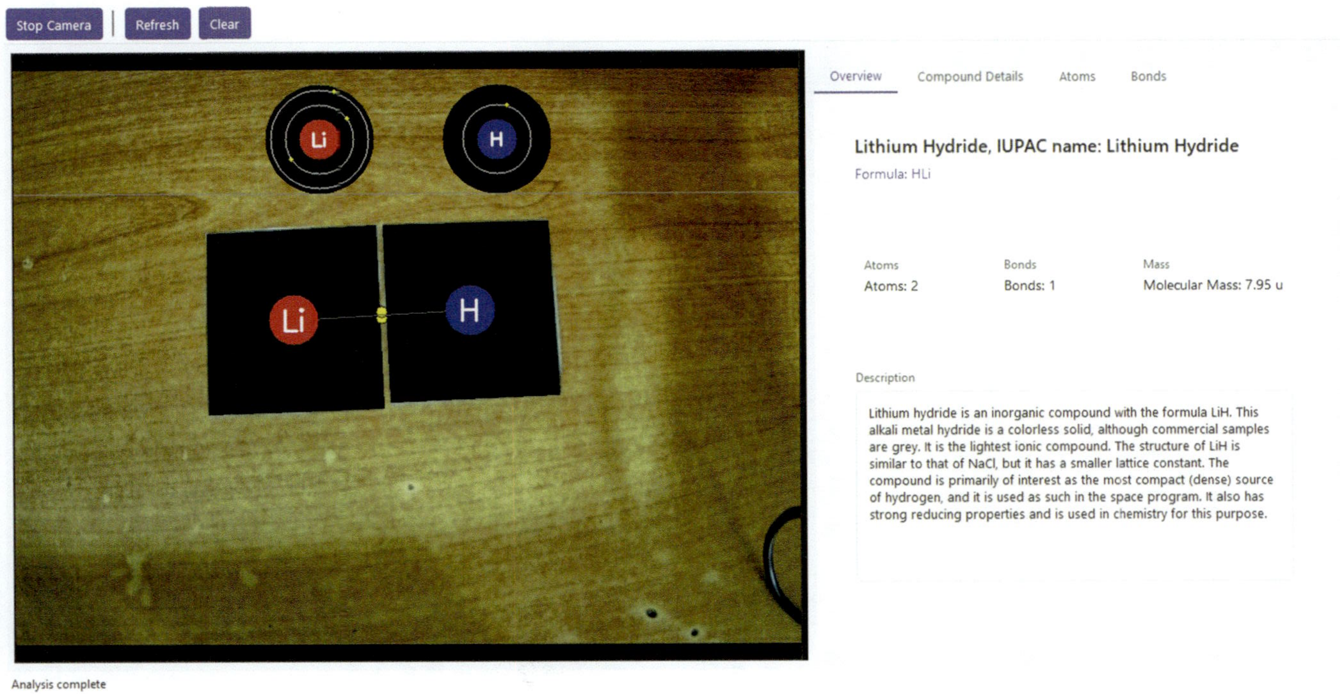

FIGURE 4.14 GenAI-enabled digital molecular model and structural overview of lithium hydride (LiH), showing atomic configuration and bonding between lithium (Li) and hydrogen (H).

4.7 CONCLUSION

GenAI has the potential to improve accessibility in STEM education when designed responsibly significantly. By offering multimodal supports, it helps students with visual, hearing, or speech impairments overcome barriers. Key tools include alt-text and MathML for equations and diagrams, sonified charts, accessible captioning for symbols, conversational tutoring via text or AAC, and advanced TTS or voice synthesis. The most significant impact occurs when GenAI is a tool-grounded for accuracy, aligned with curricula, and personalized to individual access needs rather than following a generic model.

Effective practices combine multimodal scaffolds with formative learning support to enhance student learning. For example, image-to-text creates accessible diagram descriptions, pipelines convert visuals into tactile Braille outputs, sonification translates charts into audio patterns, and real-time captioning captures technical notation. Step-by-step hints, error feedback, and adaptive practice items also reduce cognitive load while preserving rigor.

However, reliable governance is critical. Systems must utilize verified tools, clearly highlight uncertainty, and maintain human oversight for high-stakes work. Accessibility standards (WCAG/ARIA/MathML), privacy safeguards, and equity measures such as multilingual, low-bandwidth, and affordable options are essential. Despite challenges, such as the quality of tactile graphics, sign language accuracy, and limited benchmarks, a roadmap of co-design, piloting, educator training, and governance can ensure that GenAI complements teaching while making STEM more inclusive and effective.

NOTES

1 AAC-supported responses refer to communication outputs produced using Augmentative and Alternative Communication (AAC) systems. These systems can range from low-tech methods such as gestures, pictures, and written symbols to high-tech tools like speech-generating applications and computerized devices.
2 SVG is a graphics format based on XML (Extensible Markup Language) that describes images using geometric shapes, like lines, curves, and text, rather than pixels.
3 gTTS is a Python library and online service that allows programmers to convert written text into spoken audio using Google's Text-to-Speech engine.
4 https://speechtechnology.web.illinois.edu/uaspeech/.
5 https://www.cs.toronto.edu/~complingweb/data/TORGO/torgo.html.
6 https://sites.research.google/euphonia/about/.

REFERENCES

1. Şule, K. (2023). The evolution and global significance of STEM education in the 21st century. *The Journal of International Scientific Researches*, 8(3), 410–415. https://doi.org/10.23834/isrjournal.1342255
2. Li, X., & Li, Y. (2023). Individualized and innovation-centered general education in a Chinese STEM University. *Education Sciences*, 13(8), 846–846. https://doi.org/10.3390/educsci13080846
3. Alexandru, M., & Singh, C. (2023). Helping students become proficient problem solvers Part II: An example from waves. *Education Sciences*, 13(2), 138–138. https://doi.org/10.3390/educsci13020138

4. Quayson, C., Ankrah, K. T., Koranteng, E., & Hanson, R. (2022). Chemistry teacher trainees' use of molecular models in learning Spiro and Bicyclic compounds. *Science Education International*, 33(3), 291–295. https://doi.org/10.33828/sei.v33.i3.4
5. Evdokia, V. (2025). Lefteris moussiades a systematic review of AI, VR, and LLM applications in special education: Opportunities, challenges, and future directions. *Education and Information Technologies*. https://doi.org/10.1007/s10639-025-13550-4
6. Buzzi, M., Giuditta, P., & Leporini, B. (2025). How artificial intelligence is impacting the STEM education of students with disabilities: A five years. *CSEDU*, 1, 323–330, https://doi.org/10.5220/0013267900003932.
7. Sakowicz, M., & Hamidi, F. (2025). Exploring the role of generative AI in supporting students with disabilities, through the lens of universal design for learning, 15, 1–22, https://doi.org/10.32674/yeyaaq64
8. Yang, C., & Taele, P. (2025). AI for accessible education: Personalized audio-based learning for blind students. arXiv preprint arXiv:2504.17117.
9. Ainary, B. (2025). Audo-Sight: Enabling ambient interaction for blind and visually impaired individuals. arXiv preprint arXiv:2505.00153.
10. Schauer, S., Simbeck, K., & Schüßler, L. (2025). Generating Accessibility: Using AI to Improve Higher Education for the Visually Impaired. *Proceedings of the 17th international conference on computer supported education* (pp. 15–25). https://doi.org/10.5220/0013136300003932
11. Acosta-Vargas, P., Belén, S.-A., Novillo-Villegas, S., Sarantis, D., & Salvador-Ullauri, L. (2024). Generative artificial intelligence and web accessibility: Towards an inclusive and sustainable future. *Emerging Science Journal*, 8(4), 1602–1621. https://doi.org/10.28991/esj-2024-08-04-021
12. Korada, L., Sikha, V. K., & Siramgari, D. (2024). AI & accessibility: A conceptual framework for inclusive technology. *International Journal of Intelligent Systems and Applications in Engineering*, 12(23s), 983.
13. Taljaard, J. (2016). A review of multi-sensory technologies in a science, technology, engineering, Arts and Mathematics (STEAM) classroom. *Journal of Learning Design*, 9(2), 46–55. https://eric.ed.gov/?id=EJ1117662
14. Sanfilippo, F., Blazauskas, T., Gionata, S., Ramos, I., Vert, S., Jaziar, R., Majchrzak, T., & Oliveira, D. (2022). A perspective review on integrating VR/AR with haptics into STEM education for multi-sensory learning. *Robotics*, 11(2), 41–41. https://doi.org/10.3390/robotics11020041
15. Bonfim, C. S., Mól, G. D. S., & Pinheiro, B. C. S. (2021). A (In)Visibilidade de Pessoas com Deficiência Visual nas Ciências Exatas e Naturais: Percepções e Perspectivas. *Revista Brasileira de Educação Especial*, 27. https://doi.org/10.1590/1980-54702021v27e0220
16. Hayes, C., & Proulx, M. J. (2023). Turning a blind eye? Removing barriers to science and mathematics education for students with visual impairments. *British Journal of Visual Impairment*, 42(2), 544–556. https://doi.org/10.1177/02646196221149561
17. Koehler, K. E., & Picard, K. M. (2024). Making STEM accessible for students with visual impairments: Implications for practice. *TEACHING Exceptional Children*. https://doi.org/10.1177/00400599241231211
18. Nowlin, M. T. (2025). Accessibility of Higher Education STEM Courses: Perspectives of Vision Impaired Students (Doctoral dissertation, Lamar University-Beaumont).
19. Dreamerson, J. T., & Erin (2025). The current state of literature on the education of blind and visually impaired (BVI) Students in chemistry and STEMM in higher education. *Journal of Chemical Education*. https://doi.org/10.1021/acs.jchemed.5c00269
20. Kigotho, L. W. (2016). *Barriers Faced by Students With Hearing Impairment in Inclusive Learning Environment, a Case of the University of Nairobi*. Uonbi.ac.ke. http://hdl.handle.net/11295/98908

21. Nordin, N., Md Yunus, M. E. L. O. R., Zaharudin, R., Salehi, H., Mohd Yasin, M. H., & Embl, M. A. (2015). Identifying the challenges and barriers hearing-impaired learners face in using ICT education courses. *Journal of Theoretical & Applied Information Technology*, 78(3), 327–335.
22. Mendoza, M. C., Geroso, M. J., & Maguate, G. S. (2023). Hearing the unheard: Unveiling the untold stories of hearing-impaired students in inclusive education. *International Journal of Latest Research in Humanities and Social Science (IJLRHSS)*, 6(8), 01–09.
23. Safder, M., Akhtar, M. M. S., Fatima, G., & Malik, M. (2012). Problems faced by students with hearing impairment in inclusive education at the university level. *Journal of Research and Reflections in Education*, 6, 134–143.
24. Zascavage, V. T., & Keefe, C. H. (2004). Students with severe speech and physical impairments. *Focus on Autism and Other Developmental Disabilities*, 19(4), 223–234. https://doi.org/10.1177/10883576040190040401
25. Avoiding Communication Barriers in the Classroom: The APEINTA Project. (2016). Interactive learning environments. https://doi.org/10.1080/10494820.2014.924533
26. Expectations and experiences of accessing and participating in services for childhood speech impairment. (2025). *International Journal of Speech-Language Pathology*. https://doi.org/10.3109/17549507.2011.535565
27. Muhammad, D., Amjad, F., & Qudoos, A. (2024). Academic barriers of students with hearing impairment at the undergraduate level (A Case of Two Public Universities). *Al-Mahdi Research Journal (MRJ)*, 5(4), 257–264. https://ojs.mrj.com.pk/index.php/MRJ/article/view/329
28. Gates, P. (2017). The importance of diagrams, graphics and other visual representations in STEM teaching. *STEM Education in the Junior Secondary*, 169–196. https://doi.org/10.1007/978-981-10-5448-8_9
29. Visualizations and pictures for the visually impaired and its connection to STEM education. (2024). *Journal of Mathematics and the Arts*. https://doi.org/10.1080/17513472.2024.2365086
30. Tu, Y., Chen, J., & Huang, C. (2025). Empowering personalized learning with generative artificial intelligence: Mechanisms, challenges and pathways. *Frontiers of Digital Education*, 2(2). https://doi.org/10.1007/s44366-025-0056-9
31. Mohamed, F. N., Azhar, J., Yasmeen, S., Hussain, I., & Majid Khawar. (2025). Generative artificial intelligence and personalized learning environment: challenges and opportunities. *Southern Journal of Computer Science*, 1(01), 1–36. https://sjcs.isp.edu.pk/index.php/SJCS/article/view/5
32. Boateng, F. (2025). The transformative potential of Generative AI in academic library access services: Opportunities and challenges. *Information Services & Use*. https://doi.org/10.1177/18758789251332800
33. McDermott, B. (2024). AI as an accessibility tool. *Advances in Educational Marketing, Administration, and Leadership*, 162–174. https://doi.org/10.4018/979-8-3693-0240-8.ch009
34. Bura, C., & Kumar, M. P. (2024). *Advancing Transformative Education: Generative AI as a Catalyst for Equity and Innovation*. ArXiv.org. https://arxiv.org/abs/2411.15971
35. Tang, X., Abdolrahmani, A., Gergle, D., & Piper, A. M. (2025). Everyday uncertainty: How blind people use GenAI tools for information access. 1–17. https://doi.org/10.1145/3706598.3713433
36. Phutane, M., Wright, J., Castro, B. V., Shi, L., Stern, S. R., Lawson, H. M., & Azenkot, S. (2022). Tactile materials in practice: Understanding the experiences of teachers of the visually impaired. *ACM Transactions on Accessible Computing*, 15(3), 1–34. https://doi.org/10.1145/3508364

37. Sonification of numerical data for education. (2019). Open Learning: The Journal of Open, Distance and E-Learning. https://doi.org/10.1080/02680513.2018.1553707
38. Nai, G., Zanella, A., Mascolo, L. D., Ginolfi, M., Nicolò, C., Manuncola, F. T., & Grassi, M. (2024). Evaluating the effectiveness of sonification in science education using Edukoi. *Personal and Ubiquitous Computing*, 28(5), 693–711. https://doi.org/10.1007/s00779-024-01809-5
39. Personalized stem education empowered by artificial intelligence: a comprehensive review and content analysis. (2025). *Interactive Learning Environments*. https://doi.org/10.1080/10494820.2025.2462156
40. Eramo, G., Pastore, S., Tullio, M. D., Rossini, V., Alessandro, M., & Mesto, E. (2025). The sound of science: A sonification learning experience in an Italian secondary school. *Frontiers in Education*, 9. https://doi.org/10.3389/feduc.2024.1502396
41. Elmquist, E. (2025). *Sensibly sound: human-centered integration of sonification and visualization* (Vol. 2422). Linköping University Electronic Press.
42. Gourisaria, M. K., Agrawal, R., Sahni, M., & Singh, P. K. (2024). Comparative analysis of audio classification with MFCC and STFT features using machine learning techniques. *Discover Internet of Things*, 4(1). https://doi.org/10.1007/s43926-023-00049-y
43. Leon, C., Lipuma, J., & Oviedo-Torres, X. (2025). Artificial intelligence in STEM education: a transdisciplinary framework for engagement and innovation. *Frontiers in Education*, 10. https://doi.org/10.3389/feduc.2025.1619888
44. Qushem, U. B., Christopoulos, A., Oyelere, S. S., Ogata, H., & Laakso, M.-J. (2021). Multimodal technologies in precision education: Providing new opportunities or adding more challenges? *Education Sciences*, 11(7), 338. https://doi.org/10.3390/educsci11070338
45. Petit, G., Dufresne, A., Levesque, V., Hayward, V., & Trudeau, N. (2008, October). Refreshable tactile graphics applied to schoolbook illustrations for students with visual impairment. In *Proceedings of the 10th international ACM SIGACCESS conference on computers and accessibility* (pp. 89–96). Halifax Nova Scotia Canada.
46. Nathan, M. J., Rachaya, S., Walkington, C., Wolfgram, M., Williams, C., & Alibali, M. W. (2013). Building cohesion across representations: A Mechanism for STEM Integration. *Journal of Engineering Education*, 102(1), 77–116. https://doi.org/10.1002/jee.20000
47. Gatto, S., Ombretta, G., Luca, G., & Nai, G. (2024). Accessible mathematics: representation of functions through sound and touch. *IEEE Access*, 12, 121552–121569. https://doi.org/10.1109/access.2024.3448509
48. Barak, M., & Rania, H.-F. (2012). Integrating model-based learning and animations for enhancing students' understanding of proteins structure and function. *Research in Science Education*, 43(2), 619–636. https://doi.org/10.1007/s11165-012-9280-7
49. Joo, W. (2022, June 28). Experiential graphic sonification for visual and auditory communication design and musical expression. *Vt.edu; Virginia Tech*. https://vtechworks.lib.vt.edu/items/c9fb9b81-56a7-4441-a2f3-a59447926a6e
50. Long, M. R., & Kowalske, M. G. (2021). Understanding STEM instructors' experiences with and perceptions of deaf and hard-of-hearing students: The first step toward increasing access and inclusivity. *Journal of Chemical Education*, 99(1), 274–282. https://doi.org/10.1021/acs.jchemed.1c00409
51. Jenks, A., Onufer, L., & Guberman, D. (2024). Emergent questions of access: disability and the integration of generative AI in teaching and learning. *Higher Education Research & Development*, 1–14. https://doi.org/10.1080/07294360.2024.2442611
52. Raji, N. R., Biji, C. L., & Vineetha, V. (2025). Multi-modal generative AI for people with disabilities. 271–296. https://doi.org/10.1007/978-981-96-2355-6_12

53. Corsi, F. (2025). Studying maths with A.I.: A trouble liaison for blind students. *INTED Proceedings*, 1, 998–1006. https://doi.org/10.21125/inted.2025.0340
54. Adler, H. J. (2025). Language complexities for deaf and hard of hearing individuals in their pursuit of a career in science, technology, engineering, mathematics, and medicine: Perspectives from an LSL/ASL User. *Ear and Hearing*. https://doi.org/10.1097/aud.0000000000001637
55. Oreshkina, O. A., & Safonova, Y. A. (2024). Instructional strategies for hearing-impaired students who are subjects of inclusive programs of engineering education. *2024 IEEE Global Engineering Education Conference (EDUCON)*, 1–9. https://doi.org/10.1109/educon60312.2024.10578620
56. Wang, L., & Wang, W. (2025). Empirical study on GenAI use in speech difficulty evaluation. *INContext: Studies in Translation and Interculturalism*, 5(1). https://doi.org/10.54754/incontext.v5i1.104
57. Santhana Hari, S., Harine Rajashree, R., Dharani, J., & Santhiya, C. (2025). AI-Enabled learning ecosystems. *Driving Quality Education through AI and Data Science*, 165–192. https://doi.org/10.4018/979-8-3693-8292-9.ch008
58. Ronksley-Pavia, M., Nguyen, L., Wheeley, E., Rose, J., Neumann, M. M., Bigum, C., & Neumann, D. L. (2025). A scoping literature review of generative artificial intelligence for supporting neurodivergent school students. *Computers and Education Artificial Intelligence*, 100437–100437. https://doi.org/10.1016/j.caeai.2025.100437
59. Deb, S. S., Roy, M., Bachmann, C., & Bertelli, M. O. (2022). Specific learning disorders, motor disorders, and communication disorders. *Textbook of Psychiatry for Intellectual Disability and Autism Spectrum Disorder*, 483–511. https://doi.org/10.1007/978-3-319-95720-3_18
60. Kuhn, K., Kersken, V., Reuter, B., Egger, N., & Zimmermann, G. (2023). Measuring the accuracy of automatic speech recognition solutions. *ACM Transactions on Accessible Computing*, 16(4), 1–23. https://doi.org/10.1145/3636513
61. Georgiou, G. P. (2025). Transforming speech-language pathology with AI: Opportunities, challenges, and ethical guidelines. *Healthcare*, 13(19), 2460–2460. https://doi.org/10.3390/healthcare13192460.
62. Martin, A., MacDonald, R.L., Jiang, P.-P., Ladewig, M., Cattiau, J., Heywood, R., Cave, R., Tobin, J., Nelson, P.C., & Tomanek, K. (2025). Project Euphonia: Advancing inclusive speech recognition through expanded data collection and evaluation. *Frontiers in Language Sciences*, 4. https://doi.org/10.3389/flang.2025.1569448.
63. Kim, H., Hasegawa-Johnson, M., Perlman, A., Gunderson, J. R., Huang, T. S., Watkin, K. L., & Frame, S. (2008, September). Dysarthric speech database for universal access research. *Interspeech*, 2008, 1741–1744.
64. Balaji, M. T. M., Balajiraja, N., Uma, M. P., & Nair, M. S. P. (2025). *Generative AI Tools: Concepts, Applications, and Innovations*. Academic Guru Publishing House.
65. Carmona-Galindo, V. D., Ung, H., Zeng, M., Broussard, C., Taranenko, E., Daneshbod, Y., Chappell, D., & Lorenz, T. (2025). Generative AI as a sociotechnical challenge: Inclusive teaching strategies at a hispanic-serving institution. *Knowledge*, 5(3), 18. https://doi.org/10.3390/knowledge5030018
66. Dong, Y., & Payandeh, S. (2025). Hand kinematic model construction based on tracking landmarks. *Applied Sciences*, 15(16), 8921. https://doi.org/10.3390/app15168921

5 AI/GenAI and the Metaverse for Inclusive Distance STEM Education

5.1 INCLUSIVE STEM LEARNING IN THE METAVERSE

Integrating GenAI and the metaverse[1] into distance STEM education represents one of the most significant opportunities to advance inclusive education in the twenty-first century [1, 2]. The vision is not merely about transferring existing classroom practices into digital formats, but rather about reimagining learning spaces where participation barriers dissolve, allowing learners with functional immobility, chronic illness, or other disabilities to experience parity in access, interaction, and achievement. Central to this vision is the belief that education is a matter of knowledge transfer and a practice of belonging and empowerment. The transformative power of GenAI and the metaverse lies in their ability to create immersive, adaptive, and personalized environments that respond to individual learner needs while maintaining rigorous standards of STEM education [3, 4, 5]. As shown in Figure 5.1, the integration of GenAI and metaverse technologies into distance STEM education is structured around three foundational principles: equity of access, universality of design, and authenticity of experience.

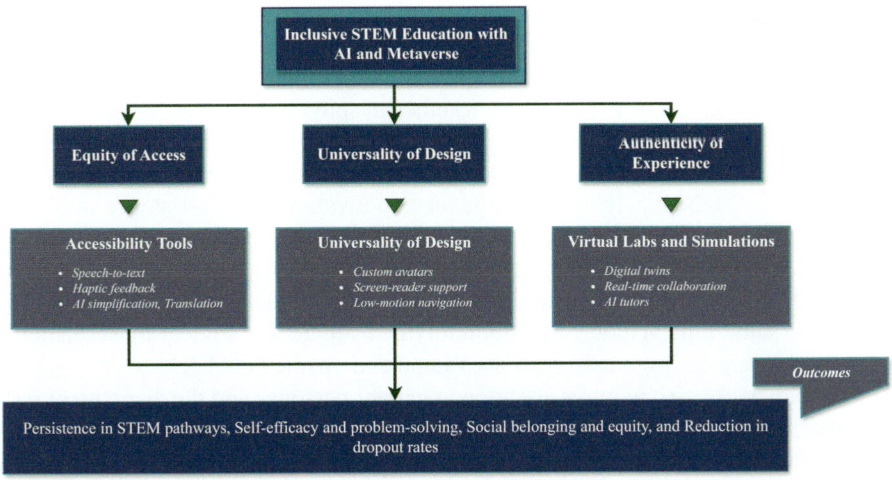

FIGURE 5.1 The integration of GenAI and the metaverse into distance STEM education.

DOI: 10.1201/9781003641490-5

The rationale for introducing GenAI and the metaverse into distance STEM education is rooted in the long-standing inequities faced by students with mobility limitations. Laboratory work, field experiments, and collaborative design sessions, which are often hallmarks of STEM disciplines, remain inaccessible to many learners who cannot physically attend or manipulate equipment in person [6, 7]. In traditional distance learning platforms, these experiences are either omitted or presented in a highly abstracted manner, leaving students at a disadvantage compared to their peers in physical settings. GenAI and metaverse technologies directly address this problem by creating digital twins of laboratories, simulating complex environments, and utilizing avatars or robotic proxies that enable real-time participation. Through these tools, learners can engage in authentic inquiry, collaborate with peers, and contribute meaningfully to shared projects, regardless of physical constraints [8–10].

An inclusion framework for this vision is based on three foundational principles: equity of access, universality of design, and authenticity of experience. First, equity of access ensures that learners with diverse functional abilities have the necessary entry points into educational activities. This involves not only physical accessibility, such as STT or haptic feedback systems, but also cognitive and linguistic accessibility, including AI-driven simplification of technical content and multilingual translation. Second, the universality of design requires inherently flexible platforms, enabling users to adjust visual, auditory, and interactive modalities to suit their preferences. Features such as customizable avatars, low-motion navigation modes, or screen reader-friendly interfaces demonstrate how universal design principles must be embedded into every system layer. Finally, authenticity of experience requires that the virtual or AI-mediated learning activities reflect the richness and complexity of real-world STEM practices. Virtual laboratories should not be watered-down versions of experiments but instead provide realistic, interactive, and even enhanced opportunities for inquiry, including scenarios that may be unsafe or impractical in physical settings [11–13].

Another rationale for this framework lies in the connection between accessibility and identity formation in STEM. Research has consistently shown that students' sense of belonging in STEM disciplines is shaped by their ability to participate in core practices: experimentation, collaboration, and problem-solving. When learners are excluded from these experiences, whether by physical barriers or inaccessible pedagogies, they often internalize a sense of deficiency, leading to disengagement and attrition. Conversely, when inclusive technologies allow learners to engage in these practices authentically, their confidence, motivation, and persistence in STEM pathways increase. GenAI and the metaverse provide the scaffolding necessary for such inclusive participation. For example, an AI-driven tutor can detect hesitation or errors in real time, offering supportive feedback tailored to a student's learning profile. At the same time, a metaverse laboratory can situate that student in a collaborative group where their contributions are valued and visible [14–17].

The framework also requires attention to learner personas and the diversity of barriers they face. Students with functional immobility may need full virtual lab experiences, while those with chronic illness may benefit from asynchronous, AI-supported modules that adapt to fluctuating energy levels. Neurodivergent students may require environments with adjustable sensory inputs to prevent overstimulation. At the same time, learners in rural or low-resource settings may face bandwidth or device limitations that necessitate lightweight, scalable solutions. An inclusive design must anticipate these variations and provide multiple pathways for engagement without stigmatizing or segregating learners. Here, GenAI can dynamically adapt instructions, simplify or expand explanations based on learner responses, and facilitate collaboration in ways that are sensitive to individual needs [18–22].

Significantly, the inclusion framework must extend beyond technical design to encompass social and cultural equity dimensions. Accessibility is not simply a matter of functional support but also ensures that digital spaces are culturally responsive and welcoming. Avatars in the metaverse should allow for diverse representation, including mobility aids, cultural dress, and gender expressions, so learners see themselves authentically reflected in the environment. AI-driven communication tools should be trained on diverse linguistic and cultural datasets to avoid exclusionary biases in feedback or assessment. By embedding cultural responsiveness, the metaverse becomes more than a neutral platform; it becomes a space where marginalized voices are validated and amplified [23–25].

The role of policy and ethics in this vision cannot be overlooked. Inclusive education mediated by GenAI and the metaverse raises concerns about data privacy, algorithmic bias, and surveillance [26, 27]. Students with disabilities may be particularly vulnerable to misrepresentation if AI systems misclassify their behaviors or needs [27, 28]. Thus, any inclusion framework must mandate transparency in AI decision-making, provide students with control over their data, and establish accountability mechanisms for detecting and remedying bias. Furthermore, institutions must adopt procurement policies that prioritize accessibility compliance and open standards to prevent vendor lock-in and ensure the long-term sustainability of inclusive practices.

This vision's LOs and equity goals extend beyond simple knowledge acquisition. GenAI and the metaverse aim to cultivate persistence in STEM pathways, enhance self-efficacy in problem-solving, and prepare individuals for higher education or workforce participation by enabling authentic engagement in STEM practices [29, 30]. Equitable participation metrics, such as representation in collaborative tasks, parity in contribution rates, and reduction in dropout among learners with disabilities, should guide the evaluation of these initiatives. At the same time, the inclusion framework emphasizes the importance of social-emotional outcomes: reducing feelings of isolation, enhancing a sense of belonging, and fostering resilience in the face of academic challenges [31–33].

Ultimately, the vision, rationale, and inclusion framework for GenAI and the metaverse in distance STEM education articulate a future where functional immobility is no longer a disqualifying factor in education, where immersive digital environments serve as bridges rather than barriers, and where inclusive design becomes the default rather than the exception. The goal is not to create parallel learning tracks for students with disabilities but to build a unified ecosystem where diversity is seen as an asset, and where all learners, regardless of ability, can engage, contribute, and thrive in pursuing STEM knowledge. This approach recognizes that inclusivity not only strengthens the learning experience of marginalized groups but also enhances the overall quality and resilience of STEM education. By embracing GenAI and metaverse technologies with an intentional inclusion framework, educators and institutions can move closer to realizing the long-promised ideal of equal education for all.

5.2 SYSTEM ARCHITECTURE AND TECHNOLOGIES

Designing an inclusive distance STEM education ecosystem supported by GenAI and the metaverse requires a strong pedagogical vision and a robust system architecture. Such an architecture must align accessibility, scalability, and security with the immersive and interactive features that STEM disciplines demand [34, 35]. The stack is layered: from the core AI and XR components that power the system, to the interaction interfaces enabling learners with diverse abilities to engage, to the data and interoperability mechanisms that connect with institutional infrastructures, to the trust and safety protocols that ensure responsible use, and finally to the scalability and cost models that determine sustainability [36, 37].

5.2.1 Core Components

The backbone of the inclusive metaverse learning ecosystem consists of several tightly coupled components that work in unison to replicate, and in some cases enhance, the traditional STEM classroom and laboratory experience.

Figure 5.2 illustrates the layered architecture of the inclusive metaverse STEM system, showing how the different technological components are orchestrated to deliver an accessible and immersive learning environment.

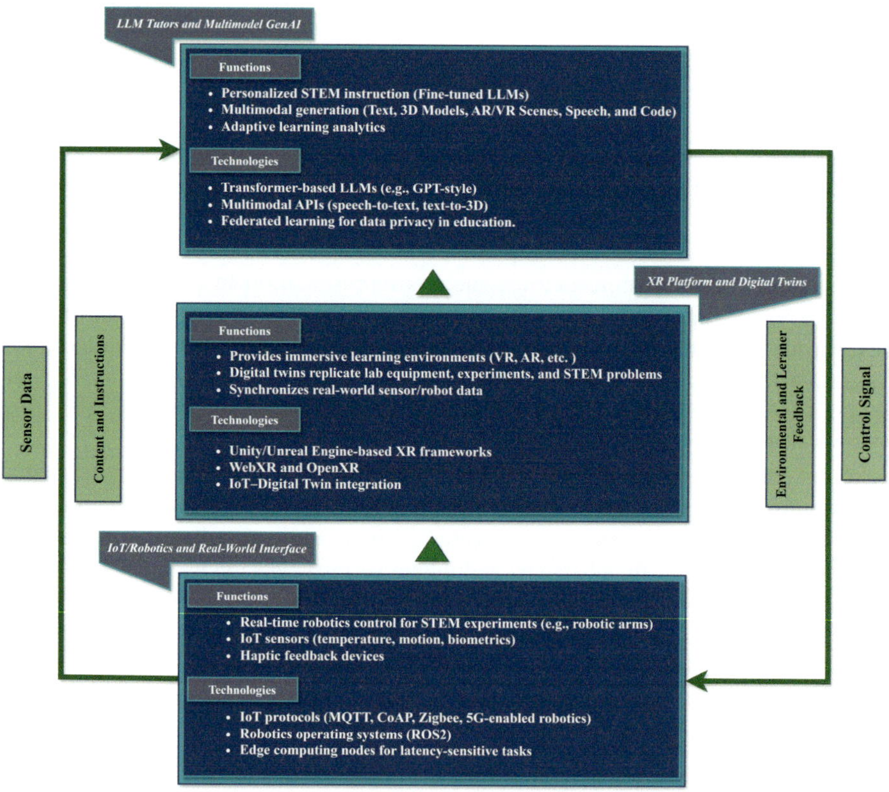

FIGURE 5.2 Core components of inclusive metaverse STEM system.

5.2.1.1 LLM-Driven Tutors and Copilots

LLMs are increasingly integrated into metaverse environments as intelligent tutors and collaborative copilots for learning and research. Within these immersive spaces, their capacity to interpret learner queries in natural language enables students to explore complex scientific and technical concepts through intuitive, conversational interaction. This lowers the entry barrier for newcomers while sustaining intellectual rigor for advanced users [38, 39].

Unlike static educational tools, metaverse-embedded LLMs generate adaptive, context-aware responses. A beginner might receive a guided, step-by-step walk-through of an experiment, while an expert could engage in higher-level theoretical reasoning or data interpretation, all within the same shared virtual space.

A defining strength of these AI tutors lies in their ability to provide multimodal explanations. They can generate not only text-based feedback but also 3D visualizations, interactive diagrams, or spatially anchored simulations that make abstract principles tangible. Acting as translators of technical jargon, LLMs convert dense scientific language into clear, engaging explanations without sacrificing precision [39].

When embodied as avatars or conversational agents, LLMs foster a sense of presence and collaboration. For example, in a virtual chemistry lab, a student who notices a solution turning blue can ask the LLM-avatar why this occurs. The AI might respond by visualizing the molecular reaction, proposing follow-up experiments, and linking the observed phenomenon to real-world contexts such as industrial dye synthesis or biomedical diagnostics. Through this kind of immersive, adaptive interaction, LLMs transform the metaverse into a dynamic ecosystem for experiential learning and scientific exploration.

5.2.1.2 Multimodal Generative AI

While LLMs excel in handling text and code, multimodal GenAI expands learning into richer territories by incorporating images, 3D models, simulations, and interactive artifacts. This broadens the scope of educational engagement by allowing learners to read or hear about concepts and visualize, manipulate, and even simulate them. For example, multimodal AI can generate three-dimensional molecular structures on demand or produce virtual physics apparatuses that replicate real-world experiments [40, 41].

Automation also plays a role in enhancing productivity. These systems can generate lab reports automatically, complete with diagrams, data visualizations, and plots that align with the student's experimental activity. They can even translate spoken input into annotated code or mathematical expressions, providing a seamless bridge between verbal reasoning and formalized problem-solving [40, 42].

Accessibility is another critical advantage of multimodality. Visually impaired learners can benefit from haptic or audio renderings of 3D models, while deaf students may interact with signed avatars or auto-captioned instructions. In this way, multimodal AI ensures inclusivity, allowing diverse learners to access the same depth of educational content regardless of their physical abilities.

5.2.1.3 XR/Metaverse Platforms

At the heart of this ecosystem lies XR, which integrates VR, AR, and Mixed Reality (MR). These technologies transform the traditional classroom into a shared immersive environment where learners engage with knowledge spatially and interactively.

In a metaverse-based class, students can conduct experiments using virtual lab equipment that mirrors the precision of real-world instruments [43, 44]. They can also collaborate in problem-solving exercises within immersive group settings, breaking free from physical space limitations.

Lectures in XR environments differ significantly from conventional teaching methods. Instead of static slides, instructors can present interactive 3D simulations. A physics teacher, for instance, can demonstrate gravitational forces in real time, allowing students to manipulate variables and observe changes directly [45]. Rather than passively absorbing information, learners actively engage with dynamic models, making abstract concepts intuitive and experiential.

5.2.1.4 Digital Twins of Lab Equipment

Digital twin technology creates virtual replicas of real laboratory instruments, enabling learners to interact with high-fidelity simulations of complex tools. For students who cannot access physical laboratories, digital twins provide an equitable alternative [46, 47]. Virtual microscopes, spectrometers, or robotic arms can be operated with remarkable precision, allowing students to practice experimental techniques and data collection in simulated environments. Figure 5.3 shows the VR objects in a real-life laboratory environment. The illustration features a microcontroller, a USB connector, a book, and a personal computer, all of which are utilized in the metaverse remote lab scenario.

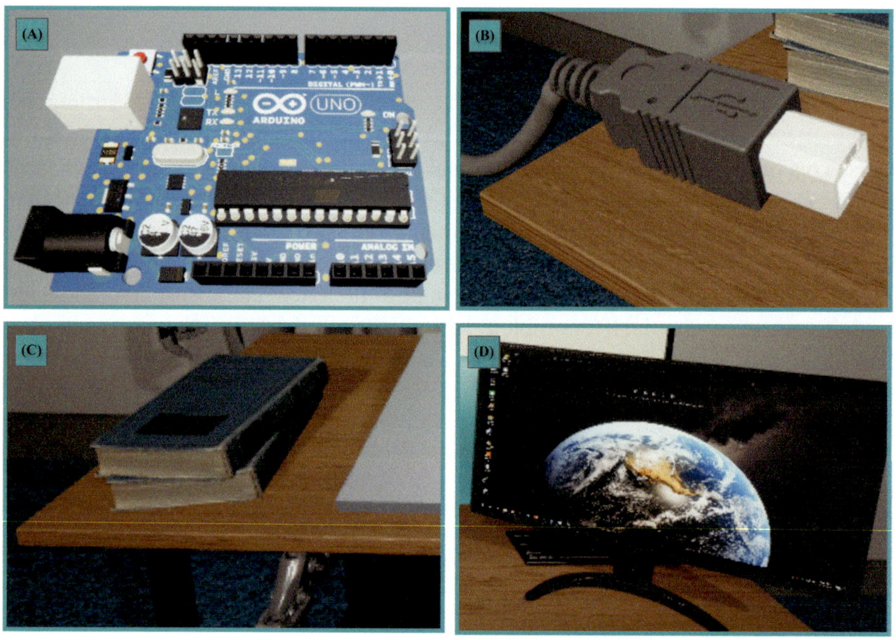

FIGURE 5.3 VR objects from a real-ife laboratory environment (a) Arduino microcontroller, (b) USB connector to the Arduino, (c) books, and (d) personal computer.

The data generated from digital twin interactions can be exported for further analysis using statistical or visualization software, ensuring continuity with professional scientific workflows. This helps students build technical skills and ensures parity between remote learners and their peers who may have direct access to physical labs. Digital twins thus democratize scientific education by making costly or geographically restricted resources universally available.

5.2.1.5 IoT and Robotics Teleoperation

While digital twins provide high-quality simulations, some educational contexts require direct engagement with physical equipment. This is where IoT-enabled robotics and teleoperation become invaluable. Students can remotely control real laboratory apparatus through the metaverse interface, bridging the gap between virtual presence and physical experimentation [48, 49].

Consider the case of a learner with limited mobility. By logging into a metaverse lab, they could manipulate a robotic arm to mix reagents in a real laboratory thousands of miles away. The entire process is mediated by IoT sensors, which stream data back to the XR environment in real time. This data can then be annotated by GenAI tutors, providing immediate interpretation and feedback. Such hybrid models blur the boundary between digital and physical realities, creating a flexible learning environment that benefits students through simulated and real-world exploration. Integrating IoT and robotics makes education more inclusive, scalable, and engaging [50, 51].

As shown in Figure 5.4, the proposed metaverse lab blends high-fidelity digital twins with IoT-enabled teleoperation to bridge virtual presence and physical experimentation. Students, including those with limited mobility, issue commands through an XR interface to a remote robotic arm, while IoT sensors (e.g., temperature, pH, force) stream data back over a real-time messaging bus. Multimodal, LLM-driven

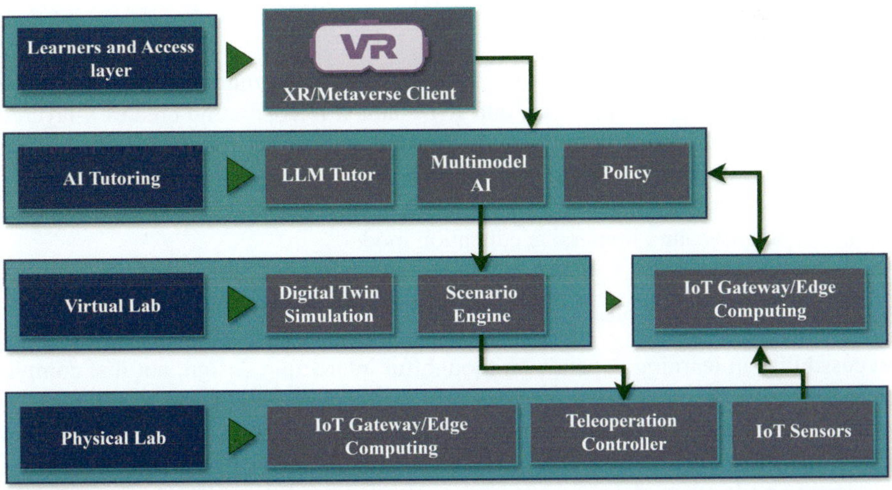

FIGURE 5.4 IoT-enabled teleoperation and digital twin learning ecosystem.

TABLE 5.1
Summary of Emerging Technologies in AI-driven Education, Illustrating How LLM Tutors, Multimodal Generative AI, XR/Metaverse Platforms, Digital Twins, and IoT/Robotics Teleoperation Enhance Learning Experiences, Accessibility, and Experimental Engagement

Component	Core Functionality	Example Use Case	Accessibility Benefits
LLM-driven Tutors and Copilots	Interpret queries, generate adaptive explanations, and act as avatars in the metaverse	Explaining chemical reactions and suggesting follow-up experiments	Simplifies jargon and offers multimodal hints
Multimodal GenAI	Generate text, images, 3D models, simulations, and lab reports	Auto-generating lab reports with diagrams and annotated code	Haptic/audio 3D models for the visually impaired; signed avatars
XR/Metaverse Platforms	Provide immersive learning through VR/AR/MR environments	Simulating gravitational forces in a physics class	Shared virtual spaces for collaborative problem-solving
Digital Twins	Virtual replicas of lab instruments for realistic experimentation	Operating a virtual spectrometer and exporting data for analysis	Equitable access for students lacking lab resources
IoT and Robotics Teleoperation	Remote control of real lab equipment via XR and IoT integration	Using a robotic arm to mix reagents in a distant lab	Enables participation for students with limited mobility

tutors interpret these streams to overlay safety guidance, explanations, and formative feedback, yielding a holistic, inclusive model that scales access to sophisticated laboratory equipment while preserving the benefits of both simulated practice and real-world experimentation.

As shown in Table 5.1, integrating LLM-driven tutors, multimodal GenAI, XR/metaverse platforms, digital twins, and IoT-enabled teleoperation creates a layered ecosystem of educational innovation. Each component addresses specific challenges in learning environments, from simplifying scientific jargon to enabling remote access to sophisticated laboratory equipment. These technologies form a holistic, inclusive, adaptive, and immersive education model.

5.2.2 Interaction Layer

Accessibility in learning depends on thoughtful interaction design, not just compliance. Effective design ensures learners can engage with confidence and dignity by making experiences perceivable, operable, and understandable across diverse needs. This "interaction layer" treats accessibility as a creative driver of better pedagogy, supporting multiple modalities so learners can switch between speech, text, gesture, or simplified interfaces depending on context [52, 53].

It adapts dynamically, adjusting controls, timing, and cues based on input methods or cognitive load, while giving clear, layered feedback and safe undo options. Features like progressive disclosure minimize overwhelm, while privacy and agency remain core through portable preference profiles and universal consent controls. Collaboration is equally inclusive, allowing mixed modalities to work together in shared environments. Ultimately, the interaction layer harmonizes inputs, feedback, and layouts to create a learning experience that is immersive, supportive, and truly universal [54, 55].

5.2.2.1 Input Modalities

An accessible learning environment requires multiple flexible input methods to accommodate diverse needs. The platform supports speech, text, gesture, eye-tracking, and switch inputs, each optimized for accuracy, recovery, and low cognitive load. Speech enables natural language commands with privacy safeguards and feedback cues; predictive assistance, minimal-distraction modes, and customizable shortcuts enhance text entry. Gestures use stabilization and snapping to reduce precision demands, always paired with text or speech equivalents. Eye-tracking allows adjustable gaze-based navigation with safeguards against accidental actions, while switch inputs empower learners with severe motor impairments through adaptive scanning and pacing cues [56–59].

Consistency across modalities ensures shared semantics and seamless handoff between inputs, while errors are gently recoverable. Tutorials and micro-lessons support learning each method, and preferences follow the learner across contexts, preserving agency and adaptability over time.

5.2.2.2 Output Modalities

The platform treats output as a driver of understanding, not decoration, using haptics, spatial audio, and adaptive UI skins, alone or layered, to meet learners' sensory and cognitive needs. Haptic gloves and controllers transform abstractions into tangible experiences (e.g., bonds as snaps, resistance as force, vectors as tugs) with adjustable intensities, ramps, and vibration/force swaps, and every cue is mirrored in both visual and audio channels. Spatial audio places voices, tools, and alerts in 3D space to aid orientation, with tuned reverb, distance, and ducking for intelligible speech. Adaptive skins dynamically reshape visuals, featuring high contrast themes, simplified layouts, dyslexia-aware typography, and sign-language overlays that can be pinned near relevant content, persisting per activity. Feedback is intentionally multimodal yet lightweight (a soft thrum, a brief chime, a clear on-screen toast), and warnings escalate gradually with clear exits and explainers. The system continuously adapts to user preferences and fatigue, throttling animation and swapping haptics for gentle visual pulses. It also supports collaboration with shared spatial audio and presence indicators, while rendering skins per client to ensure consistent meaning across all clients. Documentation and assessments follow suit, offering theme-aware guidance and accepting multimodal evidence. Overall, the architecture offers a range of input/output modalities that align with accessibility requirements, transforming inclusivity into a core capability that enhances comprehension and reduces friction for every learner [60–63].

TABLE 5.2
Accessibility Interaction Options in the Metaverse STEM Environment

Learner Need	Input/Output Modality	Example Use Case
Limited hand mobility	Eye-tracking, switch inputs	Selecting virtual lab tools via gaze fixation
Visual impairment	Haptic feedback, spatial audio	Feeling molecular shapes or hearing graph readings
Hearing impairment	Captions, sign-language avatars	AI avatar signs instructions in real time
Cognitive load management	Simplified UI skins, step cues	Sequential guidance during multi-step experiments

A critical dimension of the system architecture lies in its ability to accommodate the diverse interaction needs of learners with functional impairments. As shown in Table 5.2, inclusive metaverse environments must provide a spectrum of input and output modalities, each aligned with specific accessibility requirements.

5.3 DESIGNING ACCESSIBLE LEARNING EXPERIENCES

Designing accessible learning experiences requires a careful blend of inclusivity, adaptability, collaboration, and thoughtful evaluation. In immersive environments, accessibility removes barriers and creates opportunities for all learners to thrive. This includes accounting for sensory differences, language diversity, cognitive load, and equitable participation in individual and collaborative tasks. Below, we examine key principles and design practices that support accessible, inclusive, and effective learning in digital and XR environments [64].

5.3.1 Inclusive World-Building

An accessible learning world begins with sensory inclusivity. Features such as low-motion modes can help prevent discomfort for learners who are sensitive to motion sickness or vestibular strain. Adjustable contrast ensures that text, visuals, and interfaces are legible to those with visual impairments or color blindness. Captions and subtitles support learners who are D/HH, benefiting multilingual participants and those in noisy environments. Spatial audio can guide attention by helping learners distinguish between overlapping conversations, cues, or instructions, while tactile and haptic feedback provides an additional sensory channel for learners with different needs. Looking further ahead, sign-language avatars could serve as real-time interpreters within virtual spaces, broadening participation for deaf communities. Together, these design practices create a world where learners can engage through multiple sensory pathways, tailoring the environment to their preferences and needs [65, 66].

5.3.2 Adaptive Scaffolding with Generative AI

GenAI can serve as a dynamic scaffold, adapting instruction in real time to meet learners where they are. Personalized hints can gently redirect a learner without providing the complete answer, preserving autonomy while reducing frustration. AI systems can also diagnose common misconceptions, such as confusing velocity with acceleration in physics labs, and provide clarifying explanations to intervene and correct them. In practical simulations, stepwise lab guidance can offer structured, just-in-time prompts, allowing learners to progress at their own pace. Importantly, multilingual translation and language simplification open doors for learners who might otherwise be excluded due to linguistic barriers. Instead of static, one-size-fits-all instructions, AI enables a responsive, personalized learning approach that respects individual progress and cultural diversity [10, 20, 27].

5.3.3 Virtual Laboratories and Simulations

Accessible learning thrives in environments that allow safe exploration and experimentation. Virtual laboratories and simulations serve as digital twins of wet labs, physics rigs, or electronics benches, offering realistic yet risk-free environments for learners. These environments encourage "what-if" experimentation, allowing students to test scenarios, adjust variables, or intentionally make mistakes without fear of wasted materials or safety hazards. The reproducibility of digital protocols further enhances accessibility, allowing learners to revisit experiments multiple times, compare results, and build confidence before transitioning to physical labs. Such designs are especially valuable for learners with disabilities or limited access to physical facilities, ensuring equitable participation in hands-on scientific inquiry [37, 46].

5.3.4 Collaborative Presence

Learning is inherently social, and accessibility must extend to collaboration. Accessible avatars give learners the agency to represent themselves in comfortable and inclusive ways. Role assignment within teams, such as leader, recorder, or technician, helps distribute responsibility and ensures that diverse strengths are recognized and utilized. Virtual whiteboarding tools and versioned notebooks facilitate collective knowledge building, while social moderation features foster respectful interaction and mitigate the risk of exclusion or harassment. When thoughtfully designed collaboration tools foster inclusive communities of practice where all learners feel valued contributors, regardless of ability or background [66, 67].

5.3.5 Cognitive Load Management

Managing cognitive load is central to accessibility. Overwhelming learners with complex interfaces or too much information at once can create barriers to understanding. Chunking content into manageable units supports comprehension and retention. Just-in-time tooltips offer lightweight assistance without overwhelming the learner with instructions upfront. Pace control enables learners to adjust the speed of instruction or simulation, accommodating individual differences in processing speeds. With opt-in analytics, systems can even monitor signs of fatigue, prompting learners to take breaks before performance declines. These strategies respect the cognitive diversity of learners, enabling each individual to engage deeply without unnecessary stress or burnout [68–70].

5.3.6 Assessment of Process and Product

Accessible learning design must also extend to assessment, ensuring that evaluation captures both outcomes and the processes that lead to them. Auto-generated rubrics provide transparent criteria, reducing ambiguity and bias. Code and data provenance tracking enable the visualization of how learners approached problems, not just whether they arrived at the correct answer. Reflective prompts encourage metacognition, allowing the learners to articulate their reasoning, struggles, and areas for growth. Oral defenses conducted in-world provide alternative assessment modes, allowing learners to demonstrate understanding verbally or interactively rather than solely through written tests. These practices create a fairer and comprehensive portrait of learner progress and achievement [71, 72].

5.4 INSTRUCTIONAL MODELS, ASSESSMENT, AND ACADEMIC INTEGRITY

5.4.1 Innovative Course Models for Immersive STEM Learning

In GenAI- and metaverse-enabled distance STEM courses, course organization must move beyond digitized lectures toward designs that center on inquiry, iteration, and collaboration. A flipped exploration model repositions direct instruction as pre-class microlearning. At the same time, students use AI copilots to probe virtual phenomena, such as manipulating molecular dynamics or electromagnetic fields; therefore, synchronous sessions are devoted to sense-making and critique. Research on flipped learning across disciplines has consistently associated the approach with improved performance and engagement when the "class time" is repurposed for active learning, rather than merely substituting video. Meta-analytic and survey syntheses underscore these gains, as well as the precondition that in-person (or synchronous) time be allocated for problem-solving, group work, and feedback, precisely what immersive worlds afford at scale [73]. Problem-based learning or PBL also benefits from shared virtual spaces: teams can co-design prototypes, run simulations, and iterate with AI mentors, while studio-style critiques allow learners to present artifacts (e.g., 3D scenes, code notebooks) for multimodal commentary. Systematic reviews of PBL demonstrate gains in critical thinking, transfer, and self-directed learning, outcomes that align with the metaverse's affordances for authentic, open-ended tasks [74, 75]. Finally, via digital twins and teleoperation, remote practicums enable students to demonstrate procedural competence on realistic instruments, regardless of mobility or geography, complementing the safety and repeatability of virtual labs, where controlled scenarios have been shown to support cognitive and noncognitive skill development [76].

5.4.2 Competency Mapping and Standards Alignment

To ensure rigor and recognizability, virtual tasks should be mapped to explicit laboratory competencies and safety outcomes, with performance criteria articulated in advance and aligned to credentialing requirements. UDL provides a normative framework for this mapping: competencies are fixed, but means of engagement and expression are varied, allowing learners to meet the same standard through different accessible modalities (e.g., gesture, eye-tracking, or text). This preserves comparability while widening participation, a core tenet of inclusive assessment design [77]. In practice, institutions can define capability statements for each metaverse lab (setup, operation, troubleshooting, safety) and verify them through observable behaviors in simulations or teleoperated sessions, making explicit the equivalence to on-site lab expectations.

5.4.3 Capturing Evidence of Mastery in Virtual Contexts

Assessment in immersive environments should privilege performance evidence over proxy indicators. High-fidelity simulations can capture decision paths, parameter choices, and error recovery, yielding trace data richer than a static lab report. Complementary learning portfolios curate artifacts such as 3D models, narrated experiment walkthroughs, code repositories, and annotated notebooks; these demonstrate growth, reflection, and reproducibility. Micro-credentials (digital badges) can then certify discrete, employable skills (e.g., "operates a digital spectrometer," "implements Proportional–Integral–Derivative [PID] control in simulation"), providing stackable recognition beyond course grades. Higher-education analyses highlight micro-credentials and competency-based assessment as converging trends for online learning, particularly where institutions aim to recognize granular, skills-level mastery. Evidence from virtual-lab research suggests that scenario-based experiences can equal or exceed passive methods in terms of LOs, supporting the validity of performance-oriented assessment in simulated contexts [76]. To ensure the portability of evidence, assessment events should emit Experience API (xAPI) statements to a learning record store, enabling cross-platform analytics and auditability for accreditation purposes.

5.4.4 Safeguarding Academic Integrity and Promoting Safe Practice

Academic integrity in AI-rich, immersive settings requires layered, instructional, and protective controls. Identity assurance and risk-adjusted proctoring can be embedded at in-world checkpoints for summative tasks; empirical comparisons of proctored versus unproctored online exams show meaningful differences in score distributions, underscoring the need for appropriate supervision in high-stakes contexts [78]. For computational work, code-similarity systems such as Measure of Software Similarity (MOSS) remain effective deterrents and detection tools when paired with transparent rubrics and iterative submission models that teach proper collaboration and citation [79]. Safety is equally central: sandboxed procedures in virtual labs should prevent hazardous actions and provide just-in-time explanations of why an operation would be unsafe if performed physically, turning integrity and safety mechanisms into learning opportunities rather than purely punitive controls. Combining these safeguards with clear expectations about AI assistance (what is permitted, what must be original) helps students develop professional ethics around tool-mediated work.

5.4.5 Learning Analytics as a Tool for Equity and Inclusion

Bias-aware learning analytics close the loop from pedagogy to improvement. Because immersive platforms and AI tutors generate rich interaction traces, institutions can monitor equitable participation (e.g., talk turns in critiques, role rotations in PBL teams, distribution of tutor attention) and deploy early-alert nudges when disengagement patterns emerge. To avoid algorithmic harm, such as misclassifying eye-tracking or switch-based input as low effort, dashboards should foreground contextualized indicators and allow instructors to drill into underlying evidence rather than accept black-box flags. The xAPI data model is well-suited to this purpose because it captures heterogeneous experiences, including AR/VR simulations and serious games, enabling accessibility-relevant analytics alongside traditional outcomes. When combined with UDL-aligned course policies, such analytics shift evaluative culture from mere completion toward participation with parity, making inclusion a measurable dimension of quality rather than an aspirational add-on [80, 81].

5.5 THE MECHALAB: ROBOTICS VIRTUAL LAB (SLTC, SRI LANKA MECHATRONICS VIRTUAL LAB EXPERIMENTAL)

The Robotics Virtual Lab at the Sri Lanka Technology Campus (SLTC) was conceived to enable students to perform authentic mechatronics practicals entirely within a metaverse setting while maintaining a verifiable link to physical hardware. The lab mirrors a real university mechatronics space on a 1:1 scale. It brings together a robust development stack (Unreal Engine 5.3, SteamVR/Pico Link), high-fidelity assets, and a custom "robotic twin" that synchronizes a 3D-printed arm with its virtual counterpart. This blend delivers immersion, repeatability, and safety, without sacrificing the tactile truth of robotics practice.

5.5.1 Infrastructure and Tools

To ensure smooth rendering and real-time interaction, the SLTC lab is equipped with an AMD Ryzen 5 3600 processor, an NVIDIA GTX 1080 graphics card (8 GB VRAM), and NVMe Solid-State Drive (SSD) storage. This configuration maintains a minimum of 60 FPS in VR, which is essential for user comfort during extended sessions, and keeps load times low when swapping large meshes and textures. A Pico Neo 3 Link headset connects wirelessly via Wi-Fi 6, eliminating cable drag while preserving low-latency head tracking and controller input for natural movement in the lab. These choices strike a balance between visual fidelity, responsiveness, and cost in a teaching environment.

On the software side, Unreal Engine 5.3 offers Nanite geometry and Lumen lighting, enabling the creation of realistic scenes without compromising frame rate.

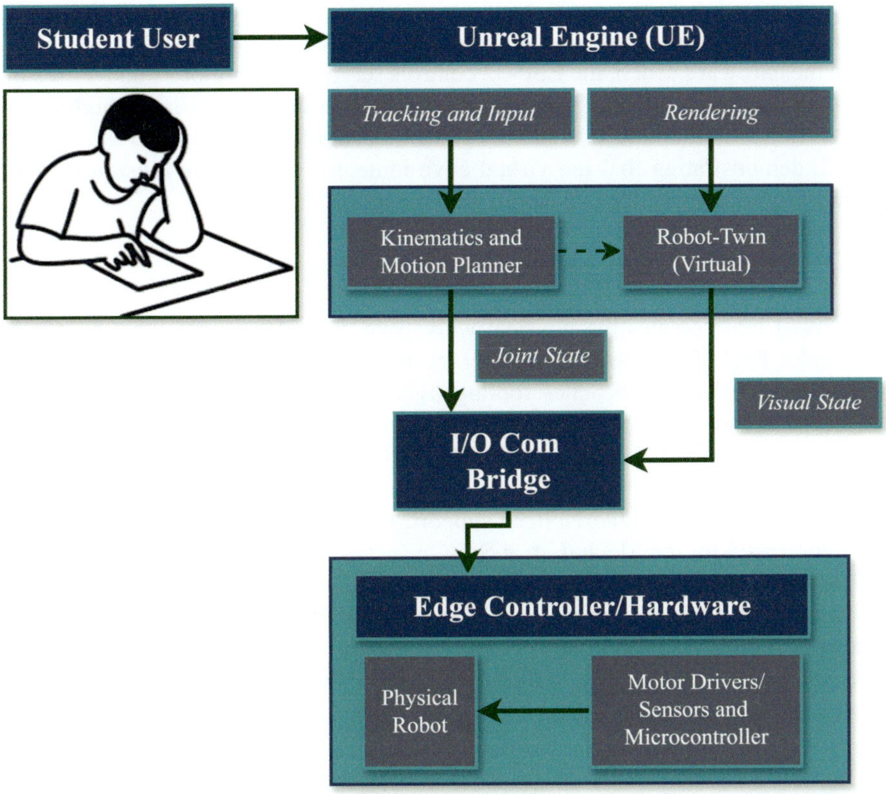

FIGURE 5.5 Methodology of the proposed system.

SteamVR and Pico Link bridge engine output to the headset with a <20 ms latency target. Development alternates between C++ (for performance-critical routines) and Blueprints (for rapid iteration, event orchestration, and readability). This dual-track approach proved especially helpful for quickly adjusting pedagogical flows while maintaining the efficiency of the kinematics and I/O layers.

Figure 5.5 shows the methodology of the proposed design of the virtual and physical lab.

5.5.2 Virtual–Physical "Twin" Robotics

A centerpiece of the lab is the Robotic Twin System. Students operate a virtual arm that mirrors a 3D-printed physical arm in real-time via serial communication; joint angles and base rotation remain synchronized, allowing learners to see how software changes propagate into real hardware behavior. The arm is modeled and rigged in Unreal, utilizing inverse kinematics (IK) and the FABRIK solver to ensure smooth, accurate end-effector placement while respecting link lengths and joint constraints. The course uses a 2-Degrees of Freedom (DOF) planar manipulator with a rotating base for targeted exercises, enabling students to focus on core kinematics while experiencing realistic constraints, such as reachability and singularities.

On the hardware bench, the ESP-32 controls servos/stepper motors and parses the incoming pose stream from the engine. In practice, this set-up produced high agreement between virtual and real joints, 97.12% accuracy on Joint 1 and 95.17% on Joint 2, demonstrating that the virtual environment is not merely illustrative but a faithful rehearsal space for real-world manipulation.

5.5.3 Environment Fidelity and Guidance

The virtual lab recreates the physical workspace using Marketplace assets, Chairs and Tables Pack, High Tech Pack, Storage Pack, and Loft Office, combined with Quixel materials to build benches, tooling, lighting, and circulation paths. Point lights are placed to mirror the physical lab's ambiance, helping learners carry over spatial memory. An in-world, AI-driven guide delivers just-in-time prompts, explains task goals, and orients students to safety and workflow conventions, reducing instructor load while preserving individualized support. Figure 5.6 shows the virtual environment developed for the MechaLab at SLTC.

To scaffold beginners from fundamentals to applied manipulation, the curriculum follows four stages: Arduino basics, LED control, 180° hobby servos, and kinematic control of a tabletop robotic arm. Each stage couples core concepts with hands-on tasks and a consistent setup, a compact arm, push-button interface, and workstation, so skills transfer smoothly across levels (see Figure 5.7).

FIGURE 5.6 A lab environment was developed for the VR MechaLab. This environment is very much identical to the real mechatronics laboratory at the Sri Lanka Technology Campus.

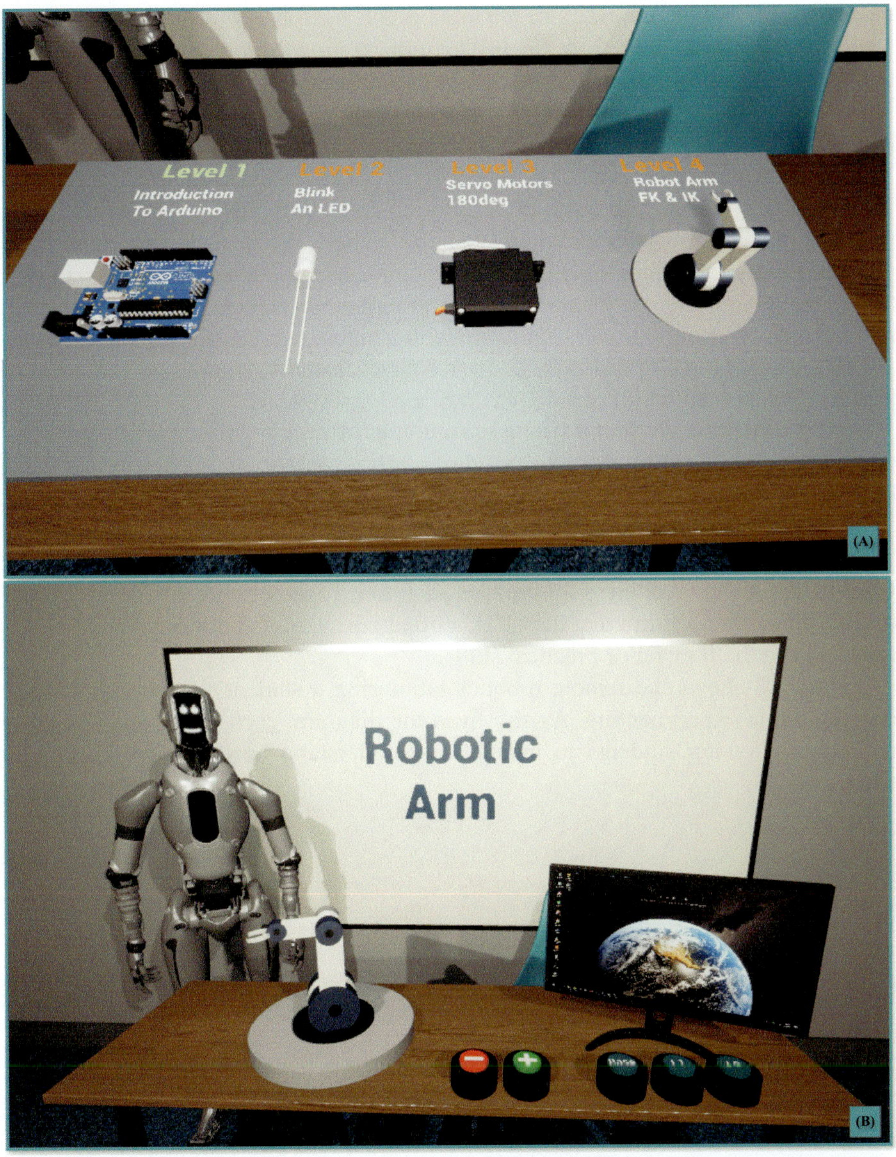

FIGURE 5.7 (A) Overview of the four-level sequence used in the lab: Level 1: Introduction to Arduino; Level 2: Blink an LED; Level 3: 180° servo motors; Level 4: robot arm control with forward and inverse kinematics (FK/IK). (B) Lab workstation for the robotic-arm module.

A typical practical unfolds as follows: (1) students enter and receive a brief orientation from the guide; (2) they open a Blueprint-driven panel to set end-effector targets (x, y, θ); (3) the UE control rig computes inverse kinematics and previews the motion; (4) on commit, the engine streams joint angles to the physical arm; and (5) students observe deviations, diagnose sources (e.g., backlash, compliance, quantization), and iterate. Because the logic graph is exposed in Blueprints, learners can inspect the event flow, from BeginPlay initialization through tick-based updates, to understand timing, states, and data paths in a real-time application.

5.5.4 Performance, Safety, and Accessibility

The lab targets 60 FPS and a sub-20 ms motion-to-photon latency to minimize sickness and maintain trustworthy hand–eye coordination. Wireless operation increases physical safety, no tether snags, and virtualizing hazardous steps (power circuits, torque spikes) allows early-stage students to explore confidently. Because the virtual lab runs on commodity PC hardware with a mainstream Head-Mounted Display (HMD), it can be replicated or scaled for cohorts, satellite campuses, and at-home practice, where bandwidth permits Wi-Fi 6-level throughput.

A 100-student study found strong usability and learning gains. Participants, predominantly 20–27 years old, rated guidance, visual fidelity, and educational value highly, and post-session knowledge scores shifted dramatically toward the top end (with ~89% scoring 4–5 after training). Navigation was widely reported as "easy" or "very easy." The platform earned high recommendation intent, suggesting positive word-of-mouth and readiness for broader adoption. Together with the joint-accuracy results, these data confirm that the SLTC virtual lab supports both conceptual understanding and the transfer of practical skills.

Figure 5.8 shows the remote robotics lab during a student's forward kinematic training while experimenting. As shown in the diagram, each angle was plotted in real time, allowing students to interact and understand how forward kinematics works.

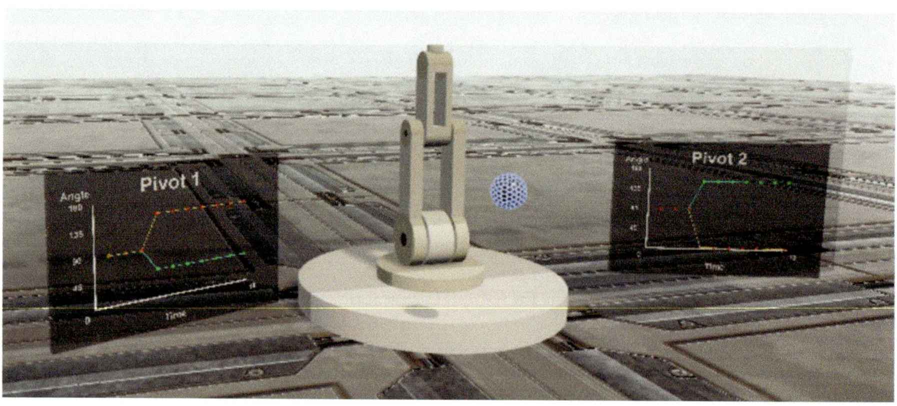

FIGURE 5.8 VR training platform for Robotics remote lab.

5.5.5 How SLTC-Mechatronics Lab Enhanced Inclusive STEM Education through Virtual Robotics Labs

The SLTC Robotics Virtual Lab has become a strong example of how immersive technologies can expand access to STEM education for diverse learners. The lab eliminates many traditional barriers, such as cost, space, and safety concerns, by shifting robotics practice into a virtual environment while synchronizing it with physical hardware. This design allows students of all abilities to engage with robotics concepts in a low-risk, repeatable, and customizable way. Learners can explore kinematics, programming, and real-time problem-solving without fear of equipment damage or injury, which is particularly important for those needing more time or confidence-building experiences.

Inclusivity is embedded in the lab's design through flexibility and adaptability. The virtual space can be tailored to different learning needs with adjustable visuals, multiple modes of guidance, and scaffolded workflows. For example, abstract mathematical concepts like inverse kinematics become more tangible when students see virtual arms moving in response to equations, helping those who struggle with symbolic learning. The environment also aligns with UDL principles, offering multiple ways to engage, represent information, and demonstrate understanding. This ensures that advanced learners can dig deeper into technical detail while beginners or students with learning differences can progress through guided tasks at their own pace.

Collaboration and equity are also enhanced. The lab facilitates group work, allowing tasks to be distributed according to each student's strengths, such as coding, documentation, or observation, so that everyone contributes meaningfully. Accessibility features, such as narration, captions, and visual cues, support learners with hearing or language challenges. At the same time, the ability to repeat experiments from home widens participation for rural students or those unable to attend in person. Teachers benefit from built-in assessment tools that capture student progress and problem-solving strategies, helping them provide targeted support without singling out individuals.

The SLTC-Mecha Lab redefines robotics education as a more inclusive and empowering experience. Blending immersive virtual spaces with real-world hardware gives every student – regardless of background or ability – the chance to engage deeply with STEM learning. This approach develops technical skills and fosters confidence, collaboration, and a more profound sense of belonging within the scientific community.

5.6 CONCLUSION

This chapter concludes that leveraging GenAI and metaverse technologies for distance STEM education is not speculative but an ethically urgent and practical step toward inclusion. Rather than framing access as mere entry, we defined it as belonging, the ability for learners facing mobility limitations, chronic illness, sensory differences, or bandwidth constraints to participate fully in authentic STEM practices: hypothesizing, modeling, experimenting, and collaborating. We demonstrated how this vision takes shape through layered system design. LLM tutors and multimodal

AI provide adaptive scaffolds, while XR spaces and digital twins recreate laboratories without reducing complexity. IoT-enabled teleoperation extends access to physical instruments, ensuring students engage in rigorous practices rather than parallel alternatives. Accessibility was shown to be foundational, embedded in multimodal interaction, including speech, gesture, eye-tracking, haptics, and adaptive skins, which reduce cognitive load and improve outcomes for all. Open standards, LMS/LRS integration, and secure identity management enable the integration of immersive environments into institutional infrastructures, preserving privacy and scalability.

Trust is earned through transparency, including privacy-preserving analytics, on-device inference, auditability, and human-in-the-loop safeguards. Instruction translates these technical layers into project-based inquiry, competency-aligned practicums, studio critiques, and portfolio assessment, emphasizing validity, reproducibility, and collaboration. Implementation requires governance, procurement guided by accessibility-by-design principles, faculty development, content workflows, and equitable support, such as device lending and progressive rendering. Evidence must be multidimensional, spanning access, learning gains, affective impact, and persistence. We also identified pitfalls, motion discomfort, device stratification, over-automation, and content drift, along with strategies to mitigate them. Institutions can scale responsibly through hybrid deployment, continuous audits, and open-source collaboration. Finally, we outlined a research agenda on adaptive assessment, career outcomes, AI-teacher orchestration, and interoperability standards.

Ultimately, the promise lies in aligning UDL with transparent governance. When done well, GenAI and the metaverse can shift distance learning from accommodation to excellence, enabling excluded learners to build authentic STEM identities and transforming inclusive education from an exception to the norm.

ACKNOWLEDGMENT

The MechaLab at the Sri Lanka Technology Campus was developed by the Computational Intelligence and Robotics (CIR) Research Laboratory. Mr. Shehan Hettiarachchi developed the system under the supervision of Eng. H.M.K.K.M.B. Herath, Ms. Kasunika Guruge, and Dr. S.L.P. Yasakethu.

NOTE

1 The metaverse is a collective virtual space that merges physical reality and digital environments, essentially a shared, immersive 3D world accessed through the internet [1].

REFERENCES

1. Herath, H. M. K. K. M. B., Mittal, M., & Kataria, A. (2024). Navigating the metaverse: A technical review of emerging virtual worlds. *WIREs Data Mining and Knowledge Discovery*, 14. https://doi.org/10.1002/widm.1538
2. Yıldız, T. (2025). The future of digital education: Artificial intelligence, the metaverse, and the transformation of education. *İstanbul Üniversitesi Sosyoloji Dergisi/İstanbul University Journal of Sociology*, 44, 921–940. https://doi.org/10.26650/sj.2024.44.2.0664

3. Behera, S. K., Sorayyaei Azar, A., Curle, S., & Dials, J. G. (Eds.). (2025). *Transformative approaches to STEAM integration in modern education*. IGI Global.
4. Basyoni, L., Qayyum, A., Shaban, K., et al. (2025). Generative AI-driven metaverse: The promises and challenges of AI-generated content. *IEEE Open Journal of the Computer Society*, 1–19. https://doi.org/10.1109/ojcs.2025.3616501
5. Wang, Y., Wang, L., & Siau, K. L. (2025). Human-centered interaction in virtual worlds: A new era of generative artificial intelligence and metaverse. *International Journal of Human–Computer Interaction*, 41(2), 1459–1501. https://doi.org/10.1080/10447318.2024.2316376
6. Rossi, M., Ciletti, M., Melchiorre, L., & Toto, G. A. (2025). The impact of generative artificial intelligence (GenAI) on education: A review of the potential, the risks and the role of immersive technologies. *Education Sciences and Society*, 400–415. https://doi.org/10.3280/ess2-2024oa18464
7. Saputro, E. A., Afuan, L., Noor, M. H. M., et al (2025). Interdisciplinary collaboration in AI and metaverse. *Advances in Computational Intelligence and Robotics*, 139–162. https://doi.org/10.4018/979-8-3373-0340-6.ch007
8. Tang, M., Mikhail, N., Alrefai, A., & Kumar, A. (2025). Metaverse and digital twins in the age of AI and extended reality. *Architecture*, 5, 36–36. https://doi.org/10.3390/architecture5020036
9. Huang, Y., Zhang, J., Chen, X., et al. (2024). From simulation to prediction: Enhancing digital twins with advanced generative AI technologies. 490–495. https://doi.org/10.1109/icca62789.2024.10591881
10. Gebreab, S., Musamih, A., Salah, K., et al. (2024). Accelerating digital twin development with generative AI: A framework for 3D modeling and data integration. *IEEE Access*. 185918–185936. https://doi.org/10.1109/access.2024.3514175
11. Pless, N., & Maak, T. (2004). Building an inclusive diversity culture: Principles, processes and practice. *Journal of Business Ethics*, 54(2), 129–147. https://doi.org/10.1007/s10551-004-9465-8
12. Shrivastava, A., Anand, G., & Shrivastava, A. (2024). A study on principles, processes and practice for building an inclusive diversity culture. *Routledge EBooks*, 359–370. https://doi.org/10.4324/9781003501374-26
13. Kunwar, R., & Adhikari, S. (2023). An exploration of the conceptualization, guiding principles, and theoretical perspectives of inclusive curriculum. *Journal of Contemporary Research in Social Sciences*, 5(1), 1–13.
14. Møgelvang, A., & Nyléhn, J. (2023). Interdependence between perceived cooperative learning, sense of belonging, and generic skills in undergraduate STEM EDUCATION. https://www.ntnu.no/ojs/index.php/njse/article/view/4949. https://doi.org/10.5324/njsteme.v7i1.4949
15. Danielson, M., & Ivar Björkman. (2025). Project-based learning in social innovation—developing a sense of belonging in online contexts. *Education Sciences*, 15(7), 907–907. https://doi.org/10.3390/educsci15070907
16. Tan, A.-L., Ong, Y. S., Ng, Y. S., & Tan, J. H. J. (2022). STEM problem solving: inquiry, concepts, and reasoning. *Science & Education*, 32(2), 381–397. https://doi.org/10.1007/s11191-021-00310-2
17. McCurdy, R. P., Nickels, M. L., & Bush, S. B. (2020). Problem-based design thinking tasks: Engaging student empathy in STEM. *The Electronic Journal for Research in Science & Mathematics Education*, 24(2), 22–55.
18. Hassmén, P., & Hindman, E. (2025). Sensory sensitivity and strengths in Autism. 101–126. https://doi.org/10.1007/978-3-031-95433-7_5

19. Osifo, O., & Terashima, M. (2024). Addressing barriers in the university campus environment for neurodivergent students. *Studies in health technology and informatics*. https://doi.org/10.3233/shti240952
20. Anderson, J. E., Nguyen, C. A., & Moreira, G. (2025). Generative AI-driven personalization of the Community of Inquiry model: enhancing individualized learning experiences in digital classrooms. *International Journal of Information and Learning Technology*. https://doi.org/10.1108/ijilt-10-2024-0240
21. Karpouzis, K., Pantazatos, D., Taouki, J., & Meli, K. (2024). Tailoring education with GenAI: A new horizon in lesson planning. *2022 IEEE Global Engineering Education Conference (EDUCON)*, 1–10. https://doi.org/10.1109/educon60312.2024.10578690
22. Hirpara, N., Weber, M., Szakonyi, A., Cardona, T., & Singh, D. (2025). *Exploring the role of GenAI in shaping education*. Lecture notes in computer science, 121–134. https://doi.org/10.1007/978-3-031-88881-6_10
23. Zhang, J., & Juvrud, J. (2024). Gender expression and gender identity in virtual reality: Avatars, role-adoption, and social interaction in VRChat. *Frontiers in Virtual Reality*, 5. https://doi.org/10.3389/frvir.2024.1305758
24. Ribeiro, A., Arouca, M. G., Amorim, A. M., Pestana, M. C., & Vieira, V. (2024). Towards inclusive avatars: A study on self-representation in virtual environments. 13–27. https://doi.org/10.5753/sbsc.2024.238056
25. Sharma, A., Kumar, S., Singh, S. K., Jawla, S., Arya, V., & Chui, K. T. (2025). Virtual identity and self-expression in the metaverse. *Unveiling Social Dynamics and Community Interaction in the Metaverse*, 93–110. https://doi.org/10.4018/979-8-3693-8628-6.ch005
26. Tabassum, A., & Qadir, J. (2024). A critical AI approach for managing the risks in educational metaverses. *EDULEARN Proceedings*, 1, 9578–9586. https://doi.org/10.21125/edulearn.2024.2318
27. Tabassum, A., Elmahjub, E., Padela, A. I., Zwitter, A., & Qadir, J. (2025). Generative AI and the metaverse: A scoping review of ethical and legal challenges. *IEEE Open Journal of the Computer Society*, 6, 348–359. https://doi.org/10.1109/ojcs.2025.3536082
28. Adel, M. M. (2025). Challenges and opportunities of educational AI in the metaverse era. *Advances in computational intelligence and robotics book series*, 1–20. https://doi.org/10.4018/979-8-3693-6165-8.ch001
29. Swargiary, K. (2024). *Beyond classrooms: How generation beta will redefine formal education*. US: ERA.
30. Indumathy, I., & Mujra, P. (2025). Sustainable learning. *Smart education and sustainable learning environments in smart cities* (pp. 381–402). Hershey, PA, USA: IGI Global.
31. Bauman, G. L., Bustillos, L. T., Bensimon, E. M., Brown, M. C., & Bartee, R. (2005). *Achieving equitable educational outcomes with all students: The institution's roles and responsibilities*. Washington, DC: Association of American Colleges and Universities.
32. Thomas, L. (2015). Developing inclusive learning to improve the engagement, belonging, retention, and success of students from diverse groups. *Elsevier EBooks*, 135–159. https://doi.org/10.1016/b978-0-08-100213-1.00009-3
33. Salmi, J., & D'Addio, A. (2021). Policies for achieving inclusion in higher education. *Policy Reviews in Higher Education*, 5(1), 47–72. https://doi.org/10.1080/23322969.2020.1835529
34. Garg, S., Dev, R., Singh, A. K., Sahani, S., Kumari, K., & Bandyopadhyay, A. (2025). Edu-Metaverse: A structured architecture and workflow model for digital and blended learning. 514–519. https://doi.org/10.1109/isacc65211.2025.10969320

35. Strousopoulos, P., & Sgouropoulou, C. (2024, October). Architecting immersive education: Designing. In *Novel and Intelligent Digital Systems: Proceedings of the 4th International Conference (NiDS 2024)* (Vol. 1170, p. 346). Springer Nature.
36. Bhambri, P. (2025). Virtual and augmented reality for immersive learning experiences. *Advances in Web Technologies and Engineering*, 17–46. https://doi.org/10.4018/979-8-3693-2973-3.ch002
37. Zhang, X. (2025). Internet of things and cloud computing-powered virtual laboratories for enhanced STEM education. *Journal of the Institution of Engineers (India): Series B*. https://doi.org/10.1007/s40031-024-01192-y
38. El Hajji, M., Ait Baha, T., Berka, A., Ait Nacer, H., El Aouifi, H., & Es-Saady, Y. (2025). An architecture for intelligent tutoring in virtual reality: Integrating LLMs and multimodal interaction for immersive learning. *Information*, 16(7), 556. https://doi.org/10.3390/info16070556
39. Shahzad, T., Mazhar, T., Tariq, M. U., Ahmad, W., Ouahada, K., & Hamam, H. (2025). A comprehensive review of large language models: issues and solutions in learning environments. *Discover Sustainability*, 6(1). https://doi.org/10.1007/s43621-025-00815-8
40. Behravan, M. (2025). Generative AI framework for 3d object generation in augmented reality. arXiv preprint arXiv:2502.15869.
41. Yeganeh, L. N., Fenty, N. S., Chen, Y., Simpson, A., & Hatami, M. (2025). The future of education: A multi-layered metaverse classroom model for immersive and inclusive learning. *Future Internet*, 17(2), 63–63. https://doi.org/10.3390/fi17020063
42. Horvath, A., & Goldschmid, R. (2025). Extended abstract—immersive education: Utilizing the potential of immersive technologies in computer science higher education. 162–167. https://doi.org/10.56198/508qgt70
43. Chang, C.-C. (2025). Metaverse-enabled collaboration for practical case handling: Triangulation authentication of performance, perceptions, and behavioral patterns. *Education and Information Technologies*, 30(13), 18679–18703. https://doi.org/10.1007/s10639-025-13510-y
44. Sidhu, M. S., Mousakhani, S., Lee, C. K., & Sidhu, K. K. (2024). Educational impact of Metaverse learning environment for engineering mechanics dynamics. *Computer Applications in Engineering Education*, 32(5). https://doi.org/10.1002/cae.22772
45. Vichare, P., Paudel, S., Rimal, B., Adhikari, S., Panchenko, V., Rijal, R., & Dahal, K. (2023). Traditional, video and extended reality (XR) assisted flipped classroom teaching methods: An approach and comparison. *2023 15th International Conference on Software, Knowledge, Information Management and Applications (SKIMA), 18*, 298–305. https://doi.org/10.1109/skima59232.2023.10387350
46. Yang, S., Mirahmadi, S. A., Zhu, E., & Solanki, B. (2025). Live digital twin with virtual reality for accessible and immersive manufacturing education. *The International Journal of Advanced Manufacturing Technology*, 136(7-8), 3577–3590. https://doi.org/10.1007/s00170-025-15078-w
47. Sakkas, K., Ntagka, N. E., Spyridakis, M., Miltiadous, A., Glavas, E., Tzallas, A. T., & Giannakeas, N. (2025). Multiplayer virtual labs for electronic circuit design: A digital twin-based learning approach. *Electronics*, 14(16), 3163. https://doi.org/10.3390/electronics14163163
48. Khaleghi, E., & Rayner, R. (2025). Revolutionising education through digital twins: Case study and applications. *Mechatronic Futures*, 393–414. https://doi.org/10.1007/978-3-031-83571-1_21
49. Alghamdi, S., Yoon, H. Y., & Song, Y.-T. (2025). Digital twins in education applications, *Challenges, and Future Directions*, 225–232. https://doi.org/10.1109/sera65747.2025.11154576

50. Kostadimas, D., Kasapakis, V., & Kotis, K. (2025). A systematic review on the combination of VR, IoT and AI technologies, and their integration in applications. *Future Internet*, 17(4), 163–163. https://doi.org/10.3390/fi17040163
51. Adel, A. (2024). The convergence of intelligent tutoring, robotics, and IoT in smart education for the transition from industry 4.0 to 5.0. *Smart Cities*, 7(1), 325–369. https://doi.org/10.3390/smartcities7010014
52. Mercier, S. (Ed.). (2025). *Design for all learners: Create accessible and inclusive learning experiences*. American Society for Training and Development.
53. Singh, A. V., & Saxena, A. S. (2023). Designing for accessibility: Creating inclusive spaces in architecture. *International Journal of Science and Research (IJSR)*, 12(5), 1255–1271.
54. Lowgren, J., & Stolterman, E. (2007). *Thoughtful interaction design: A design perspective on information technology*. MIT Press.
55. Hartson, R. (2003). Cognitive, physical, sensory, and functional affordances in interaction design. *Behaviour & Information Technology*, *22*(5), 315–338. https://doi.org/10.1080/01449290310001592587
56. Li, Q., Luximon, Y., Zhang, J., & Song, Y. (2023). Measuring and classifying students' cognitive load in pen-based mobile learning using handwriting, touch gestural and eye-tracking data. *British Journal of Educational Technology*, 55(2), 625–653. https://doi.org/10.1111/bjet.13394
57. Chen, F., Ruiz, N., Choi, E., Epps, J., Khawaja, M. A., Taib, R., Yin, B., & Wang, Y. (2012). Multimodal behavior and interaction as indicators of cognitive load. *ACM Transactions on Interactive Intelligent Systems*, 2(4), 1–36. https://doi.org/10.1145/2395123.2395127
58. Šola, H. M., Qureshi, F. H., & Khawaja, S. (2024). AI eye-tracking technology: A new era in managing cognitive loads for online learners. *Education Sciences*, 14(9), 933–933. https://doi.org/10.3390/educsci14090933
59. Li, S. (2025). The development and application of emerging interaction technologies in human-computer interaction. *Journal of Computer, Signal, and System Research*, 2(4), 1–10.
60. Endow, S., Moradi, H., Srivastava, A., Noya, E. G., & Torres, C. (2021, June). Compressables: A haptic prototyping toolkit for wearable compression-based interfaces. In *Proceedings of the 2021 ACM designing interactive systems conference* (pp. 1101–1114), Virtual Event USA.
61. Rumsey, F. (2012). Spatial audio. In *Routledge eBooks*. Informa. https://doi.org/10.4324/9780080498195
62. Zhang, R., Ji, P., Wang, J., & Zhang, B. (2025). Creative design and visual effect simulation of IoT dynamic interfaces by fractal algorithms and artificial intelligence. *IEEE Transactions on Consumer Electronics*, 1–16. https://doi.org/10.1109/tce.2025.3609538
63. Bhowmik, A. K. (2024). Virtual and augmented reality: Human sensory-perceptual requirements and trends for immersive spatial computing experiences. *Journal of the Society for Information Display*, 32(8), 605–646. https://doi.org/10.1002/jsid.2001
64. Sharma, S. (2024). Enhancing inclusive learning environments: Strategies for curriculum adaptation and modification. *Future of Special Education in India*, 109, 109–122.
65. Hutson, J., & Hutson, P. (2024). Inclusivity & environment. 85–125. https://doi.org/10.1007/978-3-031-43615-4_3
66. Velásquez, V. L. Z. (2023). *Teaching for inclusivity*. Sustainable development goals series, 309–320. https://doi.org/10.1007/978-3-031-36302-3_23
67. Gregg, N., Chang, Y., & Todd, R. (2012). Social media, avatars, and virtual worlds: Re-imagine an inclusive learning environment for adolescents and adults with literacy barriers. *Procedia Computer Science*, 14, 336–342. https://doi.org/10.1016/j.procs.2012.10.038

68. Falloon, G. (2009). Using avatars and virtual environments in learning: What do they have to offer? *British Journal of Educational Technology*, 41(1), 108–122. https://doi.org/10.1111/j.1467-8535.2009.00991.x
69. Clark, R. C., Nguyen, F., & Sweller, J. (2011). *Efficiency in learning: Evidence-based guidelines to manage cognitive load*. John Wiley & Sons.
70. Nelson, B. C., & Erlandson, B. E. (2007). Managing cognitive load in educational multi-user virtual environments: reflection on design practice. *Educational Technology Research and Development*, 56(5-6), 619–641. https://doi.org/10.1007/s11423-007-9082-1
71. Durgungoz, A., & Durgungoz, F. C.. (2025). Exploring effortless AI-generated gamified quizzes in an online special education module: Evaluating question quality, student engagement, and its potential to identify at-risk students. *Education and Information Technologies*. https://doi.org/10.1007/s10639-025-13765-5
72. Dobson, S. R., & Fudiyartanto, F. A. (2023). *Transforming assessment in education: The hidden world of language games* (Vol. 10). Springer Nature.
73. Strelan, P., Osborn, A., & Palmer, E. (2020). The flipped classroom: A meta-analysis of effects on student performance across disciplines and education levels. *Educational Research Review*, 30, 100314–100314. https://doi.org/10.1016/j.edurev.2020.100314
74. Zakaria, M. I., Maat, S. M., & Khalid, F. (2019). A systematic review of problem-based learning in education. *Creative Education*, 10(12), 2671–2688. https://doi.org/10.4236/ce.2019.1012194
75. Rehmat, A. P., & Hartley, K. (2020). Building engineering awareness: Problem-based learning approach for STEM integration. *Interdisciplinary Journal of Problem-Based Learning*, 14(1). https://doi.org/10.14434/ijpbl.v14i1.28636
76. Al-Nakhle, H. (2022). The effectiveness of scenario-based virtual laboratory simulations to improve learning outcomes and scientific report writing skills. *PLoS One*, 17(11), e0277359. https://doi.org/10.1371/journal.pone.0277359
77. CAST. (2018). Universal design for learning guidelines version 2.2. - References - Scientific Research Publishing. https://www.scirp.org/reference/referencespapers?referenceid=3284682
78. Alessio, H. M., Malay, N. J., Maurer, K., Bailer, A. J., & Rubin, B. (2017). Examining the effect of proctoring on online test scores. *Online Learning*, 21(1). https://doi.org/10.24059/olj.v21i1.885
79. Schleimer, S., Wilkerson, D. S., & Aiken, A. (2003). Winnowing. *Proceedings of the 2003 ACM SIGMOD international conference on management of data* (pp. 76–85). https://doi.org/10.1145/872757.872770
80. Blake-Plock, S., Hoyt, W., Casey, C., & Zapata Rivera, D. (2020). Data analytics and visualization for xAPI learning data: Considerations for a GIFT strategy. *Design Recommendations for Intelligent Tutoring Systems*, 8, 163–171.
81. São Mamede, H. (2025). From data to action: How AI and learning analytics. *AI and Learning Analytics in Distance Learning*, 229.

Index

Pages in *italics* refer to figures, pages in **bold** refer to tables, and pages followed by "n" refer to notes.

B

C

D

E

I

K

L

W

X

Z

For Product Safety Concerns and Information please contact our EU representative GPSR@taylorandfrancis.com Taylor & Francis Verlag GmbH, Kaufingerstraße 24, 80331 München, Germany